Thank you

A massive thank you to my editor Claire and my proof-readers Martin and Peter. They contributed so much work and skill, and this would be a far poorer book without their efforts.

Thank you to Thom, Manda and James who stepped up as my test readers, dealing with my freak-outs when I realised my work was finally going to be read and experienced. Your feedback and patience was exactly what I needed, so thank you.

Amongst all the teachers who showed me important steps on the path, I would particularly like to thank Jonathan Snell, Mac Macartney, Dr Peter Vardy and the late Rev. Roy Dorey. Without these teachers of exceptional vision, I would not be the man I am today.

Thank you to all of my clients who continue to come to me in their moments of upheaval, ambition, change or crisis, who trust me to be their guide, and who boldly open their minds to new possibilities and their hearts to healing. I learn from you every day, and your inspiring determination is all the motivation I need.

A big thank you to so many dear friends and companions who have shared their expertise and insights, debated deep truths with me late into the night and given me the love, inspiration and support I've needed. In particular, thank you to Jessica, David, Ben, Barney, Simon and Sara.

Thank you to my loving parents, Maddie and John, and my big sister and ultimate hero, Corinna.

And to the little island of Iona, out on the blustery Irish Sea, where I first began to put words to page, thank you...

Throughout this book, the author refers to a form of transformational personal coaching called Deep Coaching. This is an original creation by Alexander Butler and is based on the 12 Core Principles of Deep Coaching (summarised by the 12 Words). The author has no affiliation to other organisations or approaches with a similar name.

Deep Joy

1. CHOICE

I have the freedom and the power to choose,
and my life is the result of my choices

2. NEED

I understand and accept my own needs,
and I take responsibility for meeting them

3. AUTHENTICITY

I take care not to solve adult problems with childhood answers

I am grateful for the solutions that have taken me this far in my life,
even when I choose not to use them any more

4. INTEGRITY

My choices, words and actions are aligned with integrity and with
my personal sense of honour

5. LIBERATION

At this time, we are a broken people

6. WILDERNESS

The land remembers who I am

7. ADVENTURE

Peace is only found in the storm - I must engage with risk,
adventure and change in order to find peace

8. COURAGE

I will never be ready

9. COMPASSION

I cannot save anybody else. That's not my job

10. RESILIENCE

Nobody else can save me.
I will save myself with fierce self-love.

11. CONNECTION

I find deep connection when I combine
vulnerability with clear boundaries

12. COMMITMENT

I will never "get there" - my life is a sacred journey

Contents

Part 1: Understanding

Part 2: The 12 Words

Part 3: Integration

Deep Joy

Part 1

Understanding

Deep Joy

A beginning

This is a book about how to thrive in challenging times. How to be strong, happy and deeply connected. It's about the fullness of human potential and how to explore your own.

Imagine for a moment that you had the perfect childhood. Your earliest memories are of your loving parents who were always there for you. They were happy and they felt content and fulfilled by their lives. They were always calm and wise and always knew how to guide you as you learned about the world. You were also parented by a wider community and you learned from all of the adults about how to grow and learn, how to be. You had all the play-time and fun with other children that you could possibly want. Your community had a strong cultural heritage, with stories and myths that taught you what was expected of you as an adult, and how to relate to other people with kindness, clarity and balance. You grew up with a spiritual tradition and with an emotional connection to the place where you were born. You reached adulthood with confidence, strength, vitality and a bold courage to explore this wild and free adventure called life.

How many of us felt like this when we were growing up? How many of us feel like this now?

What actually happened was that we each grew up in a culture that isn't suited to human flourishing. We weren't taught how to be comfortable with ourselves, how to relate healthily to others, how to feel strong and proud of ourselves because of the way we live. We were given the bare essentials of how to function and then thrust into adulthood, surrounded by other struggling people. The level of stress, worry and confusion that we carry is now so common that it's considered normal. It's become strange and unusual to even notice how crazy our world has become and how uncomfortable and unsatisfied we each feel.

This book is about learning the fundamental building blocks of a happy, healthy and whole life.

Because, unless we commit ourselves to a life of personal discovery and development, we will tend to fall a long way short of our true potential. I have spent most of my adult life working in personal development and transformation, and what I've been shown over and over again (sometimes to my complete surprise) is that every single person is naturally confident, naturally healthy, naturally curious and open-minded. We are each born to be happy, fulfilled, deeply connected with people and with the world. We naturally give and receive love. We naturally tend towards emotional, physical, mental and spiritual wholeness. It takes significant, sustained effort to un-learn how to be and to do these things. That effort was called our upbringing and our education.

When I talk about this with my coaching clients, I talk about a tree growing from a seed. Imagine a new seed falling to the ground, hopefully into deep and fertile soil. This seed begins to grow, pushing its roots deep and starting to reach upwards for the nourishing light. Left to its own devices, a seedling will surge upwards, growing leaves and branches until it becomes a mighty, beautiful, healthy tree. But imagine that our seed landed in poor soil, or that a stone rolled onto the seed while it waited in the earth. The seedling reaches upwards and finds something blocking the light, keeping it from its natural growth. It will still reach towards the light, but it will have to find a way around the stone before it can continue to grow. This weight upon the seedling won't stop it forever, but it'll stunt its growth and it might leave a mark on the tree's trunk.

We naturally reach for the light. It takes an outside force to smother us and leave us with doubts, confusions, low confidence, neuroses or insecurities. We continue to reach for the light for the rest of our lives. Sometimes we just need to remember how.

This book is about coming home to who you were always meant to be. This is a book about the real you, who has been waiting to be freed, to explode into life, to surge into fullness and feel good simply about being alive. It is about discovering yourself to be a brave, powerful, wonderfully complex being who knows what they want and how to get it.

Three paths of the one journey

Your personal journey, and indeed all moments of life, can be broken down into three aspects: Being; Doing; and Relating. As you walk the one journey of your personal awakening and empowerment, you will need to walk these three paths, and at times one trail will seem more important than the others. So many of my clients tell me how much easier this would be if they could just put two paths on hold while they focus on one of them: their career; their family; their relationship or their personal development. But it doesn't really work like that. Each depends upon the other, and you will go further, faster, by accepting that you need to walk all three at once.

The path of **Being** is the path of your relationship with yourself. It is your inner work, your psycho-spiritual, physical and emotional development. It is coming to know yourself deeply and feeling comfortable with your own strengths, foibles and eccentricities. It is being at home in your own skin.

The path of **Doing** is your outer work. It relates to your place in the world, the effects your life has, the kind of work you're doing and what you choose to do with your time. It is the contribution you make to the world around you. Your career, your home, your hobbies and activities. It is as important to work on developing your outer world as it is to grow your inner self.

The path of **Relating** is about how you meet other people. How do you relate to friends, family, lovers, partners, colleagues and strangers? Are you balanced and fair or do you tend to emphasise their needs or yours? Do you tend to get what you want out of relationships? Are you bringing your mature, empowered self to relationships or do you tend to bring a more infantile version of yourself? This is also your interpersonal relationship with the living world itself, with the wildness that exists inside you and out on the land, with plants and animals, with the seen and the unseen.

Walking one of these paths without the others will significantly stifle your growth. As much as we might want to put our career on hold to work on ourselves, our inner work cannot be completed without an outer world to relate to. To grow as a person but not in relationship will leave your relationships fractured and unfulfilling. To make strides in your work life but not in your inner development will risk finding yourself financially fulfilled but emotionally hollow.

The paths reinforce one another. Nothing in life is harder than deeply relating to another human being with a mature balance of vulnerability and clear boundaries, and by learning these skills we grow ourselves enormously. Your work will be significantly different if you bring an emotionally resolved, empowered, ambitious version of yourself to it. Beautiful and interesting things happen when the three trails of our lives touch one another, and we notice a cross-over in our personal growth.

So, as you walk your journey, be aware of the three paths that you are treading. What is most important for you, right now? Are the paths closely aligned with one another, going in the same direction, or are they pulling you apart? Which are you most committed to right now? Where do you need to grow, develop and change? This awareness will serve you through this book and through your own personal journey.

How to use this book

This book, then, is a guide to a certain kind of life. The shape of that life will be determined by you. Above all I want you to feel empowered and capable of shaping your life, so I will simply be offering you ideas and tools. You will be taking the steps to create the life of your longing. I will invite you to consider questions and possibilities, and to consider abandoning your old solutions and answers, so that you can transform your experience and come home to the life you were always meant to live.

I encourage you to read the book from beginning to end, rather than jump from place to place. Once you've read the whole book, feel free to dip back into the parts that feel most helpful for you. The book is divided into three parts...

Part 1, which you're currently reading, asks the question WHY? Why should you read this book, why should you reconsider the way that you live, why is any of this important? We'll explore the nature of the prison that tends to keep us trapped in place, we'll build up a common language about what the human person really is beyond the shallow model that our upbringing offers, and we'll explore what a new way of living might feel like. Parts of this journey are going to be hard, so it's good to be clear on why we're doing it at all, and what exactly we're trying to achieve together.

Part 2 will introduce you to the 12 Principles of Deep Coaching. The question here is HOW to live in a way that's fulfilling and satisfying? These are the 12 essential affirmations that this book is based around. They are intended to be helpful reminders of the most important truths on your journey of personal awakening.

Part 3 asks WHAT NOW? A great many of my coaching clients have undertaken powerful journeys of awakening, only to find that the way they feel, the way they relate to people, the way they think and the things they choose to do with their time have all changed. Their old life feels a bit weird, a bit uncomfortable and a bit alien. Part 3 is an exploration of the kind of life that might serve you once you've unlocked the hidden truths inside yourself.

FIRST INVITATION

I invite you to consider that you may be at the beginning of a great journey of awakening and transformation. What lies ahead is an adventure, with a massive array of possibilities and opportunities for change, growth and prosperity.

Chapter 1: A beginning

Deep Joy

Why are we trapped?

There is so much beauty, joy and wonder waiting for each of us to experience. Life can be a positive, exciting adventure full of prosperity and success. We can each feel calm in ourselves, confident and in control, ready to greet whatever the day brings.

But on a bad day, these things can feel a world away. An unsatisfying life can feel like a prison cell. We look at other people living happier, better lives, but it can be easy to feel like we can never have the lives they have, never be so happy, content or successful.

So many of us spend years living lives that leave us sad, frustrated, and uninspired. Why?

Deep Coaching, the unique form of personal coaching that I have developed over 20 years of research and 9 years of practice, is about finding freedom and happiness by asking deep, probing questions that take us into difficult places. From there, we find the answers we need to transform our lives. When it comes to understanding the prison that keeps so many of us trapped, stuck and deeply frustrated, the key questions are: what's forcing us to live these unsatisfying lives; and what skill do we need to pick up to let us thrive and find deep joy?

In this book we're going to explore a powerful, holistic approach to life that will give you the tools and knowledge to break out of the prison. But it's useful to understand exactly what keeps some of us trapped in painful or unfulfilling place in our lives.

There are always practical reasons to stay where we are...

- This job may not nourish my soul, but it's good enough, and I can't afford to make changes right now anyway.
- My friends don't really get me, but it's better than not having

friends.

- My relationship hasn't felt exciting or passionate for years, but it's nice to have someone to come home to and besides, we have a home together and disentangling things could be messy, painful and expensive.
- I could start a training course or head in a new direction in my life, but I don't really know what I want to do and I wouldn't know what to choose.

Often our emotions are a big part of this. We can be afraid of all sorts of things. Being unable to provide for ourselves or our families. Being alone. Doing things that seem too big or frightening to handle. Being afraid of ourselves and what we might find if we dig too deep, if we break out of the rigid pattern of our lives.

I want to begin by talking about non-human animals, because they can give us a clues about what's going on in human animals.

Imagine you're visiting a farm. You see cows and sheep gently grazing in the fields. Are they energetic and rushing around or do they plod from place to place with nowhere to go? Animals in every farm I've ever visited have been basically placid and content with their situation. If a gate is left open, the animals might wander out but this is less a desperate bid for escape and more the plodding meander of an animal looking for food. They're calm, docile creatures. They're also dependent on us. They wouldn't survive for very long without the humans who bring them food, or tend to their medical needs, or keep them safe from predators. Some of our farm animals have become so dependent on us that they will quickly die without human support.

We've bred these animals over time to make them dependent and docile. They have no idea that their lives exist to feed the people they depend on. They just chew the grass and accept that this is the way things are.

Chapter 2: Why are we trapped?

Wild animals are different from their domesticated cousins. A wild animal is more alert, more curious and more aware of its surroundings. It has to be – food might be scarce and it might need to hunt around for food. Predators could wait in the shadows or around the next corner. Death is a constant companion, never very far away. A wild animal is wary, cautious and forced to explore and experiment. Its senses are sharper and its mind more alert. It lives on the edge between life and death and it makes no assumptions about how tomorrow might be.

A wild animal will also tend to be more sociable, especially animals like horses, wolves, elephants or dolphins. They will play, compete, mate, travel, hunt and scrap in ways that you won't see in a field of sleepy cattle. In some species there are leaders that make the decisions. Relationships are strong and animals will recognise each other and pick up their relationships after being separated. Wild animals display emotions more obviously and more freely than their docile counterparts. The social structures in wild herds, packs or pods exist in part to stop this wildness, this freedom, from running out of control.

Many wild animals can't bear being confined in a small space. A wild animal in a trap will often hurt itself or even kill itself in its desperation to escape. It needs freedom, and space to run, fly, forage and nest. When locked into a small space with others of its kind it has a much lower tolerance for being pressed-up against other animals. A herd of cattle will stand patiently in a pen with dozens of other cows, albeit with plenty of mooing. Put only a couple of wild horses into the same pen and they'll become stressed and anxious, lashing out to break free.

Humans are the only species that have domesticated themselves. We've trained ourselves and our children to be calm and ok with feeling trapped. Have you ever had a hard day and you just wanted to shout or scream or smash something, but of course you were at work, or with family or in a public place so you just had to hold it in? Have you ever been in a bustling crowd and just wanted to be somewhere else so you can breathe? Even people I meet who are really, desperately fed up with their lives don't actually spend that much of the day thinking about it. We're too busy. We have jobs to do, kids to feed, bills to pay, complicated lives to organise. We have telly to watch, friends to hang out with, people to take care of. We simply don't have time to reflect too much on the things that are hard.

Just like other domesticated animals, we've become dependent on the systems that keep us alive. We go to work so we'll have the money to provide for ourselves. We buy our food pre-prepared in shops, our wealth is managed by banks, our conversations are often electronic, our medicines are issues by doctors and the way we raise our children is directed by tradition and by the school system.

Somewhere, hidden in this life of comfort and dependence, is the true nature of the prison that stops us breaking free and building hugely more nourishing lives for ourselves.

The thing that keeps us stuck and trapped is an attitude. I tend to call it: 'just the way things are'. It's the attitude that most people use, most of the time. You might feel that you hate your job. But doesn't everyone? Always panicked about money or trying to make it from one payslip to another? That's normal, isn't it? Sex is boring or rare? That's just the way things are, right? Feel too shy to speak your truth? Working long, exhausting hours? Enduring fights or persecution at home? That's just the way things are.

In the end, our domesticated minds will turn anything into 'just the way things are'. In the end, it is this human ability to normalize hurtful things that has caused the most suffering in history. It's happening right now. Every day we endure lives that aren't right for us, that don't bring us the full bounty of joy and wonder that is our birth-right. We accept this because we've normalized it. In the same way, we walk past homeless people every day, or we buy products that we know were made by people who are suffering, or we hear the droning of politicians that clearly worsens the suffering of vulnerable people, and we shrug it off.

'Just the way things are' begins early in life. Unless we were incredibly lucky, our parents lived the same way. Confronted with questions that challenge their own 'just the way things are', our parents tended not to know how to handle it. Maybe they distracted us, maybe they gave us the only answers they knew, or maybe they shamed us into silence. As adults, they had learned to stop asking deep questions.

School does its part in teaching you 'just the way things are'. By now you're expected to have stopped asking a lot of the inconvenient questions, and you'll be given good marks for playing by the rules, memorising facts and reproducing them in the right ways. None of this is done maliciously: for the teachers this is also 'just the way things are'. They provide the learning and the structure that shows us how things are, and we enthusiastically join in, enforcing rules and social structures, resorting to bullying and mocking anyone who stands out or who still has a wild, curious edge. You might have been one of the people who failed to learn the rules quickly enough, or you might have been one of those who enforced the social norms. Either way, you learned 'just the way things are' sooner or later.

For most of the rest of our lives, we can have this feeling of being weirdos or outsiders if we continue to ask questions. The French philosopher Albert Camus wrote the book *The Outsider* all about this feeling of not fitting in with the template that society expects of us.

People around us seem to be ok with the way things are, and it doesn't occur to them to wonder if they could be otherwise. Often what's going on under the surface for these people is that they also feel uncomfortable and trapped, but their anger and urge to change has turned inwards, becoming bitterness and resentment towards those who continue to ask, to challenge, to try to find a better life.

So, from within and without, we are encouraged to believe that this is all there is. Maybe you can imagine another life, but it's just a dream. It's just fantasy. Here and now is what's real. We tend to feel free, but this learning goes deep, far deeper than just deciding what to do with our day. It tells us, in subtle ways that we hardly ever notice, how to think, how to feel, what to believe in, what to trust, things that are good and things that are bad.

That's the prison. Anyone in this prison who feels trapped, overwhelmed, disappointed or frustrated has the ability to break free. What holds us back is a deeply ingrained belief that things cannot change. That even trying to change certain things is pointless.

In this book I'll be asking you questions and inviting you to consider things from new perspectives. But more than anything else, this book is about restoring the power that is rightfully yours. Nothing can stop you if you are focused and determined. Whatever it is that you want, you can have, if you are willing to step forwards and do the inner and outer work to make it happen.

What if everything could change? What if your thoughts could change? What if the emotions you feel could be different? What if the way you talk to people and the way they treat you could change? What if you could be doing radically different work that makes you feel good? What if you could connect to people in new ways, transforming your friendships and your relationships? What if sex could be better and more fulfilling than you ever knew? What if you could feel like you're a positive force in the world, that you're part of something significant and important?

What if you could rediscover yourself as a free, wild animal?

Chapter 2: Why are we trapped?

If you spend time with successful entrepreneurs, or successful artists, or indeed anybody who stands out as strong, creative and open-minded, you'll find an entirely different attitude to 'just the way things are'. You'll find a person who has rediscovered much of their wild nature, a person who doesn't allow things to become normal, a person who is always curious, always learning.

Right now you don't need to know how to fully embrace your power, or what to do with it, or even what it really means. At the beginning of your journey of personal awakening, I invite you simply to allow the possibility that if you ever feel trapped, stuck, squashed, frustrated, or unsatisfied, it's because on some level you've chosen to let that happen to you. The choices that we make have consequences. As we'll explore later in this book, power and responsibility go hand-in-hand. You cannot truly have one without the other. If you want to shake up your life and break through into a new way of feeling, being and living, then it begins with looking at the life you have now and saying:

"My choices brought me here, and as long as I continue to choose the things I've always chosen, my life will continue to look the same way."

Deep Joy

Attitude is everything

The word 'success' means different things to different people. For some of us, success might be the outcome of a long-term plan or strategy. Some of us want material wealth and prestige. Some of us would call success a happy family and healthy children. For some people, simply living with peace and happiness would be their idea of being successful.

Whatever it is that you're looking for, success is the result of a process. Things that are worthwhile tend to take time and sustained effort to achieve. Good choices build on good choices, moments build on moments, effort builds on effort until eventually you reach your goal. Like climbing a ladder, each rung is a minor achievement in itself, but success lies at the top.

One thing that tends to hold us back from success, or which convinces us to aim for smaller goals than we're actually capable of, is a lack of consistency in our lives. Life is a complicated and messy business that sometimes knocks us off-course. We lose momentum or become distracted, and this makes it that much harder to set ourselves back on the path to achieve our goals.

The way you feel every day will change, as will the things you think about. If you remember where you were ten years ago and what you were doing, were the same things important to you then as they are now? Your thoughts and emotions will adapt and change over time. So many things influence us: the opinions and attitudes of the people we spend time with; our lifestyle and the shape of our day; the stresses and obligations that we live with; the way we eat and exercise; the beliefs and customs of our culture. Things can happen in your day that that leave you feeling excited and happy, or which leave you exhausted, miserable or feeling negative.

Change is the only sure and constant companion we can expect in our lives. 'This too shall pass', no matter what 'this' is. A good feeling or a bad one. A friendship or relationship. Our health. Our very lives. Everything that has a beginning has an end.

Throughout our lives we develop experience and skills. For example, if you start a new job you might feel clumsy, confused or overwhelmed by all the new things you're expected to do. But within a short time you'll learn and develop competence, efficiency and skill. One of the most common things that holds people in careers that no long satisfy them is how comfortable they've become with their expertise in very specific tasks. If I feel really good at what I do, even if it's not what I really want to be doing with my time, it's tempting to stay and enjoy my hard-won expertise.

We can apply the same logic to other things. We get to know a partner really well, so that we anticipate their words and moods. We synchronize our lives with theirs. Long after the relationship has ceased to be fulfilling and nourishing, we don't want to make any changes because it's familiar and comfortable. We do the same with friends, with how we treat ourselves, or with our daily routines.

Expertise in things we know well and do often will tend to look a lot like general expertise. What I mean is that if you know your daily routine very well, doing each task effortlessly, from making breakfast to getting ready to leave the house to doing your job well, all the way through to your bedtime routine, you will look and feel very competent indeed. You're the master of your world. You do things quickly and efficiently, even if they're complicated and difficult tasks. You make tens of thousands of individual decisions every day and, in general, you handle them very well. They're so familiar that you can make decisions quickly and without a second thought.

Our culture encourages us towards efficiency and routine. There is so much to do, and if you want time to relax at the end of the day then you have to be pretty organized in completing the tasks of the day. Your boss will praise you or promote you, if you demonstrate efficiency and smooth competence at work. If you want to meet with your friends at the weekend, then you're going to need to balance your diary. Our lives tend to be structured, organized, measured and calendarized. We tend to know what we need to do, and how to do it, and how to do it quickly, efficiently and properly.

This is a significant problem for those of us who want to change something important in our lives.

Attitude

Søren Kierkegaard was a philosopher in Denmark in the 19th Century. He liked to say that most people live like a drunken peasant on a cart, mostly asleep, letting the donkey wander where it will. Unless we have done some personal development work and made some serious commitments, we tend to meander from place to place, buffeted by life, unaware of where we're going and unconscious of our power to direct our lives. Even those of us who try to make resolutions and positive decisions can easily find ourselves knocked off centre again.

Kierkegaard encouraged his readers to dedicate their lives to something, to become focused on an overall goal or mission. He said that that life can be *intentional* rather than accidental. Plato, one of the biggest names in the whole of philosophy and wisdom, said that an unreflected life is not worth living.

The attitude that I'm going to offer you in this book is contained in the 12 Principles of Deep Coaching. It includes these concepts:

- Personal power – the idea that we can and should approach our lives with the knowledge that we can choose the shape our life takes
- Personal responsibility – all of our choices have consequences and we cannot truly claim our personal power without also owning the results of the things we choose
- Growth into true adulthood – the distinction between child and adult life and the determination to manifest an adult self
- Letting go of unhelpful attachments – not waiting for somebody or something else to save us or empower us, but taking the initiative to empower ourselves

But at its heart, the attitude of Deep Coaching holds two core values: determination and curiosity.

Determination

In her inspiring poem, 'The Invitation', Oriah Mountain Dreamer says:

I want to know if you can live with failure, yours and mine, and still stand at the edge of the lake and shout to the silver of the full moon, 'Yes.'

It doesn't interest me to know where you live or how much money you have. I want to know if you can get up after the night of grief and despair, weary and bruised to the bone and do what needs to be done to feed the children.

When the wellbeing of our children is at stake, we get up and do what's necessary. It's a matter of priority. When something utterly precious to you is in danger, you keep moving. There isn't any question about it. You enter a different mindset, where our personal hurts and limitations simply aren't as important as the task at hand. No matter how bruised you might be, even though you know that you won't show up at your best, even though you know you're bound to make mistakes, you adopt that simple resolution to keep moving. There is no other possibility.

On days when you feel good, energised, inspired or happy, be determined to apply yourself fully to the challenges of your life. Let your energy flow into your actions and let your choices be positive ones that build towards the life you want. Use this time to plan, to vision the life you want to build, to dream and to get excited about possibilities that might exist for you.

On days when you have less energy, or when you feel overwhelmed, unsteady or filled with doubt, be determined to do what you can. Even if they are very small, take positive steps and make positive choices. The size of the step is not the most important thing. What's important is that you begin to manifest in your life a potent and unrelenting determination to reach your goals. Momentum is important, so keep it pointed in a direction that's positive for you.

It is not a matter of 'if'. It is simply a matter of 'when'.

Or in the words of master Yoda: "Do, or do not. There is no try."

Curiosity

The attitude of Deep Coaching is unusual because it joins the ferocity of a determined spirit with a kind of playfulness and a light touch. Happiness and lightness of spirit are powerful life skills, and to be gently curious about anything and everything lends us that lightness. Genuine curiosity says: I want to know more. I want to investigate and play with this thing, and I'm not really attached to the outcome. I just want to understand.

The French philosopher Paul Ricoeur suggested something called the Second Naivety.

In our youth, we are genuinely naïve. We don't know how the world works, so we're curious about everything.

Then we gain knowledge and we believe we know how the world works. Often, people will get very attached to their knowledge and become rigid, stuffy and lose their sense of wonder or appreciation for the mysteries and miracles that are happening around them all the time. Life for these people becomes a dry and lifeless place.

So we have the option of evolving to a more engaged state. We can choose to maintain the knowledge that we've gained, but to re-learn the curiosity and wonder that we had as children. In this state we find ourselves much more emotionally present and more appreciative of simple things. We're also much more likely to learn. We relinquish our attachment to our hard-won expertise and the single perspective that we've developed, and we welcome information and learning from every possible source.

We become a more flexible, adaptable person by embracing a curiosity about life, and we end up stronger and more successful as a result.

Our determination keeps us grounded in our personal values and priorities and keeps us steadily and relentlessly moving in a positive direction.

Our curiosity ensures that we don't take ourselves too seriously, and are always open to learning and growing.

Know thyself

One thing I've learned in my years of studying psychology, motivation and philosophy is that we humans are much more complex and nuanced than we tend to realise. I've helped so many people break out of frustrating, unhappy lives into effortless creativity, confidence and fulfilment. When this happens, things become easy and simple. But getting there often requires learning a lot of things about who and what we are, and unlearning a lot of bad lessons.

Our culture is not designed to help us understand ourselves.

A word about gender

I'm going to talk about gender quite a lot throughout this book. The very idea of gender is an important conversation at the time I am writing this book. The rights and identities of people who identify on a broad spectrum of definitions of gender, and people who reject notions of gender altogether, are a significant challenge for our culture. In some parts of the world, people who are exploring this question are subject to fear, persecution or violence. Even in the West, there is a lot of intolerance towards anyone who feels that they need to explore their own gender identity.

If you're navigating this challenge yourself, I want you to know that when I'm talking about gender, I am not dictating to you how you should be or what you will find when you explore yourself.

However, whether we see gender as a biological thing or whether it's simply something deeply ingrained in our society, stories, myths, language, education, and cultural identity, it is a fundamental building block for people's identity, in one way or another. I will be using a lot of language about masculine, feminine, male and female in this book.

Deep Joy

The modern human is a highly-strung, often-stressed animal. In a search for identity and belonging, we encourage those around us to behave themselves in all sorts of subtle ways. This leads to predictable people who don't cause us further stress and worry. As soon as you understand the masks you wear in order to keep yourself and others in safe, predictable boxes, you will become free and powerful, and this is going to be alarming to those who are not free and powerful. What we tend to do instead is make a deal with each other. It's better, we say to each other, to have a shared status quo, a world of people wearing masks and following pre-defining patterns of words, choices and behaviour. We all know where we stand and we are not disturbed. In my experience, this shared reality came about because of all the things we fear to meet if we stop wearing our masks. So we all walk around, trapped in simplified, limited versions of ourselves that we've been taught our whole lives. We did this to ourselves, and we continue to do it to ourselves every day. We create for ourselves a restricted, truncated, stunted, constrained version of who we could be. We do this from a deep need to be loved.

To wear a mask is normal, and if I am normal then perhaps I will be accepted and loved.

Unfortunately, it's an illusion. Throughout our lives we find moments of clarity where we're shown the bizarre nature of the masks we wear. Sometimes these moments are brief: an overheard conversation, a moment of seeing people living another way. Sometimes they come about through times of trauma or moments of bliss (which I call 'peak experiences'). But, tragically, it's most often found at the very end of life. The profound trauma and dread as we approach death is, in fact, the unveiling of a lifelong need: the need to exist, to be our true selves, to truly exist in a moment, a place, amongst a people who love and accept us for who we really are.

We are all naturally drawn to undertake a journey of personal awakening. The very fact that we have to make time for this work, separate from our employment and daily life shows just how profoundly our culture fails to meet our most fundamental needs.

The beginning is awareness and understanding about the self. Without knowing what you are, you won't know how to bring yourself into the world in ways that truly nourish you. You'll keep feeling held back by the limitations that have always blocked your growth. Individually and collectively we will continue to re-enact the cycles of our past.

We carry intrinsic, inescapable needs that yearn to be met. I'll be naming some of them later in this book. We can either do this consciously, with awareness and understanding, or we can ignore them. But either way, our needs will find ways to be satisfied. Our fundamental needs exert a lot of pressure on our choices, pushing us to make decisions that are more likely to get those needs met. If we continue to resist, they might compel us to do things that will hurt us or hurt the world around us until we recognise what they want from us and then actively take control. Without this level of control we end up flailing about, often without noticing, desperately trying to feel ok, pulled and pushed by motivations we don't quite understand.

There is a kind of joy that can only be known by those who have done this work. A feeling of fierce and powerful aliveness and presence, a certainty of purpose, a deep joy and a series of heartfelt connections with other people, with the place where we belong, with the purpose to which we feel called and to which we have dedicated out lives. A freedom, a focus, a sense of being awake and aware. The relaxation and calm that comes from being only who we truly are. Delight from simple things.

Self-image

Self-image is a thing that you already have. For many of us, it's a deeply precious thing that we work hard to maintain and protect.

Self-image is the person you think you are. It is the image you have of yourself in your mind, in your feelings and in your body. It is the person you believe that you are, that you feel you are, that you know you are.

You say to yourself: I know who I am because recognise these things about myself. It's how I know who I am.

I do these things, I believe these things, I talk like this, I can do these things, these are my limitations.

Self-image is your idea of who and what you are. It may be completely wrong.

The building blocks of self-image

This idea of self-image is build from a lot of things.

For example, your memories and experiences form part of your idea of who you are. You draw on all the moments of joy, pain, triumph, failure, disappointment, satisfaction, gladness and desolation that you've lived. Your memories are part of how you define who you are. You remember how you handled situations, how you reacted, what happened to you, and this informs who you believe yourself to be.

Self-image also comes from how you currently relate to people around you. Are you the kind of person who, when arriving in a room full of people, will feel excited to go around shaking hands, exchanging names, making new connections? Or does this situation make you tremble or feel uncomfortable? Do you put huge effort into just a few, precious relationships or do you get happiness and satisfaction from knowing a wide range of people who you prefer to keep at a bit of a distance? Perhaps a bit of both? When intimate with someone, do you want to throw yourself in deep, becoming an open book, sharing all that you are, or do you prefer to keep a part of yourself withheld and just for yourself? These kinds of instincts in relationships are part of the way you identify yourself.

The person you imagine yourself to be is also defined by the work you do, how you do it, and how you are regarded in the eyes of society at large. You define yourself this way. Do you earn well, in a job that brings you respect and approval? Do you work hard, gaining satisfaction from the quality of your work? Is work a secondary thing for you, just a thing that has to be done in order to pay the bills? Do you avoid work entirely? Are you prevented from working by something? Do you do something else with your time, which you struggle to label as 'work'? Do you see yourself as a success or a failure? What would other people say?

Another thing that informs your self-image is the things you think of yourself as skilled or unskilled at. From baking to driving, from making coffee to making conversation, from dancing to painting, from IT to gardening, from meticulous planning to the ability to truly and deeply let go and relax. There are so many things that you might believe you're good at, and so many that you probably believe you do badly. These beliefs all contribute to our image of ourselves.

You receive aspects of your self-image from your culture. We think of ourselves as coming from a country, with certain laws, traditions, customs and language. We will tend towards a certain view of the world, of history, of believing people from other countries, languages and traditions are better or worse than we are. People from the same culture tend to dress similarly, tend to display wealth and prosperity in certain ways and tend to have similar ideas about education, how politics should work, how human beings should relate to the natural world. We might be very proud of our country or feel ashamed of the way it behaves. We might work hard to fit in with rules and expectations or we might try to break them. Whatever your relationship with the culture around you, it will feed into how you think and feel about who you are.

Self-image is physically embodied as well. The way you hold yourself when you walk and stand, your body language during conversations, the way you breathe, where and how you hold tension in your body. Do you see yourself as graceful and aware of your body, or is your body just a clumsy thing that carries your consciousness around? Do you tend to breathe in short, shallow gasps, or do you breathe fully into the whole of your lungs with slow and purposeful breaths?

These are just some examples of things that contribute to your sense of who you are.

The crucial thing to understand about self-image is that it's not who you are. It's who you think you are.

You will have a mental picture of yourself as someone who does some things, doesn't do other things, speaks in a certain way, thinks in a certain way, breathes in a certain way. This is a deeper level of the 'just the way things are' story from chapter two.

A vital step in coming home to the person you were meant to be is to begin discovering your own authentic self-image. Abandoning labels and images that you've been given and searching for your own idea of who you are. This will allow you to begin unlocking your awareness of your genuine self.

This curiosity and willingness will open up the opportunity for you to change your self-image, and thus redefine the limits of what you can achieve.

This chapter is about exploring the levels and aspects of who and what we are. I want to offer you a model of the human person that will give you ideas and inspiration to deepen and broaden your search for your own identity. It's not going to deliver your true identity to you, because your answers are unique to you and you will find them through your own inner work. We'll be doing a lot of that work in Part 2 of this book. But I've learned that people are people, and there are a lot of things that we all share, simply by virtue of having bodies, being human and growing up with shared cultural stories. In this chapter I'll unpack some important distinctions and establish a language that we can use for the rest of the journey that we're going to take together.

Compassionate non-judgement

In this journey of empowerment and awakening, we're going to meet uncomfortable or challenging things. There are always parts of us that we'd rather not look at, things that we've done that we feel ashamed of, things that we find unacceptable but which exist deep within us. Everybody has this. Over the course of this book we'll examine why, but I just want to offer you some reassurance that if this happens for you, it's not a bad sign. It's entirely normal.

Equally, there are things we are very fond of in ourselves. Maybe you're particularly gifted at something, or perhaps you're very proud of a certain thing that you do. It can be very tempting to look at these things for a long time and just bask in the feeling of pride. That's not a bad thing, but it can stop us from wanting to dig deeper into the whys and the underpinning truths. I'm going to be inviting you to dig deep during our journey together. We're looking for a radical honesty with ourselves.

Other things inside us might be boring, frustrating, frightening, painful or feel dangerous or reckless.

The skill that we all need to develop in order to safely do this inner work, is the skill of compassionate non-judgement. This skill also tends to dramatically improve our relationships with others. I'll be offering you ideas and resources to develop your own sense of compassionate non-judgement.

We are explorers in an inner landscape, and as explorers we don't judge what we find. We simply observe and understand. The best attitude to adopt in this work is one of compassion. If I learn that a part of me is petty, or selfish, or wants to hurt other people, then I regard that part of myself with compassion and just seek to understand it. I don't label it as good or bad, because I know that any labels are going to limit my ability to understand. Things within ourselves are neither positive or negative: it's their effects and the actions that they lead us to perform that we must learn to control, and our self-control will grow with our knowledge. What lies beneath simply is.

Similarly, if I notice parts of myself that are beautiful, courageous, graceful or noble, then I regard them with exactly the same kind of non-judgemental compassion. I cultivate a deep curiosity about the whole of myself, from the very 'best' parts to the very 'worst' parts. This complex and multi-faceted being is who I am, and judging or suppressing parts of who I am does not stop them being true. It just limits my ability to learn.

Later in this book we'll look at what we're going to *do* with all this stuff that we find. For now, we are simply exploring and trying to understand. I believe, having spent hundreds of hours of my life with people exploring this landscape, that our deepest and most fundamental motivations are basically good, and that the negative and harmful things that we find within ourselves are all attempts to meet forgotten or neglected needs, where the attempts have gone wrong somehow. So I invite you to trust that your inner landscape rests on healthy foundations, and that underneath things that might be uncomfortable or difficult, even frightening, we will find beautiful and good roots.

I want to add that nothing in this book should be taken as judgement upon you. I offer you the same kind of compassionate non-judgement that I encourage you to offer yourself. I will be showing you things that might be challenging or emotionally triggering, but these too are delivered without judgement.

The tree of self

We exist on many levels. When I choose to do something, or when I do something without noticing, there will have been a reason for it. We do nothing without a reason, even if that reason is as simple as: I scratched because I had an itch. Some of our reasons don't even exist any more: something was right for us once, and we keep responding in the same way. But each time we recycle choices which have ceased to be relevant for us, we have the option to choose to do something else instead. Everything is choice: some part of us chose to say that word, or perform that action, or think that thought, or make that choice.

However, some motivations sit closer the surface than others. Some impulses are shallow and we tend to be pretty aware of them. When we take the time to examine these motivations, we tend to find that they sit upon other, deeper and more fundamental ones. Often, these sit upon deeper still and more profound reasons.

As an example, I'm going to look at the choice to make an effort to look nice. One day, I choose to wear nice clothes, take care with my personal grooming, get a nice haircut. It's something we all do sometimes – some of us do it more often than others. But it takes effort: it's an active choice.

The obvious surface motivations are that it feels good, and I like the responses I get from others. People might comment on the way I look. I catch a glimpse of myself in the mirror and I like what I see. Perhaps somebody is attracted to the way I look and a new connection is formed that brings all kinds of possibilities with it. By taking this action, I get a range of positive, warming sensations which all came about because I made a certain choice. I hoped these things would happen, which is why I made the choice I did.

But is that it? Does that tell us everything about the reason I choose to make an effort with my appearance?

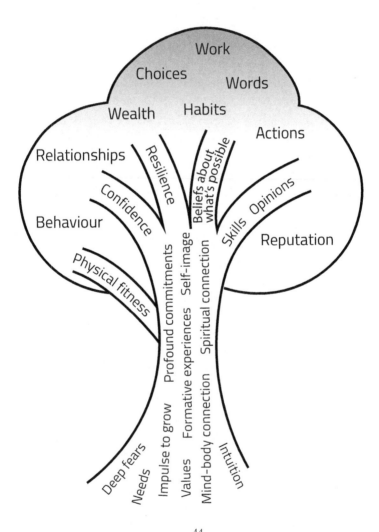

Chapter 4: Know thyself

I like to think of the image of a tree. At first we notice the branches of this tree. In this example our branches are called positive self-regard, words of affirmation from others, and possibilities for intimacy and connection. Those are the reasons for the choices I've made.

The branches of a tree are supported by its limbs, boughs and trunk, and the same goes for our motivations. Under every surface impulse are deeper reasons. The deeper we understand our reasons for doing things, the more awareness we have of ourselves and the more power we have to change. If we've been stuck in patterns of behaviour for our whole lives then it will take some courageous, deep searching to uncover why, and then choose to do something different.

We've identified the surface motivations in our example of choosing to make an effort with appearance, so what do they rest upon? What deeper reasons hold the branches of positive self-regard, words of affirmation and intimacy?

It may be that I am masking my insecurities. I may carry a sense of shame or a dislike of myself, and it's important for me to make an effort to mask this. Perhaps I believe that my ability to succeed in the ways that are important for me depends on the way I look. Maybe my parents drilled into me the importance of appearance based on their own experiences or insecurities, and I've just carried their priorities through my life. Maybe I was shamed or attacked once for not looking right, so I dress carefully to avoid more conflict or shame. What if there's somebody in particular that I want to impress? Or perhaps I am trying to shore up a certain kind of prestige or model of success: people who succeed dress like this, don't they? When I'm stressed and struggling, looking nice might be the only way I have to reassure myself that I'm doing well. It could be that I don't even notice the clothes I wear, and I'm confused or annoyed that people respond to me differently depending on how I look. It could even be that I don't get to choose what I wear: perhaps work or my situation in life dictates the way I dress, and that leaves me feeling in a certain way.

These are just some possibilities that exist for this one choice.

Judgement and self-deceit

Often, self-image will be deeply cherished. It can feel very important to know who we are, to know what we're good and bad at, to know how we relate to people and how people see us. Even if we believe that we're incompetent, or bad, or a failure, or some other negative thing, it's still basically comfortable. We know where we stand.

We're heavily invested in these ideas of ourselves and our place in the world. It gives us security and reassurance. Often, we will have invested so much time, energy and intention in fighting to protect this version of ourselves. We don't want all that energy to have been a waste!

It's understandable that we might work hard to protect our sense of self-image. Many people go to great lengths to protect themselves from being challenged in their beliefs about themselves. Perhaps they immediately reject somebody's ideas if they don't fit how they see themselves. Perhaps they only spend time with a certain kind of person, or go to places that feel familiar. Perhaps they avoid using their bodies in new ways, and would reject an invitation to a gym, a dance class, a meditation retreat or a martial arts hall. Perhaps they judge people who dress differently. Perhaps they only spend time with people of a similar age group or political persuasion.

We get settled into patterns of behaviour very easily. It's the 'just the way things are' story again. We will often fight fiercely to protect our ideas about ourselves. Here are some of the things we say to fend off suggestions that we might loosen our grip on a fixed idea of who we are:

'I'm just not like that!'
'I don't do things like that!'
'I'm too shy for that.'
'I'm too good for that.'
'What a stupid thing for somebody to do.'
'Oh I could never do that!'
'I just don't have the time.'
'Well that's fine for some people but it's not right for me!'

Judgement is the ultimate defence against a challenge to self-image. We can become so attached to our ideas about who we are that we feel we need to attack those who are different, to prove to ourselves and other that we aren't like them. This need to judge people, to categorize them in broad and sweeping ways that erase individuality and turn complex and interesting people into just a member of a group, is a demonstration of basic insecurity. The weaker and less explored your self-image, the more likely you are to be judgemental. Something challenges an aspect of our self-image, and we fear its loss, so we remove the challenge by turning the person saying it into something non-human, something easily dismissed. We might groups them as 'idiots', 'fools', 'posh people', 'rich, privileged people', 'hippies' or 'drop-outs'. We might judge them as much less intelligent than we are. We might judge them as failures, or people who have made stupid mistakes in their lives. They might be the wrong religion, the wrong class, the wrong colour, the wrong political affiliation or the wrong sexuality. Whatever we decide they are, we stop them being a challenge to the nice, reassuring things we believe about ourselves by removing their humanity and assigning them a label instead.

We might also go to great lengths to deceive ourselves, to build up a self-image that has very little to do with reality. Are you really as smart, skilled and competent as you think you are? Or perhaps you think the opposite: are you really as stupid, as unskilled and as incompetent as you think you are?

One of the core messages of this book is that self-image can change. You do not have to be who you have always been. But more than that: holding tightly to a fixed idea of who you are will stifle your growth and will encourage you to judge others and miss out on great opportunities.

I invite you to treat the person you think you are as an idea. Hold it lightly. Investigate it. Allow yourself to be surprised. Be willing to confront the parts of yourself that have stagnated or held you back. For some people in our culture, there's an illusion that it's a virtue to be stubborn, unyielding and unwilling to change. In my experience, the opposite it true. A person who is strong and successful, who is real and present and dependable, is somebody who is able to shift and change over time. They have become conscious and aware of who they truly are through a programme of challenging inner and outer growth. But they are always willing to learn more, to discover that they were wrong about themselves, and to make changes in the light of new information.

This is true strength.

The three paths on the one journey

There are three paths that you will need to walk on your journey of awakening and empowerment: Being (your inner development), Doing (the effect you have on the world) and Relating (how you relate to other living beings).

Uncovering your current self-image (the person you think you are) will involve exploring all three paths. In this chapter I'll be looking at the inner aspects of your self but we'll come back to self-image throughout this book, and we'll look at how Doing and Relating contribute to who we think we are. For now, here are some simple ideas of things from the Doing and Relating paths that go into self-image:

The outer path:

- The work you do
- Your hobbies and how much energy you devote to them
- How you relax, how often you rest
- Your exercise routine
- The things you own, collect, accrue and how you use them.
- Your car
- Your home
- Your daily routine, like the route you take to work
- Your holidays

The path of relating:

- Your intimate partner
- The rituals of love that exist in your relationship(s)
- The depth of your trust and vulnerability with others
- The way you are intimate
- The way you are romantic
- How you interpret and expect love
- The friends you have, how often you connect with them and what these relationships are like
- The levels of contact and sharing that exist throughout your life

Inner aspects of self

The rest of this chapter will set out a common language for us to speak about aspects and areas of ourselves. Each of these areas offer you new opportunities for discovery, awakening and personal growth. Some people find one aspect so compelling, or so in need of their attentions, that they'll dedicate their entire lives to its study. But more often, we each need to delve a little into each aspect of ourselves. I have never met anyone who did not need to explore each aspect below, at least a little. There are certain signs that you are called to delve into a particular aspect of your self. As you read, observe your own responses. Practice the compassionate non-judgment that we've spoken about. Watch out for feelings of annoyance, boredom, anger, discomfort, inadequacy, yearning, fascination or excitement. Any of these might be a sign that you are called to explore this aspect of yourself more fully.

Language is very important. Since humans began using it to structure the way we think, our thoughts and intentions have been bound up with the meaning of the words we use. A subtle difference in the way that we speak about ourselves can transform the way that we feel and the way we appear to others. Confusion, conflict and poisoned relationships arise from the wrong words. So at the beginning of this journey together, I will lay out some language that we can be sure we both understand.

Mind

Depending on where you grew up, you'll understand your mind in completely different ways. Eastern religions, particularly Buddhism, have a very different understanding of the mind from the one we have in Western countries. If you'd grown up in certain parts of India, Nepal, Tibet or Thailand, your 'just the way things are' would include a radically different experience of mind. Buddhism can reasonably be called a two-and-a-half-thousand-year-old scientific enquiry into the nature of the mind. Unfortunately, in the West we tend to enshrine the mind as a thing of great value without really trying to understand it. We confuse the mind with the brain, and we confuse the mind with consciousness. *Thinking about* something is often confused with *being* something.

An old teacher of mine, a Buddhist who had dedicated his life to travel and to meditation, studying with gurus in India and Tibet, would refer to the mind as a 'repeating engine'. The mind is something that repeats things it's already learned. In the minds of many people there is a constant babble and chatter which is made up of old conversations, old ideas, old memories or parts of songs. This chatter is so normal to us that we barely notice it most of the time. In busy lives spent in busy towns and cities, there is almost always noise going on and we mirror this with our internal noise.

In my experience, and in the experience of everyone I've met who has explored their own relationship to their mind, the mind is the part of us that thinks things through, that orders and aligns the world to make sense to us, that makes plans and lists, that imagines future scenarios, that uses logic, that solves problems. It is a complex, organic calculator that uses information we've learned and retained in order to solve the problems that we meet. The mind is not the brain. Modern science has shown that the brain is probably the organ that gives rise to most aspects of the mind, but the mind is a thing we experience. I feel my mind, I do not feel my brain. That said, there are a lot of features of the brain that carry over into the nature of mind. For example, the brain tends to form pathways, which it strengthens over time if it uses those pathways a lot, like a worn path that becomes a road that becomes a highway as it used more and more. These become the most efficient routes between two places: well-worn and neurologically developed. So it is with the mind. When we become used to thinking in certain ways, we tend towards repeating those thoughts again. The mind likes to repeat things, and only with sustained effort to shift our thinking to a new place will we let go of our old patterns of thought.

As far as personal development and awakening are concerned, the most important things to know about the mind are:

- thinking is addictive, and
- we are not our minds.

A meaningless babble goes on in the mind a lot of the time. Generally, we don't notice it. But if you've ever tried to clear your mind after a busy or stressful day, you'll notice how loud the babble has become. We tend to get attached to these thoughts and pay them a lot of attention, and we tend to take them very seriously. We play along with the memories and join in the conversations. We talk to ourselves. We can become just as emotionally triggered by an old conversation or an imagined situation in the future as we can from a real situation. For anybody who struggles with anxiety, you'll know the dread of something that hasn't even happened yet, and might never happen. But none of this exists, here and now. We only truly exist in a single moment that we call 'now'. That is the most real thing we can experience. Why is it, then, that we can find things in the mind impact us so strongly?

We'll be focusing a lot in this book on the toxic nature of modern culture. One way that it hurts us is by massively over-inflating the value of the mind. Remember that the mind is just a repeating, planning, thinking engine. Very useful for problem solving, but that's all that it does. There is an old phrase: "to a man with a hammer, everything looks like a nail". In a thinking-addicted culture, everything looks like a problem to solve. We have developed jobs, entertainment, an education system and a language that is heavily skewed towards using the mind. Our money and wealth are ideas far more than they are tangible things. This is a major reason why we cause so much harm to the natural world that we depend on for our lives: we are not really here! We are not rooted in the moment, connected with the living world and with one another. We are not feeling, experiencing or being. We are away in our minds, chasing a thought, a memory or an imagined future. We think, we plan, we remember, we fantasize.

Thinking is addictive, and if you were brought up in addiction and if you've never known anything else, it's hard work to shake the habit. Somebody asks you to plan something at work: you need to think. You want to socialize with your friends so you go to see a movie: you're taken out of your body into a fantasy of the mind. Entire relationships can be spent between two people who barely notice each other, but are caught up in their imagination about what's actually happening in the relationship. Old friends meet and repeat the same ideas at each other. We tend to wake up thinking, spend most of the day in the mind, and unwind at the end of the day by doing mind-led things.

This has become so ubiquitous and so normalised that we rarely stop to notice that we are not actually our minds. The mind is a thing that you have. A very useful, very distracting aspect of self which wants to snare your attention. The mind is jealous of your attention and wants to keep as much of it as possible. So the boundaries between consciousness and mind are forgotten or ignored. The 'I', the part of us that exists in the moment and oversees our whole selves, is drowned out by the babble of the mind.

In the 16th Century, René Descartes wrote "I think, therefore I am". He was talking about what we can prove and what we can be sure of. So much of what we believe or experience cannot be *proven* to exist, but one thing must be true: in order for somebody to wonder if the world exists, in order for there to be a consciousness capable of asking any of these questions or observing anything at all, there must be an 'I'. If I am having thoughts, I must exist. Hence: I think, therefore I am.

But it seems to me that there's a problem with this phrase. Descartes' famous phrase only exists if you believe you are your mind. If he'd been able to spend some time with a Tibetan Buddhist of his time, already far more advanced in the science of the mind, he might have written his most famous phrase differently. He might have written 'I observe, therefore I am.'

He might even have written, 'I think, therefore I am not.'

We tend to confuse the 'I', the conscious awareness that allows us to perceive anything at all, with the mind.

At this point, at the boundary between thinking and being, language begins to fail us because language is a construct of the mind. Thankfully, the tools that allow us to directly witness the difference between mind and consciousness are becoming very popular and easily accessible.

Your own exploration

The scientific study of mind, passed down to us through the Buddhist tradition, has given us a process to be able to observe our own minds without attaching to the thoughts and losing our identity once more amid its babble. This tool is called meditation.

There are dozens of kinds of meditation and each tries to achieve something different. Some are reflections on a certain topic, like the Sufi Muraqabah. Some are mystical rituals that try to access things normally hidden from us. Buddhism itself is fragmented into many branches and traditions, from the semi-magical traditions of Tibet to the ascetic traditions of Zen. The problem is that all of these approaches to meditation carry a set of beliefs and values with them. They carry with them the expectation that you are going to buy-in to a belief structure.

There is value to this, but here we are trying to understand the nature of the mind and begin teasing apart the conscious self from the thinking self. So I tend to recommend a modern tradition called Mindfulness, which one meditation master I learned from called "Buddhist practice without the Buddhism" or "Buddhism Lite". Mindful meditation is becoming very popular. You will probably find a local Mindfulness group or class, you can find Mindful meditations available online and there are free apps that you can download. Some businesses bring in Mindfulness experts or teachers to support their staff.

We'll look at Mindfulness in more detail later in this book, but it's so easily accessed that you can start exploring it as soon as you want. It uses simple techniques like body scanning and listening to the breath to lure your conscious attention away from its fascination with the mind. Given enough time and a sustained, determined practice you'll begin to notice how separate the mind is from the part of you that's doing the observing. This is, for many people, a transformational awakening in itself, and it opens up many possibilities.

In order to discover the nature of 'I', the core self that sits at the heart of the kaleidoscope that is you, you will need to relinquish attachment to the idea that you are your mind. This can only be done through experience, and Mindfulness meditation is the best experience I know to allow you to learn about the nature of mind. It may not happen quickly – the greatest benefits of Mindfulness happen over time. If you haven't already, I invite you to explore the nature of mind by committing to a regular Mindfulness practice.

Emotion

Emotion is utterly separate from mind. Where mind is a repeating engine and a mechanism that is removed from the here-and-now, emotions exist in the present moment. While philosophers, psychologists and neuroscientists have been writing about how we feel for a long time, they've generally done it from the perspective of a thought-addicted culture. For this reason, several things have confused our exploration of the nature of emotion. The first is a very old prejudice around gender. In our culture, women are believed to be emotional where men are rational. Second, and linked to the first, is the idea that thinking is superior to feeling. These two prejudices work together to create a lot of judgements around gender and emotion: women are irrational; men should be emotionless; emotional people are stupid and useless; emotionless people are intelligent and reliable. If you listen carefully, you'll hear these prejudices behind all sorts of things that people say.

Beliefs like this grow out of confusion and fear. Most women who enquire into the sacred basis of their menstrual cycles will come to understand that yes, at certain times of the month they will tend towards stronger emotions of one kind or another. This is a fairly predictable pattern and grants women an insight and perspective that men can struggle to reach. But this kind of insight has generally been lost and is only now being rediscovered through things like the Red Tent movement and the political awakening of Menstruality. Tragically, many girls and women in our culture continue to be taught to consider their monthly cycles as annoying, debilitating, messy and useless. Medication now exists to eliminate the cycle altogether, allowing a woman to be a bit more like a man. A bit more rational. A bit less silly and unpredictable.

Men are equally afflicted by outdated patriarchal ideas of the rational, emotionless ideal. We'll be looking at this in more detail in Part 2 of this book. Men are expected to be 'blokes', to be tough, to be practical, to be stable and rational and certainly not to be emotional. Boys are told that boys don't cry. Men who are emotional tend to be shamed and mocked for it, and in their unfamiliarity with emotion they'll tend to use the only approach to emotion that they've seen, which tends to be from a female role model. Thus we saw the emergence of the 'new man' in the last decades of the 20th Century: a man who is very emotional, very empathetic, but one with little resilience or fire.

Our mind-addicted culture, caught up in thoughts and plans that don't exist here and now, does terrible damage to the natural world. Mountains levelled for the minerals they contain. Rivers polluted. Ecosystems ravaged. Entire species exterminated. Islands of plastic floating in the oceans. Rising global temperatures that threaten runaway destruction. Realistic projections are forecasting a very difficult future for our children. This is the final result of a culture that thinks rather than exists. Emotions are a way back to sanity. So I invite you to leave behind your preconceptions about emotions. They have been badly misrepresented.

Emotions are messengers from deep and wise aspects of ourselves. They are at once fairly simplistic, and possessed of a great deal of information. Each emotion exists to serve you in a specific way, to bring your attention to something that's happening, to restore some imbalance in your life.

They are simplistic because they simply do what they do. They are not malleable in the way thoughts are, we cannot mould them into convenient shapes because we don't like the shape they already have. Anger feels like anger, fear will always feel the way fear feels and happiness will continue to feel happy no matter what you do. Situations happen, and when we don't meet those situations from our deepest awareness and with profound wisdom, our emotions respond to help us. Nobody has the awareness to always respond perfectly to every situation, so the flow of emotions within us act like guardians and helpers to bring us back to the moment and attend to it properly.

Emotions are not always convenient or well behaved. If we are living in ways that don't fulfil all our needs, our emotions will remind us about this regularly. If we make choices that are harmful, or which don't honour the true being that we are, our emotions might be chaotic and confusing, as each feeling tries to respond to some aspect of our bad decisions. If you find your feelings confusing, uncomfortable or baffling, I strongly encourage you to begin learning to listen out for what they're telling you. For many of my coaching clients, learning the messages carried by their emotions was the most radically freeing and exciting thing they'd ever done. It all finally made sense, and guided by the wisdom of their emotions they naturally began living more empowered, happier, calmer lives.

Emotions bring us the skill of empathy. Where mind fails to understand another person, empathy connects us. Where words are clumsy and wrong, empathy communicates without language. Through empathy we come to know another person in a deep and compassionate way without knowing specific facts about them. When I see a person who is suffering, and I allow myself to connect empathetically, I am with them in their suffering. From this place I will relate to them with far more skill and kindness than I would by merely observing their struggle. With a connection of empathy, we allow emotions to flow, to be witnessed, to be grounded, and to be released.

Emotions are supposed to flow into our lives, share their message, be recognised and understood, and then flow on, leaving us calm.

Emotions are profoundly wise because they are constantly offering us information that will drop us more deeply into the present moment. Karla McLaren, author and teacher, is a world-renowned expert on the subject of emotions. Her book, *The Language of Emotions*, is a practical guide to the origin, nature and function of each major emotion, and of developing skills in emotional awareness and empathy. I have used her ideas with men to help them break out of the emotional straight-jacket that our culture puts on men, and with women to legitimize the role of emotion in living, learning and healing, restoring it from the cultural judgements of silliness, confusion or irrelevance.

Further exploration

The work of un-learning old stories about the nature of emotion, and of learning to respect and listen to the messages carried by each emotion, is a massive challenge for most of us, but one that we must each engage with to overcome our personal patterns and to begin making better, more consistent choices in our lives.

I know of no better place to start than Karla McLaren's book *The Language of Emotions*. I also recommend that you begin to observe your language and beliefs around your feelings and the feelings of others. Are you carrying outdated ideas about the value of emotions? Do you judge or mock people for the emotions they feel? Do you judge or persecute yourself when you feel things that are inconvenient?

Body

For a mind-addicted culture, the body is the thing that you see when you look down. There are two functions for the body: to do all the unimportant biological stuff that's necessary so that we can keep thinking; and to carry around the consciousness so we can do all the things that we've thought about. As we've become aware of the obesity epidemic, and of rising levels of certain lifestyle-related diseases, we've realized that we need to put more effort into keeping the body healthy so that it can keep fulfilling its two basic functions. We're also fully aware of good and bad sensations that the body gives the mind to work with. We want more of the good experiences (things like tasty food, nice sensations, sex, the positive feelings when somebody says our body looks nice) and we want less of the bad experiences (physical pain, stiff joints, embarrassment, disease, limited freedom and death). That is about as far as most people's relationship with the body goes.

However, we're becoming aware that the body does its own thinking and has its own consciousness. My body is as much 'me' as my thoughts or feelings are. The body notices and experiences things, which it passes to the mind to reflect on. Some of these things are obvious (it's cold outside today), but some are subtle and packed full of genius (my gut tells me something's wrong here). We tend to associate the mind with the head and the emotions with the heart. But the gut has a lot to tell us, and so does the rest of the remarkable physical organism we live inside.

Our body is a big part of our memory. Whereas the mind can just replay events from the past, the body lives them. The body remembers how to do things that the mind doesn't. The body stores feelings for us. Many emotions have a physical sensation and, often, a location in the body. The body is there with us, experiencing our feelings. The body stores stresses and traumas for us, doing its best to limit their impact on our lives. We might go through a very difficult time, or experience a sudden shock or trauma. Losing somebody we love, or being involved in a car accident or some other sudden physical trauma, or suddenly losing an aspect to our lives that we loved and needed. We need to go on, we need to keep functioning, so the body does its best to help. It holds our hurt and upset, it tries to heal physical wounds, it tries to keep us safe, stable and functioning until the danger or shock passes.

What we find when we begin to explore the nature of the body is an incredibly rich ecosystem and consciousness. For many people, this journey only happens when the body has taken all that it can and begins to break down. It's held memories of trauma for decades, but it just can't go on. Now you feel pain where there hasn't ever been an injury or you find yourself unable to do things you used to do. Maybe a doctor diagnoses you with a serious condition. Maybe you just suddenly find that you have no energy at all. Your body, this remarkable friend who has been with you throughout your whole journey, is asking for your attention and your help. In a culture that's addicted to the mind, where the wisdom, awareness, consciousness and compassion of the body is all but ignored, where the body is only there to serve the needs of the mind, we can be annoyed and baffled when it doesn't do what we tell it to do. But this is an invitation to learn.

Further exploration

The best ways to explore and begin meeting the body are through physical practices. Allow your attention to leave the chatter of the mind and enter the direct physicality of the body as it moves, stretches and works. This can feel scary or embarrassing for people who are used to living in the mind. For other people who more naturally feel at home in the body, it'll be easy. Yoga is perhaps the most obvious way in. Like Buddhism, it is an ancient practice that offers many levels of learning and exploration. I certainly recommend classes over learning by yourself, but any sustained engagement with yoga will help.

Other physical practices that begin to open our awareness of the wisdom of the body include qi gong, older martial arts and dancing. If you have a local 5 Rhythms dance group, this can be a wonderful way to freely express the unique, precious organism of the body.

Be open to leaving your mind behind and connecting with everything your body is and everything it can do.

If you'd like to know more about the nature of trauma and how it's held and stored by the body, I recommend the work of the psychotherapist, Peter Levine. In his book *Waking the Tiger*, Levine talks about how humans evolved into their relationship with trauma, how common misconceptions about trauma leave people feeling powerless about it, and what action we can take to release, shift and ease the impact of physically-held trauma.

It's a remarkable work and I'll be making reference to it a few times in this book.

The unconscious

A great deal goes on inside us that we're either semi-conscious of, or utterly unconscious of. That is, it's *beyond* or inaccessible to our conscious mind, except in extraordinary circumstances. Our hearts beat, our cells divide, our tissues repair and our blood chemistry is carefully regulated. These things aren't within our conscious control. In the same way, we have no awareness at all of the processing that's constantly going on in our unconscious mind. We only become aware that this is going on when it pops up into our consciousness, when it triggers an expected choice of behaviour or when we say something we didn't know we were going to say. Perhaps we wake up with a brilliant answer to a problem that we've been wrestling with. Perhaps our dreams show us images and ideas that we never knew were within us. These are examples of the unconscious making brief contact with the consciousness.

The image I like to use is a boat on a great ocean. This image has been used throughout history: it appears in the writings and poetry of ancient teachers from Greek mythology to Nordic rune lore. The boat is conscious awareness. We can see it, we can steer it, we're aware of it. Beneath us lies the depthless and unknowable ocean, full of wonders and terrors. This is the unconscious.

Marketing executives became very interested in early research into the unconscious in the early 20th Century. They used it, and continue to use it, to manipulate us into buying their products. Our deepest needs, desires, longings, fears and hopes arise from the unconscious and if these are triggered without us realizing, we buy things without noticing that we've been manipulated. Today there is a great deal of money put into things like the layout of supermarkets to ensure that we're encouraged to buy things without noticing. Our voting habits are also manipulated by combining data-mining and analysis with an understanding of the unconscious mind. Whether you know it or not, a lot of money is spent every day to manipulate you into making unconscious choices.

One reason we tend not to notice when our unconscious takes control, for example when we say something we never meant to say or when we buy something because we've been cleverly steered into buying it, is because we really want to believe that we're in control of ourselves. For people brought up in a mind-addicted culture, it can be very uncomfortable to think that conscious, rational thought only makes up a small part of who we are, and that unconscious desires and needs are having a huge impact on our decisions. When we do something that surprises us, or make a choice we don't really understand, or when we're manipulated into believing something, agreeing with something, or voting a certain way, we still want to maintain this illusion that the conscious mind is in control and calling the shots. What we'll do, in fact, is rewrite history. We'll notice something that we don't understand in our own behaviour and we'll quickly invent a reason why we wanted to do that all along. It can be tricky to notice, but if you start looking out for it you might catch yourself rewriting history to ensure you feel like you're in control.

The unconscious is a big part of who we are. It's therefore important that we know it, or at least understand its currents, tides and tempests. You will never fully explore its depths, but you can be ready for its effects. Here we begin to leave behind the familiarity of clear definitions and predictable patterns. In the world of the unconscious, intuition, association and imagery become more important that logic and rationality. Thankfully, we have inherited a tool for understanding the unconscious mind, one which we already use daily without knowing its power. Like the Buddhists devoted their attention to a study of the mind, so storytellers, saga poets and sages of the West, and especially shamanic traditions, embarked on studies of the unconscious. The famous psychologist Carl Jung made a great study of myths and their power to reveal aspects of the unconscious psyche, although it is the mythologist Joseph Campbell who stands out as the figure who restored the place of myth in the modern world as a method for personal and cultural understanding, rather than simply a form of entertainment.

Myths are stories that carry meaning. Myths are the stories that people in a culture tell one another in order to define, enshrine and renew their shared beliefs, values and priorities. Myths are written around characters who represent important aspects of the things we all believe about people. The hero in the story does what we expect heroes to do, because we all share an understanding about what a hero is. These core characters are the archetypes of our culture. A warrior is what we all know a warrior to be. A queen, a knight, a whore, a villain, a traitor, a damsel in distress, a magician or a shaman. We all know what these characters represent, feel like and mean in a story. When we simply tell the story of a trip to the shops to buy a bottle of milk, we might mention some archetypes without even realizing it. Jung called this vast reservoir of shared knowledge the 'collective unconscious', a single body of knowledge that we all use to communicate profound ideas quickly and powerfully with one another.

A study of mythology is also a study of the unconscious. Older and more mature cultures used stories of the underworld, of great quests, of the gods, angels and demons that guide our steps. Our unconscious is full of needs, drives and fears. It's a restless ocean that we can only learn about from its effects on our lives and the myths that we've told about ourselves over the millennia. Our individual unconsciousness uses myth to communicate with us. Our dreams are often made up of characters that represent aspects of ourselves, or important people (or our beliefs about important people) from our lives. It communicates with us by guiding our choices to meet our unconscious needs and excise our shadow-self (both needs and shadow are explored below).

The important thing to take from the nature of the unconscious is that it is vast, and inaccessible, and mysterious. It is, however, hugely relevant to our daily lives. The idea that the world is a rational and ordered place and that humans should strive to be rational and ordered people is the delusion of a mind-addicted culture. We can be in control of ourselves and we have ultimate responsibility for our actions. That is one of the core messages of this book. But we'll know ourselves better, and therefore have more control and power in our lives, if we understand that a huge and important aspect of us is bound up in mystery, intuition and instinct. It's necessary for anybody who wants to truly know themselves to relinquish comforting ideas of straight lines and logic and be open to mystery and wonder. The unconscious mind will pop up unexpectedly and deliver important, often brilliant or revelatory news at any time. That is normal. That is humanity.

Further exploration

To begin really understanding the hidden meaning in the myths and stories from ancient to modern time, and their relationship to human consciousness, I recommend a couple of fantastic books.

The classic in this field is *The Hero with a Thousand Faces* by Joseph Campbell. I'll talk about Campbell more later, but he was one of the great students of worldwide myths in the precious time after global travel became accessible but before our single, dominant culture stamped out older, land-based cultures around the world. He collated the great stories of different peoples and, looking at them altogether and working with some of the great psychologists and sociologists of his time, he came to see the common threads and the important messages that they hold for all people.

Martin Shaw is a modern master of myth. His book, *A Branch of the Lightning Tree*, is a way in to the forgotten art of storytelling and how to use it in the modern world.

Spirit

While I'm pretty sure that the need for spiritual connection and expression is a fundamental human need, it's a difficult thing to explore at this messy time for our culture. In my experience, every human being has a yearning to encounter an aspect of themselves which seems to go beyond the individual and transcend the ordinary. In the Christian tradition, which has influenced our culture so much, there's often the idea that a part of God resides within us. Other traditions echo this, providing a framework for the individual to find divinity within themselves, while allowing for the flawed and temporal nature of the rest of self. Some suggest that our soul is interwoven with the soul of the world so that individuality and personal identity become irrelevant and all beings become one. Some make us the children of gods. Some make us aspects of a single universal consciousness which has broken itself into many pieces to understand its own nature by experiencing separation and unique, individual perspectives. For some of us, simply being in nature, in a calm and open way, brings us a kind of peace and understanding that transcends our thought and conscious knowledge.

Today it's very hard to explore spiritual experience without either falling into the reductive, anti-religious dogma of the mind-addicted culture, or being absorbed by a religion of faith that brings a lot of extra baggage. But in between these two, and separate from both, is a rich and important seam for all of us to explore. I encourage you to be both curious and rigorous in your approach. Spirit is not entertainment, it is not escapism, it is not an emotion and it is not a thought. It is something else, and it's there for you to explore in your own way.

Further exploration

If a religious or spiritual tradition calls to you, feel free to follow that. I simply urge you not to get lost in bliss or in the reassurance of sharing a belief with others. These things are wonderful feelings, but will ultimately hold back your spiritual growth. I talk more about the pitfalls that can snare the unwary traveller in Part 3 of this book.

If no clear path exists for you, make time to explore different traditions. I would suggest at least one of the popular Abrahamic traditions (Christianity, Islam or Judaism), some time praying and spinning with the sufis, some time drumming and dancing with the shamans, some time in contemplation with Buddhists and some time in the wild vibrancy of a living polytheistic faith like those found in India.

Beware of charlatans. A scepticism and a slowness to trust will help keep your spiritual thirst from being used against you. But when you encounter Grace, allow it to teach you about yourself.

The Four Directions

In the traditions of some Native American peoples, the Four Directions are a model for the nature of reality and the nature of self. In people, the Four Directions are: **Mind**, **Emotion**, **Body** and **Spirit**.

We each feel more confident or comfortable with some of these aspects than others. Some of us are physical first, tending to be practical and confident with physical expression, but perhaps less comfortable with rigorous mental work or honest and vulnerable emotional expression. Others are naturally strong in Emotion, but less so in Body or Spirit.

Where are you most comfortable?

In order to find balance in your life, you will need to pay attention to all four Directions.

Needs

Needs reside in the unconscious, although they make themselves known to us every day.

In psycho-spiritual language, needs are things that we know are essential to be happy, healthy and whole. Each need requires one or more things in order to be fulfilled or met. An unmet need becomes a problem, and the longer it goes unmet, the more insistent it becomes. Needs will find a way to be met if we do not provide them with the thing they demand from us. Ultimately, they cannot be denied, although we can choose the way that we meet a need.

We may feel a need for food. If we're used to a diet of sugary or processed foods, we'll tend to meet this need that way. But the need for food can be met just as well by eating fresh fruit and vegetables, by having a balanced and healthy diet. It might take a while for your need to understand that it's being properly met in a new way, but it will adapt.

If we're hungry and we don't eat, the need will worm its way through our unconscious into unexpected parts of our lives. We might become angry or upset. We might become fixated on thoughts of food. We might make a series of strange choices that sabotage whatever we're trying to do, so that we stop doing it and eat instead.

Needs that are not met will find ways to manipulate or sabotage our behaviour so they become met. This isn't because they're mean or evil: every need is trying to keep you safe from something and it's working to protect you. Some of our mental and emotional needs will be the kind of thing we expect: needs for love, acceptance, safety, belonging, expression, recognition and fulfilment. Others will be things we might want to pretend don't exist: the need for revenge, to lash out or cause harm, the need to own far more than is necessary (greed), the need to be seen as perfect or special. Some of our needs will be unwelcome, and we might feel embarrassment or shame about them. These parts of ourselves are called our Shadow. The unconscious is not bound by the rules of civilized behaviour or morality, but we are. If you notice a deep and forceful need for something that's unwanted or unwelcome, you will need to find a way to allow it to be met, or some way to manage it. If you don't, your unconscious needs will manipulate your behaviour to do things that you may not expect and may not be able to fully control.

Over time, we can come to understand our needs more deeply. If we understand that a need has arisen from an early-life experience, for example, and we do the necessary healing and personal development to remove the power this event has over us, we'll find that the need becomes less imperative or vanishes altogether. Sometimes simply understanding the root of a need is enough to break its hold over us. Sadly, most people never do this work and refuse to admit that unconscious needs even exist. They remain victims of their own inner processes and never take back true control of themselves.

Further exploration

We'll look at needs more fully in Part 2 of this book. Some of the exploration needed is private, while some of it is best done with a therapist or in groups. You can probably name many of your core needs right now, but others might take a little digging to realise. You might need to ask people who know you well what they think you need from life, and which core needs most strongly drive your choices and behaviour. I'll be giving you a lot more information about needs, how to learn them and how to handle them later in this book.

Toxic shame

Toxic shame is something that's become so normal, so everyday and common, that we hardly ever notice it. It's one of the foundation pillars of our culture and it's the basis for many of our assumptions, expectations and the way we relate to ourselves and to other people. There are entire schools of psychology that study the ways that we interact with each other, based on toxic shame. We are taught to expect and accept toxic shame in our early childhoods, and we continue to use it and allow it through our entire lives. It begins with the way that our parents treat us, and the behaviour we witness in them. Mum and dad also grew up with toxic shame, and passed it on to us without realising. If you, as a little child, did something wrong then a parent who is psychologically and emotionally skilled, aware and present will respond by stopping you, laying down clear boundaries and, where appropriate, explaining why something is wrong. But in a world where our parents have little or no psycho-spiritual education and where they are exhausted, confused, depleted or overwhelmed, they will tend to use toxic shame to control our behaviour.

It might manifest as a total over-reaction to a situation. A child cries or throws a tantrum in a supermarket or other public place, and the mortified, embarrassed parent screams at their child. Or it might be a response of disgust or contempt to something the child has done wrong. 'How could you be so stupid?' 'That's disgusting, don't ever do that again!' 'How dare you behave like that?'

The parent is saying more than 'you've done something wrong'. They are throwing enormous emotional weight behind the statement. They are dumping shame, judgement, rage, or their own fears onto a vulnerable child. The experience for the child is that their behaviour has caused the parent to suddenly and violently withdraw their love. Parents, to young children, are giant figures of care and love. The child knows they utterly depend on the parent and they use the parent as a template for how to act, how to know right and wrong, how to be a person. To find that love is no longer available is one of the most terrifying experiences for a young child. The child quickly learns the terror of rejection and the withdrawal of love. They learn that their safety and security are at stake if they get certain things wrong. This lesson is reinforced as they grow up by peers, teachers and role models. What we're left with is a clear pattern of things that we want or need, but which trigger this shaming response in others.

When we internalize this pattern, we're left with a story that goes:

there is something intrinsically wrong with me, and if people really see who I am they would reject me and nobody would love me. This belief is really, really common in our culture. It says that deep down we're basically unworthy of love. It's a kind of stagnant, unchanging, unquestioned and paralyzing shame. It is the shame of being the person we believe ourselves to be, the person we've learned that we need to keep hidden. This belief sits somewhere between consciousness and unconscious. We can be aware of its effects, and if we focus on it we can realize that we know this feeling pretty well, but the feeling slips beneath the surface of the great ocean of the unconscious and has all sorts of unexpected or unintended effects on our choices, words and actions.

Toxic shame goes on to dictate our relationships. If we believe on some level that we're basically a bad person, basically unworthy of love, then our mission in life becomes developing a mask that is so attractive, lovable, impressive and complete that we will never experience the pain of rejection. People will say 'wow, what a great person!' Our society can be seen as one great competition to make the best mask. There are prizes for making a better, more convincing mask that shows all the things we think we're supposed to be. We get rewarded with good jobs that pay well, with expensive things that prove to other people how good we are. Most importantly, we are rewarded with love. Many friendships and intimate relationships in our culture are between the masks of two people, with those people never truly meeting, even in a life-long relationship.

Brené Brown, author, researcher and public speaker, who has delivered some of the most popular talks on TED.com, has studied and written extensively about shame, its effects on our behaviour, and how to overcome it. Vulnerability, she says, is the antidote to shame. As long as we keep living behind a mask in order to protect ourselves from imagined rejection, we'll never truly connect with others. According to Brené, we are "hardwired for connection". It is the thing that we most treasure and most need in our lives. If we have a belief that we should feel ashamed of ourselves, we will not truly connect with another human being. We won't let them in. So Brené explores the skills necessary to lower the mask, step into our lives with vulnerability and learn to endure the feelings of exposure and the fear of rejection.

These skills have the power to transform our personal lives and, ultimately, transform the way we function as a society.

Where Brené talks about shame, I talk about toxic shame. As we'll explore later in this book, it's been my experience that some shame is completely right and appropriate. Adult shame, where we recognise our own harmful behaviour and choices, can be a healthy and proper way to restore our behaviour to something we can feel rightfully proud of. The function of a healthy shame is to alert us to choices that breach our own beliefs of right and wrong. That's the emotion doing its job properly. But this persistent shame that lies beneath our beliefs about ourselves and our relationships isn't helpful to our personal growth and serves no good purpose. It's the remnant of the response by a child who didn't know how to do better. It lurks behind our friendships, our sex lives, our parenting, our shopping and voting habits and our aspirations for ourselves, to name just a few things. It's pernicious, ongoing and does us a lot of harm.

Further exploration

Brené Brown's work is exceptional in helping you to understand the nature of toxic shame, to identify how it's shaped your life and influenced your choices, and how to begin developing skills in vulnerability to break the hold that toxic shame has over your life. If you found yourself resonating with my description of toxic shame, I urge you to engage with Brené's work. Her book *Daring Greatly* is an excellent place to begin.

If you're curious about the ways that toxic shame has subtly shaped the way we relate to one another, you might enjoy learning about a field of psychology called Transactional Analysis. This field studies the individual 'transactions' that go on between people when they're communicating. I say something to you, hopeful to get a certain response (maybe approval or sympathy) and if you respond in the way I expect then we both feel good. A kind of transaction has happened between us.

A certain model in Transactional Analysis which looks at the three most common masks we wear to gain approval and a safe kind of identity, called the Karpman Drama Triangle, has become a big part of the work I do with my coaching clients and I'll be exploring it later in this book.

Shadow

The term 'shadow' was first coined by Carl Jung. Just as there are things that we're proud of about ourselves, that we are happy for people to know about us, there are parts of us that are secret, dark and hidden. We prefer to pretend that these parts of us don't exist. Our darker impulses, our secret desires, our longings for things that aren't ok or acceptable. The things that we feel ashamed of, the things we don't like about ourselves. You know something is part of your inner shadow if you notice yourself pushing it to the edges of your consciousness awareness, or if you try to ignore or avoid it because you feel shame, discomfort, embarrassment, fear or disgust about it. We keep these things out of the light of our everyday selves and we push them to lurk somewhere at the periphery, supressed, barely noticed, associated with darkness.

Things that reside in the shadow tend to have a strong hold over our imagination. Horror movies terrify and excite us because they show us the dark things inside ourselves. Taboos and sexual fetishes exist because we are both excited and repelled by aspects of ourselves that we keep hidden. The revulsion and the excitement feed on one another, leaving us with a potent mix of fascinating feelings.

This book is about empowerment through understanding. It's a guidebook to your inner and outer journey towards a life that's fulfilling, nourishing and under control. This book is about growing into the person you were always meant to be. As we'll explore, being that person means making choices to do things you feel proud of. But there are parts of you that want to do things that you can't be proud of, things that want to sabotage your good choices.

The most common way that we lose control is by denying the presence of something that is manipulating or influencing us. Every time we deny and reject something, or pretend it doesn't exist because it seems so unacceptable that we don't know how to deal with it, we reinforce its power over us. So it's important that you factor your shadow self into your journey of awakening. The shadow is there, in everybody. It is your fears, your loathings, your shames, your hidden longings.

A parable from Native American teachers is useful here, one that was passed on to me by Mac Macartney, who spent 20 years studying with indigenous people in North America. They call these dark impulses the 'wild dogs'. Imagine you are sitting on an open plain at night. You've build a fire and you're staring into the flames, but out in the darkness you can hear wild dogs howling, barking and yapping. They sound huge and terrible and you fear them, so you huddle closer to the fire. But what happens if you welcome the wild dogs into your firelight? Now you can see them, and perhaps you begin to realise that they aren't so great and terrible after all. Out in the unknown darkness things can sound far worse than they are. As long as we keep things squashed, hidden or pushed away they exert great control over us. But if we welcome them into the light and begin to get to know them, we begin to break their hold over us.

This isn't the same as giving them free rein. This isn't about letting all our darkest impulses loose. Control is a big part of the message of this book. Rather, this is about acceptance and awareness, so you can make good choices in full knowledge of who you are and what needs you have.

This book will offer you signposts towards a certain kind of life, and in that life you will be strong, empowered and you will make good choices. We do not allow our shadow selves to rule our lives, sabotaging our great ambitions, stifling our imagination, or making us ruin friendships, relationships or opportunities. Left unchecked, our shadow would have us hurting people, betraying trust and causing harm in the world. Indeed, that is what humanity is doing on a large scale. We have lost our ability to welcome our wild dogs in from the darkness and learn about our greatest fears – and in so doing, we have lost the ability to make consistent, good choices.

Further exploration

Books, websites and courses exist for those who want to understand and explore their own shadow. If you feel that you could do with a better relationship with your shadow, I would recommend looking for a workshop or course where a teacher will guide you through this challenging and sometimes savage experience into the inner dark. You might find things there that are deeply unsettling, so I only recommend you study this alone if you feel you'll be ok doing so.

One online resource I can recommend is exploringtheshadow.co.uk by Shadow-work expert Marianne Hill. Many of Marianne's blog entries are excellent, clear ways to understand this murky but vitally important side of the human psyche.

Some good books on this topic are:

A Little Book on the Human Shadow by Robert Bly and William Booth

Meeting the Shadow: Hidden Power of the Dark Side of Human Nature by Connie Zweig

Dark Side of the Light Chasers: Reclaiming your power, creativity, brilliance, and dreams by Debbie Ford

Wounds

I'll refer to wounds throughout this book, so I will say a few words about what I mean.

Life is not always smooth. When we are very young, we are at our most vulnerable and we can be hurt in ways that aren't always visible. We pick up psycho-spiritual scars from traumatic events that happen to us or sustained neglect of some kind. We learn bad lessons that stifle our growth or which make us repeat self-harmful patterns of behaviour. Most commonly this comes from our parents because we trusted them as our care-givers, role models and teachers. For the infant, the primary care-giver (usually mum) is god. But lots of other things can wound us. Growing up with injustice, prejudice or social inequality. Bullying or harassment at school. A violent or traumatic event that leaves a physical or psycho-spiritual wound.

In a forest, few trees grow straight and true. Most will have notches on their bark, kinks in their trunks. Sometimes we see trees that have been smashed, cracked or burned and they've continued to grow around the wounds. It's the same with people. Some wounds are physical, or have obvious effects. Others are carried in the heart and the mind and continue to influence us for years afterwards.

Many wounds can be healed. Probably more than you think. This is one of the main functions of counselling, psychotherapy and psychiatry. These professions exist, in part, help us understand, explore, process and heal wounds that we carry in our minds and in our hearts. The body gets involved in all of our mental and emotional wounds, so it too will require healing even if you didn't seem to take any physical harm. I have been lucky enough to learn about Upledger CranioSacral Therapy, which is effective at healing and releasing physically-held traumas, but a range of other physical therapies exist, from the many forms of massage to things like Shiatsu and the Alexander Technique. Part of your personal journey of awakening and empowerment may involve sampling these forms of therapy to find that one that supports you best.

Sadly, in my experience, some wounds cannot be healed in a conscious way or in a predictable time-frame, because they are too deep, or were caused too early in our lives, or because we simply hold on to them too tightly. Some wounds may take a very long time to shift even a little bit. So there are wounds we carry that we must learn to compensate for, in the way that a hurt leg is compensated with a walking stick. We learn how these wounds affect us, and we make allowances for them. Our friends or partners know about them and they adapt and forgive us because they love us. When we're overwhelmed by anxiety or fear or depression or anything else that arises from a wound we carry, it's understood. When we enter into relationships, we hope that our wounds will be accepted and eventually cherished by our partners.

But you may be surprised what can change, what can be healed. I encourage you to be open to the possibility that you may find ways to heal things about yourself that are old and seem impossible to change.

Like a notched or gnarled tree, our growth can be stunted by an old wound. The act of seeking help to heal our wounds is a profound act of self-love. It is also an act of love to those who depend on us and who care about us. Some of us tend to sit in the knowledge of our wounds, fixating on them, sure that we'll never get over them. But love is a tremendously healing thing, and as we'll explore later in this book, loving yourself in an active and committed way is one of the most important skills we all need to develop. Love opens the possibility of healing and change, and it inspires us to seek out healing when we need it.

Further exploration

Do you know your wounds? Do you know the knocks and bruises that sometimes send you off-course, and do you know the core wounds that have dictated the course of your life and defined your story?

Reflection, such as regular journaling, is an excellent way to meet and identify your wounds, and sometimes it's just your attention and your compassion that will allow them to shift and fade.

At other times, it's important to seek out professional support. Counsellors and psychotherapists are now pretty common and you'll find one near you. Investing in this is an investment in yourself and the person you might become if you could heal this part of yourself and grow beyond it. Physical therapists are also increasingly common and can be very supportive in making breakthroughs in your personal healing.

The 'I'

I've mentioned the four directions of the human person: the mind, the emotions, the body and the spirit. We have talked about the vast ocean of the unconscious, the needs that drive us, the toxic shame that suffuses our culture, the inner shadow that we all carry and the wounds that can influence our choices.

If we take all that away, if we remove the babble of the mind, the flow of emotions, the unique consciousness of the body, the inner spark of the spirit and all the other things, what do we have left?

We have a thing that simply is. We have a core of awareness, always present, never distracted. This part of us does not change, doesn't grow or get hurt, doesn't exist in the past or the future (because these are constructs of the mind). I refer to this part of us simply as the 'I'. When we deeply meditate and the mind and all other distractions fall away and we simply are, we have returned to the 'I'. We are born with this awareness and it is with us until we die. It cannot be harmed by traumatic events, and this perfectly detached part of us can be a consolation in difficult times.

In my experience, love is the natural state of life. Love is not an emotion, it is a natural and true way of being where our minds are quiet, our emotions flow naturally, we act with compassion and care and we are fully present in a moment. Two people sharing love have returned to the natural state that we inhabit before we learn all of the complicated and messy business that life requires of us.

The 'I', which never has to deal with the complicated and messy business of life, exists in love. It offers compassion to us and to the world.

In my experience, the 'I' is a hugely reassuring and comforting presence. When things are hard, or overwhelming, or lead us away from ourselves, the 'I' is always there, compassionately detached. A core part of our identity from which we observe the world. We can't live there because the 'I' can't do relationships, can't do anything, but it is a part of us, the true self, the centre of our consciousness, to which we can always return and find stillness.

Further exploration

Meditation is a necessary part of developing a relationship with your 'I', as you'll need to quieten and calm everything else to begin to notice it.

Beyond that, I simply invite you to be curious and aware of this aspect of self. It requires a stillness of being to notice and experience, but the unchanging continuity of the 'I' may be profoundly helpful at difficult times of your life.

SECOND INVITATION

I invite you to awaken and nurture a sense of care for yourself, so that your exploration of who and what you are is done with kindness, love and compassionate non-judgement.

There are things within us that we find easy to love. Other things may be hard to love. I invite you, at this time, to foster such care for yourself that you offer love to both the light and the shadow that you find.

Chapter 4: Know thyself

Deep Joy

Committing to the journey

"News of your insignificance has been greatly exaggerated. Might you consider another possibility: that you are needed?"

– Stephen Jenkinson

This book is about being real. We're offered a lot of easy fantasies to follow. We're given the possibility of becoming whoever and whatever we might imagine ourselves to be. But my belief is that there is only one true self, under layers of illusion, forgetting and wounding. This self is strong, vitally alive, deeply present in the moment and possessed of great potential to create, to connect deeply with others and with this time and this place, to experience the full flow of emotions without getting stuck on just one, to be a positive force in the world.

As we live our lives in the mind-addicted, spiritually malnourished culture into which we were born, we are given gifts that bring our attention to the truth of the moment. Most often, we would call these crises. The death of somebody we love. The end of a treasured relationship. A great failure or disappointment. The reassessments needed when we become parents, amid the exhaustion and bewilderment of a child's sudden arrival in our world. The onset of age. A profound, destabilising change to the shape of our lives. A shock or shift that leaves us shaken and calls into question everything we thought we knew.

These gifts, often painful and upsetting as they are, are part of the call of our true self. 'Come home,' they whisper, 'see through the illusions and limitations of the life you have settled for. Come home to me.'

Death, grief and rebirth are at the heart of Deep Coaching. We stand naked in the reality of who we are and the choices we have made, and we take full responsibility for what we see. We know that all things, no matter how painful or how precious, will pass. We accept the joys and the sadness, the pride and the shame, and we do our best to understand why we did what we did. Then, with the power that comes from taking ownership of our choices, we look forwards to the life we would like to create. We begin, slowly and with great care, to let go of things we have held so tight. The patterns of behaviour that have kept us safe, the beliefs and actions that were born out of our confusion, our distraction or our desire to make somebody else responsible for our lives.

Many older cultures offered their people some version of the Vision Quest. Today this ancient practice has been revived and you will find opportunities to embark on your own Vision Quest in many places. Stripped down to its basics, a Vision Quest is a few days spent alone in the wilderness without food, without distraction, without anything but yourself and nature. You will have arrived with a question or a longing, and you will be held and supported by the place of your Vision Quest to find your answers.

Each Vision Quest has three stages. This is an utterly ancient structure, and it's mirrored in myths and stories from the earliest records right up to the modern day. Movies and books continue to use this structure.

First comes the departure. You say goodbye to your old life. In some traditions, this was treated like a literal death. You would give away possessions, say goodbye to people and to your home and prepare as you would for your own death. You would take part in a ceremony of ending, of letting go. You draw a firm and definite line under the life you have lived so far and you gather your strength for the coming journey.

Then comes the quest itself, the opening to new possibilities, the adventure, the wanderings of the mind, body, emotions and the spirit.

Finally, there is the return. We come back to our lives and we are birthed into this new phase, again usually supported by a ceremony.

But rebirth cannot come without death first. That is why crises are blessings in our lives.

This book follows a similar shape. In this part of the book, you are invited to enquire into how things have been for you so far. Have you been mind-dominant? Perhaps you've neglected developing your mind or some other aspect of yourself? Do you have a feeling or an idea that your choices and words have been driven by old wounds from earlier in your life? Can you see patterns in the choices you've made so far: are you adventurous or do you tend to play it safe? Are you open-minded and experimental, or do you prefer to stick to what you know? In relationships, do you tend to seek our balance and be vulnerable with your partner, or do you either take too much or give too much, or perhaps wear masks to hide your true self?

I invite you to spend some time reflecting on these questions. Be as real as you can. Record what you find, either in writing or some other form. Think of this not as 'this is who I am' but rather, 'until now, this is who I have been'. By doing this, you allow for the possibility that everything could yet change, you could yet forge your life into a new shape. Take time to do this. Consult with friends and family who you trust and who know you well. Ask for honesty and be ready to receive it. If you think that somebody isn't being entirely honest because they want to be kind, stop them and ask them if they're doing this. Be ready to receive surprises and challenges. Be curious. Remember: you are not confined to being this person, but the more you know about who you have been so far, the better equipped you'll be to let it go and step forwards in wholeness and honestly.

When you begin to grow, evolve and step into a deeper and more conscious version of yourself, you will still be you. Do not expect for this work of death and rebirth to be total. But as time passes and if you do the work consciously and consistently, you may be surprised by the number of things that can shift, heal and change.

Pay particular attention to things that are uncomfortable, deeply treasured or which you would normally dismiss as unchangeable. We hold on tightly to some things because they bring us comfort and because they have always defined how we see ourselves and how we see the world. Perhaps these things will always be with you and perhaps they're exactly right after all. Perhaps this is your opportunity to shed old ways of being, doing and relating. Whichever is true for you, you will be best served at this time by loosening your grip on old ways. Hold them lightly. Let them be ideas rather than beliefs or needs. Let your curiosity be playful and unattached.

In the next section of the book, we'll look at the 12 Principles of Deep Coaching. These are some core truths about living, learning and loving at this time that are helpful, challenging and supportive to anyone who is seeking an empowered and fulfilling life. They won't tell you exactly how to live, but they will give you a structure and act as a series of reminders in your journey. They'll help you build a resilient attitude, an open mind and a strong heart. Read them, be with them, wrestle with them, dismiss and return to them. Do with them whatever is helpful for you. Follow your intuition. Seek to connect with the unattached, compassionate 'I' and see how it guides you. Be as open as you can be to new possibilities.

The last section of this book is the return. It's a series of helpful pieces of advice to live a life that will support the growth you have achieved. How to live in a modern world in a way that is happy, healthy and whole, without falling back into illusion and confusion.

You are not expected to be anything, or to become anything in particular. I didn't write this book only for people who can achieve great and impressive things, but neither did I write it for people of limited ambition. If, at this time, the steps that you are ready to take would appear, to an outside observer, as very small, then draw together your determination and your curiosity and take those steps, celebrating what you can accomplish. If you are ready for massive changes and big, ambitious leaps into the unknown, I invite you to leap.

Start from where you truly are, having taken an honest and real appraisal of your life, and be as brave and determined as you can be as you take steps forwards.

Adulthood and the death of innocence

Our full power lies in our full adulthood. As we will go on to explore, our culture does not provide a mechanism to move smoothly from childhood to adulthood. We slowly morph from one to the other, and usually carry with us all sorts of incomplete aspects of a confused and bewildered child self. We will need to put this inner child in a place of care and love, and remove him or her from the driving seat, if we want to take full control of our lives. We will need to assume full, adult responsibility.

This is the price of power, and the thing that you will lose on this journey. As children, we can afford not to worry about all sorts of things because an adult is there providing for us, making sure we are safe and protected, guiding our footsteps. As we step into adulthood, it's really normal to keep doing this in all sorts of unconscious and semi-conscious ways. We ignore things, or we imagine that somebody else will sort things out for us, or we avoid doing things because they're frightening or because we might be told off, or we use friendships and relationships to create a sort of replacement parent who will nurture, guide and take responsibility for our decisions and wellbeing.

None of this is compatible with being the happy, fulfilled, powerful person you are called to become.

When we become that person, filled with awareness and personal power, there is no place for the passive handing-off of responsibility to real people or imagined people. This can be hard, at first. It can feel like reliving being severed-from or abandoned by a parent. We are so used to living in a semi-adult state that setting childish ways aside for good can feel like we are losing something precious.

The theme of full adulthood runs through the whole of this book. I'll be covering what it means, how to reach it and how to maintain it. We will be exploring something called self-parenting, which is a practice that's emerged to compensate for this merging of child and adult states. We learn to identify, nurture and care for our own inner child so they feel safe and happy, allowing us to continue as empowered adults. Play and fun still happen. The person you are called to become is capable of being silly, playful, mischievous and curious. When we walk hand-in-hand with our inner child, we get to experience all these things.

But something changes. Comforting illusions and the ability to look away from inconvenient truths are lost. We live in direct contact with the realness of the world, with its wonders and its profound challenges. This is a necessary part of the growth into the fullness of our being.

Commitment and stopping short

The work we do to understand and resolve our past, to arrive wholly in the present and to form a positive, structured plan for our future is a gift that we give to ourselves. It's an act of self-kindness and self-love to give ourselves that much commitment to our own unravelling and rebirthing. It'll take as long as it takes for you to arrive at the self that you were born to be, but the attitude conveyed in this book, centred around determination and curiosity, will be very helpful in the journey. This many-layered attitude will equip you with the resources you need to persevere in your growth and to thrive in your life.

So I invite you to commit to this journey of awakening, and commit to it for as long as it takes. Give yourself that gift. Let the commitment to awareness, healing, self-discovery and unlocking the limits of your potential be a lifelong commitment. As we learn and grow, as we seek help and reconcile our past, as we take risks and discover new possibilities for ourselves, we take steps on the journey. But as we'll explore later in this book, there is always more adventure ahead. This journey isn't about a destination where everything is perfect and we get to put our feet up in the knowledge that we've finally arrived. This is about living for the journey itself, for the thrill of being alive, being healed and aware enough to see every day as an adventure. It's about always seeking, always wondering, always learning more about being, doing and relating.

The way of being that we'll explore in this book has many names. Abraham Maslow, author of the famed Hierarchy of Needs, called it 'self-actualization', and he said this about it:

> *"Self-actualizing people are, without one single exception, involved in a cause outside their own skin, in something outside themselves. They are devoted, working at something, something is very precious to them, some calling or vocation in the old sense, the priestly sense.*
> *They are working at something which fate has called them to somehow and which they work at and which they love, so that the work–joy dichotomy in them disappears."*

Some people stop short of this state, usually because they meet something that is so difficult or too deeply ingrained to overcome that they would rather settle for an unfulfilling life than confront it. You may meet hard things in yourself or in the world on your path of your own awakening. Your commitment now will help in those times. Your dedication will compel you to persist in learning, growing and healing. Your curiosity will allow you to play and dance with problems instead of becoming too entrenched or too one-dimensional in your approach.

You may get distracted by life. That's ok. As soon as you're able, return yourself to the path.

You may reach a certain point, perhaps when you've met your current goals, and decide that's far enough. That's ok. Enjoy that new place in your life, re-evaluate, explore it. But sooner or later you will be called back to the journey, or you'll long for a new goal, a new adventure or a new achievement.

THIRD INVITATION

I invite you to write down your commitment. A simple statement. What is it that you want to achieve? Where do you want to be? What do you want to let go of? Make it a single sentence, affirming your intention at this time. Avoid elaborating or explaining – it's just your intention.

If you can, put this intention somewhere in your home where you'll see it regularly.

Chapter 5: Committing to the journey

Deep Joy

Part 2

The 12 Words

Deep Joy

How to use the 12 Principles

A life that is deeply nourishing and satisfying, that brings us all the things we need to thrive and be content, is a result of a certain attitude. This attitude helps us to make good choices about what we say, do, feel and think. Over time, building on each choice with other good choices, we begin constructing a positive, successful life that can bring us the things we want. It's a process of consistently taking steps, from big and dramatic ones to simple and subtle ones, that moves us inexorably towards joy and fulfilment.

But life is a complicated and messy business. There are so many things to think about and feel, so many things that try to pull us off centre.

We also need to consider where we're going, both individually and together. Some answers that might be right for us now won't be right for us in the world that we long to live in.

The attitude we bring to our lives, then, must give us personal resilience. It must be adaptable as things change in our lives. It must be honest and true to what we want and need, but it must also be realistic about our obligations and responsibilities. It must empower us, make us feel strong and capable and able to make good choices, but it must also be realistic about the knocks and bruises we've taken in our lives and how they tend to make us act, think and feel. It should bring us to life, to make us feel awake and conscious and excited to meet each day it comes.

I have had the privilege to spend time with many wise and inspiring women and men in my life, and I continue to seek out people I can learn from at every opportunity. What I've noticed, as I've spent time with religious and community leaders, activists, academics, priests, Buddhists, Sufis, shamans and successful entrepreneurs and business leaders, is that there are certain phrases and beliefs that keep coming up over and over. I would notice the same words and ideas spoken in a teambuilding seminar that I would in a vision quest. Together with the teachings from great works of philosophy, ethics and spirituality from around the world and across recorded human history, and with the myths and stories of human cultures with strong oral traditions, I noticed that some things are common across the human experience. All of these teaching come together in my coaching work, but some of them can also be summed up in a series of phrases or affirmations.

Eventually, after 15 years of learning and seeking, I decided to write down the most common and important ones.

Each of the 12 Principles is an affirmation. Affirmations are used by people around the world every day to focus their minds and bring themselves into positive or creative mindsets. If you ever say anything to yourself that shifts your perspective and brings you feelings of strength, happiness or connection, these are affirmations.

The 12 Principles are also lessons. Each one is designed to remind us of deep, important truths about the human experience.

Some may seem obvious.
Some may seem confusing.
Some may provoke feelings of despair, despondency or regret.
Some may be warming and comforting.
Some may make you laugh.
Some may make you angry or annoyed.

Each of the 12 Principles is a gateway to a world of learning. A person could devote their entire lives to exploring and understanding the teachings hidden behind just one Principle. The 12 Principles are offered as drops of water in a still lake, sending ripples out into thought and feeling that bring about change, challenge, learning and growth. As I present each Principle, I'll explain what each means, where it comes from, what it implies and what to do about it. However, there will be much, much more to learn about it than I can share in this book. If you find that a Principle speaks to you and you know that learning more about it would really help you, then I encourage you to follow that feeling.

I particularly urge you to apply the same compassionate non-judgement that we explored in the last part of this book as you read the 12 Principles. Be curious, not just about my words and ideas but also about how you respond in thoughts and feelings. If a Principle makes you feel good, reassured, optimistic or positive, then that's interesting and perhaps it's telling you things about yourself and where you are on your own personal journey. If they annoy you, frustrate you, anger you or make you feel depressed and inadequate then try to take that as a lesson about you and where you are in your life. It's all information, and the more we understand, the more power we have to make positive changes. Some feelings may obscure others at first: annoyance might mask fear; happiness might mask challenge. There is much to be learned from these feelings and responses.

The 12 Principles are arranged into groups.

The first three Principles are about the self. We begin by mastering ourselves before we focus on how we engage with the world.

The next three Principles are about how we understand our place in the world and prepare to interact with it in a way that is conscious, empowering and positive.

Principles 7 and 8 are about how we take action in the world, creating a life that is satisfying and rewarding.

Principles 9, 10 and 11 are about creating relationships that are balanced, deeply connected and which meet our needs for love and belonging in healthy ways.

Principle 12 stands alone. It's a reminder that learning about the truths and mysteries of ourselves, and all of the things we can learn about the complex, marvellous and imposing world that we live in, are not things that we can do quickly and then forget about. We may have moments of intense learning, epiphany, realisation, awakening, crisis, collapse, or moments when it all seems to click together, but in between these peak moments is the long, concerted, determined journey into life, into self, into relationship and into consciousness. This life is far more about the journey than the destination. It's one of the most common and most unhelpful lessons of our culture that we should be solely focused on goals and outcomes. It is the spaces in between that will occupy most of our time and therefore should be something that we bring a proper attention to.

What I am inviting you into through this book is a lifelong commitment to yourself. A commitment to constantly learn, grow and enquire. A life of curious exploration, of stretching in new directions, of learning to fully occupy your mental abilities, your emotional landscape, your physical body and your spiritual experience. This does not tend to happen quickly, or in a controllable or predictable way. Many of the lessons will only be understood after we have begun to live them, and as we look back on what has shifted since we took that leap of faith to change. As the Danish philosopher Soren Kierkegaard once said: "Life can only be lived forwards, but it can only be understood, backwards".

Chapter 6: How to use the 12 Principles

Deep Joy

1. CHOICE

"I have the freedom and the power to choose, and my life is the result of my choices"

The first Principle is about choice, and about personal power. In order to create and live a life that feels great and brings you the things you need, you must have the power to make good choices and then follow through on them. From working out the things you need to change, to making plans, to putting them into action, to staying focused even when life throws you off-centre…all of this is your personal power. It's a fundamental and important part of any personal growth work, and it begins with a single choice.

It can be easy to believe that you're a victim of your circumstance. Perhaps you were born into a poor family, or perhaps into a privileged family that lacked something important that you needed in early life. Perhaps your situation in life hampers your growth and happiness: a meaningless job, a frustrating or dysfunctional relationship or a town that's just plain depressing. Perhaps you have friends or family who are negative or who need a lot from you. Perhaps you have a physical or mental health challenge that limits what you can do.

This may all be true, and if you believe that things like this dictate the limits of your ability to choose and function in the world then you're right. They do.

If you choose to believe that you are truly and radically free, then this is true instead.

Limiting factors in life are real, and can be frustrating, exhausting or distracting. That's real. I have worked with clients with profound disabilities. To pretend that these disabilities didn't exist would be fantasy. But to believe that these people were forever defined by their disabilities would be fantasy too.

Principle 1 begins with a choice. The choice is to choose to believe that you are free, and that you can make any choice that's open to you, and that you've lived a life full of choices already that have led you to where you are now.

Chapter 7: Choice

To choose to follow, to be led by others, to do what is expected of you or what you're told, or to try to please people by doing what you think they want you to do, is also your free choice. Everything you do is choice. It might be very deeply embedded, and it might take a long time of exploration and hard work to change, but it's still a choice, and you can choose otherwise.

I often get my clients writing as part of their coaching work. This can be a great way to reflect on things and begin to realise what's going on under the surface. I'll set a question or an idea, or I'll simply ask my clients to begin keeping a regular reflective diary. I remember one client who turned up to sessions over and over and said he hadn't done any of the writing, or maybe he'd done some writing but not as much as we'd agreed and certainly not as much as he'd hoped to do. I understood that this was a choice he'd made. He might be angry and frustrated about not being able to write, but he chose not to write. That choice probably came from the fear of what he might find, and the temptation of sitting in front of his TV and opening a soothing beer rather than wrestle with his deep inner processes and work to bring about change in his life. To him, it seemed like he was powerless. He wanted to write, but he just couldn't. To me, I see a man who is conflicted between his choices to face himself, and to hide in comforting distractions. It's understandable to see this as a powerless situation, but he was actually entirely free and empowered.

'Rather than bring this conflict into consciousness and choose to do the hard thing, he chose to push the choice towards his unconscious and allow the choice to be made in a passive way. He believed himself to be powerless.

I confronted him and asked why he made that choice, which allowed him to notice, understand and explore his resistance. After this, he could make a conscious, empowered choice about what he was going to do.

We tend to unconsciously give our power away to others, or to other aspects of ourselves.

We might say…

"I can't do that; my wife wouldn't like it"

"We don't do things like that in my family"

"I hate this thing, but I just can't stop doing it"

"I can't say that at work, it would upset everyone"

"I'll never get a better job, I wouldn't know how"

To step into your full adult power, you will need to leave these illusions behind. There will be genuine limitations in your life, but you choose what to do about them. You may only have a certain amount of money, but you choose how to spend it or save it. You choose how you exercise or don't, how to connect with others or don't, how much you learn or how long you stay stuck in one place. You choose to restrict yourself in order to please others, or to try to impress them, or to prove things to them.

You are free to choose whatever is available to you, and probably far more is available to you than you realise.

What have you chosen today? When you woke up, how did you feel and what did you choose to do about it? What did you choose to think about? What did you choose to eat? What did you choose to put in place so that your future will get steadily more aligned to the life you want? Did you choose to rest and recover energy? Did you choose to take brave actions?

Are you proud of the choices you made today?

You may have decided that some choices are impossible for you. Are they really? Are there things you can do to shift your situation that you avoid because they are frightening, or require lots of effort, or you fear to try and fail?

It's ok to make choices that preserve you. You are not required to be perfect, or to overcome everything in one day. It's ok to make choices to delay things, or to pace yourself, or to recover your energy when life is hard. That's alright. But it is also choice. The first Principle is not about becoming a perfect person or a powerhouse of amazing, inspiring action. It's not a matter of worth or achievement or success. It's a matter of power. We bring all the power back to the centre, back into consciousness, back to ourselves. We stop farming out our power to others, or to situations, or to other aspects of ourselves. We make conscious choices, and we do so with compassionate non-judgement for ourselves.

Some days we will consciously choose to go for a big promotion at work, or to say something important to our partners that we've avoided saying, or we'll work out a new, healthy diet plan and start putting it into action.

Some days we'll choose to rest, or ask for help because we feel overwhelmed, or to have fun, or to switch off from our worries by watching mindless entertainment.

The important thing is to realise that it's all choice. The realisation of choice will open doors you never knew existed.

I'm inviting you to risk a level of honesty with yourself that most people will avoid. Behind every choice are reasons. Understanding your reasons will be a crucial part of your personal growth. For instance, I do not believe in laziness or procrastination. They're not real. They're entirely made up concepts. They're a language that we've developed to avoid accepting the reality of our power and capacity to choose. "I can't do that, I'm lazy" is a sentence that should read "I have reasons for choosing not to do the thing, so I chose not to do it". We don't procrastinate: we make choices to avoid action.

The more deeply you understand the reasons behind the choices you make, the more you will unlock your power and your potential. Again, this process should be undertaken with compassionate non-judgement for the self. You will find things you don't like: if you liked the reasons for your choices, you'd know them consciously and admit them freely.

With power comes responsibility, which brings us even more power.

From the moment your become an adult, nobody and nothing else is responsible for the shape of your life. It is entirely down to you. All of the things you might blame, or rage against, or surrender to, are just information. They define the shape of the playing field. They are obstacles and barriers and challenges on your path. They do not define your capacity.

Since you became an adult, you've had the power to make empowered, aware choices. Nothing and nobody has ever taken away your ability to choose, except in the most extreme situations. In most situations, for most of our lives, we have to actively choose to give somebody or something any power over us. If this has happened to you, you chose to give it away. You may have had a good reason to do this, and there are times in life when it is right and proper to surrender options. Relationships, and especially our relationships with our children, involve surrendering a lot of possibilities. But we make this choice consciously. We never allow ourselves to lapse into the belief that choice was taken away. It wasn't. You can always choose otherwise, but of course you will need to accept the consequences.

Sometimes we'll choose to believe that we don't have a choice. We do this all the time, if we're not careful. There can be lots of reasons to this, but the most common reason is about living with consequences. Full adult power, where every choice is accepted as our own personal responsibility, brings with it the full weight of the consequences of our choices. So long as we pretend that things are beyond our control, we are not responsible for anything. This might be the hurt which we caused when we let somebody down in order to protect ourselves, or the harm we do our children when we continue to choose to live in addiction, or it can just be the consequences in our lives from the way we choose to live. A body shape that results from a certain diet and lifestyle. Preventable diseases. Unhealthy relationships. Being stuck in a job that's stressful, unhappy or low-income. Having a great idea for a business but never launching it. So long as we pretend that we couldn't choose otherwise, we never have to face the outcomes that of our choices.

But if we accept that everything is choice, and every choice we've ever made had reasons behind it, then the focus shifts from avoiding the reality of choice and to starting to understand *why* we continue to make that choice. It might be something near the surface. Something that is your choice, but isn't a choice that you tend to acknowledge, might arise from a fear or a dislike of something. Your first step, then, is acknowledging that you are afraid, or accepting that you don't like that thing. Bring it into consciousness. Reclaim the power instead of pushing it to the edge of your mind.

Other things might lie deeper. If you were taught a pattern of thinking or feeling as a child, it can be very hard to shift it. If you have deep fears or beliefs or anxieties, they can be hard to notice, understand or overcome. I've had a number of coaching clients who seemed to constantly relapse into weight gain through bad diet choices. They simply couldn't shift the weight and keep it off. For one man, his choices were being governed by an early-life connection between love, reassurance and food. His early life was difficult emotionally, but his mother would feed him big meals and he learned that love was expressed through eating. As an adult, he continued to feel love when he ate food. His over-eating was a longing for the love that he couldn't otherwise allow into his life. He was not powerless to fight against his urges to over-eat, he just didn't understand the choice he was making to order pizza and buy cakes. As his understanding of this underlying search for love grew, he was better able to accept the fact that eating was a choice, and he reclaimed his power to make other choices. He gained more information, he made his choices conscious, and he became more empowered. It brought him a lot of happiness to realise that he had the ability to change his situation.

The journey into your own power, which will unlock your confidence and creativity in ways you've never imagined possible, is a journey of self-understanding. It begins with accepting that everything is choice, and there is nobody to blame but ourselves for the shape of our lives. Then we begin to employ curiosity and determination, with compassionate non-judgement, as we try to understand why we have consistently made the choices that made our lives into this shape. By accepting that we caused our lives to take on this shape, we also free up the ability for them to change. We reclaim our power to be the authors of our lives. If we wrote the story of our lives this way, we could change the story at any time. We could begin making new choices.

Choosing your responses

If it's all choice, if you have the power to author your own life, then one of the things that's within your control is your responses to situations.

It's common to think of your responses to things like a rock pushed off a mountainside. When a trigger happens, the result is uncontrollable and inevitable. When he talks to you in a certain way, you can't help but feel something. When you run out of money, or when your safety is threatened, you always feel a certain way.

Often, there are cascades of responses in us. One of my clients was once talking to me about how she responded to a situation at home.

Her partner would say ask her to make a choice, and she knew that her partner expected a certain answer. Having been here lots of times before, her first response was fear, that another fight was looming. Next was the temptation to make the easy choice. Then anger that she couldn't make a genuinely free choice, that she was being manipulated to make a particular choice and there was also despair that this pattern of behaviour kept coming up over and over in their relationship.

This all happened in about five seconds, completely unnoticed, and pretty soon they were fighting. It all felt inevitable and overwhelming. Only by patiently and calmly examining what happened inside her, step by step, could she begin to understand her responses. Once she understood them, it was pretty easy to begin taking active, conscious control for the way she responded to this situation. They stopped having these fights, and a lot of other fights, and they had some big and challenging conversations and their relationship improved immensely.

The experiences of your life will be a constant stream that never stops. Some of these experiences will be predictable, some will be sudden or unexpected. Many will just pass you by, acknowledged but not triggering. Others will trigger things in you. Emotions respond in predictable ways, and we'll be looking at the nature of emotions later in this book. If you have strong beliefs or rehearsed responses to things, those will kick in. These are the unconscious expectations of the way the world is, and should be, and the lessons you've learned about how to handle all sorts of situations. These can be examined, understood, accepted or changed.

It's all choice. Ultimately, you can become conscious and in control of every single response you have to every single event in your life. But that's a long journey and for a lot of us, not actually something we want. On the way to this kind of total awareness and total control is a gradual increase in noticing, understanding, appreciating and choosing our responses. This is vital for all of us, because without conscious control of our emotional and mental responses, we will sabotage our choices, and keep us from attaining our ultimate goals.

Visioning

It can take time to fully embrace and accept your own power and responsibility. It's a thing that happens steadily over time, if you remain focused and determined to uncover all the ways that you have, until now, been giving your power away to others, or to unconscious aspects of yourself.

As you begin to return this power to the centre, you will find new choices open to you. What choices should you make? What should you do with this newfound power?

There will be very few moments in your life where one choice is going to influence the whole shape of your life. It does happen. We can all think of mistakes we've made that cost us dearly, or bold choices that we made that redefined what life looked like for us. But broadly speaking, good and nourishing lives are made up of a long chain of positive choices, each building on the last. Slowly but inexorably, we take little steps towards a better life. You can't always predict what effects your choices will have, and you will make mistakes, and sometimes you'll be tempted to stop walking your chosen path because it gets very hard, or something else seems more appealing. You will need to construct something that keeps you walking towards a really great, really fulfilling, really nourishing life.

You need a vision.

It's important to make time for visioning, and once you have one, it's important to return to it from time to time.

Begin by spending some time thinking about what's most important to you. What things nourish you and bring you to life? We'll discuss this more in Principle 2. What things are vital for you and what things are unacceptable for you? We'll discuss this more in Principle 4.

Your vision is your idea of the ideal life. Try to forget what others have told you is the ideal life: if people have told you it's about being rich, popular and successful, question whether these things really have meaning for you. What does success mean, for you? If you simply try to live somebody else's life, you're going to end up unhappy.

Then, begin constructing your vision. I like to draw and write mine, I think there's something helpful about the tactile sensation of writing with pen and pencil, but use whatever method works for you. Type it, or dictate it, or put together a vision board made of images that you find in magazines and online. Start putting together your idea of an exciting, nourishing, happy life. What does it look like? What does it feel like? Where do you spend your time? Who do you spend your time with and what are your relationships with them like? What work do you do? How much do you earn? What is your financial situation like? How do you rest and have fun? What is your daily life like? What attitude do you bring to it?

The last one on that list – what attitude do you want to bring – is really important to bear in mind. Right now, you are the person you are, the person you have grown to be. If you want to reach the things in your ambitious, amazing vision, you're probably going to need to grow and change, to become a stronger, wiser person with different skills, knowledge and understanding. We all yearn to grow, so be prepared to change and evolve as you work towards your vision. It's useful to think: who do I need to be, to get there? Who do I want to be? How do I need to change? What do I need to learn? What will help me grow and heal in the ways I need to grow?

Brené Brown, who I will mention throughout this book, makes an important point in her book, *Daring Greatly*. Brené's work is focused around cultural shame and how we can combat it, but another thing she talks about is the glorification of exceptionalism, a search for every moment to be special and different and extraordinary. We're often brought up to believe that unless a person is exceptionally good at something, they're not worth much. Equally, if a moment is exceptional or if an experience isn't wildly exciting, it has no value.

Most of our lives are not spent in peak moments. Even if we live in an intense and thrilling way, this will become our norm. Most of our lives are lived in the long stretches of 'normal' in between peak experiences. As you are constructing your vision, don't just think about making your life into one big peak moment. When you've made your vision into a reality, make sure that you enjoy living there. You can do this by thinking about the mundane. If your vision involves travel, or exciting work, or amazing relationships, or mind-blowing sex...that's great. Run with that, make sure that's in your vision. But also think about the day-to-day. What do you want 'normal' to feel like? How do you want to be when you're just walking about, or relaxing, or not doing anything exceptional? How do you want the background state of your life to be?

A vision gathers power as it becomes more real to you. A very vague vision is just a daydream, and that is a beginning. But you must pour your desire, your ambition and your hope into your vision. Let it come to life. Spend time imagining how it's going to feel to be there. See yourself living that life. When you're daydreaming, return to your vision and take yourself into it. Sometimes you'll notice things that are missing, or things that don't feel the way you expected them to feel. Use this information to refine your vision. But let it build and grow over time, becoming real, becoming a constant companion in your life.

As a guide, here are some categories that you can break your vision down into:

- Work and career
- Money, home and security
- Daily life
- Relationships
- Personal attitude
- Adventures

The really amazing stuff happens when you combine an awareness of your freedom to choose with your growing clarity of vision. Each time you need to make a decision, check in with your vision. Which option fits with your vision, and which takes you away from it? This process will introduce the incremental, step-by-step journey that will bring your vision to life. Determination really comes into play here. You'll get a lot of tempting moments to take you away from you vision, or moments where the choice that'll carry you towards your vision is intimidating or overwhelming. Stay focused. Be flexible about your methods, but don't compromise on your vision.

You can also begin breaking your vision down into a plan. Try not to let old thinking limit your planning phase. You may once have had a self-image that didn't allow you to do certain things. "Oh, I could never do that" or "I could never earn that much" or "I could never find that kind of relationship". You have the freedom to choose the shape of your life. Now you can begin using that freedom and power.

If you vision is very different to your current life, it may take time to get there, and it might require hard work and sacrifice. Parts of your life may suck while you work towards it. That's how this stuff works. You will need to factor in to your plan the ways that you'll keep yourself healthy and whole during the sucky phases. But as Mark Divine writes in his brilliant book, The Way of the SEAL, you must learn to "embrace the suck". You need to throw yourself in to the manifestation of your vision. If it's hard, that's ok. That's good. Things being hard is often a good sign. Life is a messy business and sometimes it's going to be hard. Discomfort, challenge and risk are ok. As we'll explore later in this book, that's how we grow.

You may need to plan in phases to your transition to your vision. If you want a completely different job, there might be a step or two in between here and there when you retrain, or get an intervening job, or move somewhere and need to establish a new life. Don't let your old ideas about your capabilities limit your thinking. You are free to choose. Let your ambition be big.

Free choice and the ways we protect ourselves from our deep wounds

Everything is choice. Everything you do, everything you think, everything you say and everything you choose can become part of your conscious, empowered choice. However, you need to understand the playing field before you can master the game.

If you carry certain wounds from your life, either traumas and bad lessons that were deeply ingrained when you were a child, or very shocking events from your adulthood that have left their mark on you, these are going to affect the freedom of your choices. For example, if you have been betrayed then you may jump quickly to mistrust, anger or rejection to protect yourself from further harm. Wounds tend to show up quickly in triggering situations. Deep, unconscious parts of you jump into action fast to protect you or to try to limit exposure or damage. These are learned behaviours of a specific type. They are your core psycho-spiritual wounds in action, and they can plague your life and interfere with your free choices to build a positive, nourishing life.

There are two things you should do when you notice a core wound and begin to appreciate its affects in your life.

The first is to get to know it really well. This will start of being profoundly uncomfortable and even painful, as you'll re-experience the echoes of the thing that caused the wound. Treat it lightly, use your curiosity so you don't get lost in it and use your determination to not forget it or shy away from it. Gently, over time, learn how this wound affects your life. Learn to anticipate what tends to trigger it and how you tend to respond. Know it like an old friend. Get to know the shape of the playing field, so you can adjust your strategies and still end up winning the game.

The second thing you should do is not let yourself believe that wounds and traumas are forever. Elsewhere in this book we look at the healing of traumas. So many things that my clients have believed were core, permanent parts of their personality have turned out to be the echoes of past trauma which, when understood and treated with love and care, were able to heal. There are a lot of healing professions out there. Many or all of your psycho-spiritual wounds (and we all carry them) can be healed if you are patient, curious, and you do not allow yourself to believe that it's hopeless.

The affirmation

"I have the freedom and the power to choose, and my life is the result of my choices"

Counter-affirmations

We aren't taught about our freedom and power when we're growing up. We encourage each other to blame other people, blame institutions of power, to seek permission to do things, to rely on others, to enter into complex power exchanges at work and in relationships. We avoid taking responsibility for our choices and their consequences, and as a result we surrender our power while believing that it was stolen from us.

If you lapse into this unhealthy cultural story, you might find yourself saying:

- I'm the person the world/my parents made me
- I never had the opportunity to do that
- I'm too lazy to do anything like that
- I don't do things like that
- I'm stuck – my situation is hopeless
- If I do that, my partner/friends will leave me
- It's too hard
- People like me can't do things like that

Chapter 7: Choice

Deep Joy

2.NEED

"I understand and accept my own needs, and I take responsibility for meeting them"

This book is about developing a mature, many-layered attitude. The attitude of a competent and self-aware adult. Principle 1 is about awakening your understanding and acceptance of the total freedom you have and bringing your personal power back in its proper place. Everything is choice, and so everything you choose to do or not do is within your power to change.

Deep Coaching combines this kind of radical self-honesty, where we stop hiding behind comforting illusions like our own powerlessness, with a deep compassion for self. Principle 2 calls you to another exploration. What do you need in order to be whole? What needs do you have on mental, emotional, physical and spiritual levels that must be met in order to truly thrive? Because your life will only full nourish you and feel *right* when your fundamental needs are being met. I've suggested that it's all choice. You are responsible for the shape of your life. In this Principle, we choose to assess and understand our needs and stop waiting for outside agencies to meet them.

Forgotten needs

Depending on the opportunities and encouragement you had as a child, and the work you've done since then to investigate and understand yourself and the things that make you thrive, you're going to have a certain awareness of your needs.

Again, the priority here is understanding and awareness. By asking the question 'what do I really *need*' you begin to delve deeply into things that have been forgotten. For instance, our bodies are wonderfully competent at surviving on poor, malnourished diets but they really *thrive* on a diet rich with green leafy vegetables and a full range of vitamins and minerals. Stress is a physical, hormonal, muscular and mental response to adversity and we can continue to live and function while stressed, but life *flows* more easily when we learn to shed stress so that it doesn't stay with us. We can survive by living quiet lives where we rarely connect deeply with others, but we come *alive* when we feel a sense of belonging with a people and a place. In the last chapter, I suggested that we choose our responses to things, but when we've done the work to create a life that meets our fundamental needs we enter an easy and flowing state where we're supported to make good choices and live without so many things draining our energy.

This is an invitation to deploy your curiosity and determination to truly understand what things support you and nourish every aspect of who you are so that you can easily live the life you want.

Principle 1 was about our agency and ability to choose, and returning these things back to their proper place at the centre of our awareness. In this chapter, we're going to look at doing the same for our needs. Need that are forgotten, cause us problems.

Fundamental needs – things we must have in order to thrive – are aspects of ourselves that protect what is most important to us, starting with our survival. Each need has a rudimentary consciousness of its own and when the need isn't being met, it is striving and yearning towards fulfilment. To take a simple example, hunger is the need for food and nourishment. Your body knows that it needs food, and when it notices that you haven't eaten for a while it starts taking action to ensure that you meet your need. It might begin with a gnawing feeling in the stomach, or a feeling of weakness or lethargy. If that doesn't work, it'll turn to other ways to get you to eat. Erratic behaviour or anger that leads to conflict and drama, which might get you to finally eat. The need will do what it must in order to safeguard you. It might be annoying sometimes but try to see needs for what they are: they are aspects of you trying to keep you safe.

In this book I'm mostly going to focus on psycho-spiritual needs. Your physical needs can be learned by a study of nutrition, anatomy and physiology and by being open to learning of all kinds about the incredibly complex mechanisms of the human body. What is less understood and less easily available are the subtle needs that guide and influence our choices. Unless we become conscious of those and return those to the centre of our awareness, we'll continue to feel disempowered. Wild choices, erratic behaviour or moments of "why did I do that?" are the result of unconscious needs stepping in to overrule your conscious awareness. Children can afford that: empowered adults cannot. The destructive and unkind nature of modern culture is the large-scale manifestation of this kind of ignorance. We owe it to ourselves, our friends, family and lovers and to the world to come home to our fundamental needs and choose to meet them consciously and with purpose, rather than forgetting them and let them act irrationally and erratically in the shadows of our perception.

Here is a helpful list of some fundamental psycho-spiritual needs of all humans, which when unmet cause us to act in ways that betray our fullest potential. As you read the list, I invite you to consider your own relationship with this need: are you meeting it; are you meeting it in a healthy and effective way; are you neglecting it?

Fundamental need	When acknowledged and managed by an adult self	When unnoticed, ignored or handled with immaturity
Recognition and affirmation	Knowledge of the kinds of affirmation and recognition that most satisfy me, granting myself as much as possible, seeking further affirmation from others with clear boundaries and clear asking	Structuring my life around pleasing, impressing or demanding attention from others, either real and present people or those from my past. Basing my self-worth on the judgements of others.
Connection with others	Clearly understanding what connection means for me, then picking suitable people to connect with in a conscious and honest way	Unfocused craving of connection with anyone, often working to create familiar situations where some connection is found, even at the expense of safety, dignity or self-esteem.

Clear sense of identity	A lifelong commitment to a programme of discovering the nature of self. Understanding the perils of a fragile ego and working to create strong, empowered and self-aware identity.	Basing the nature of self on an external template (parent/friend/celebrity). Semi-consciously shying away from the challenges of self-discovery. Tendency to change to fit situations and people.
Belonging	Acknowledgement of the need to belong to a people and a place, to have this as a core part of self, and understanding that our society does generally not provide for this need. Working hard to establish belonging, without surrendering own identity. Only engaging in social rituals when I know they are for my highest good.	Denial that such a need exists, insisting on an independent or hermetic life. Unconsciously reaching for belonging through other means: sporadic community or religious events; donating to a sports industry that supports injustice; travel to exotic cultures; cultural appropriation.

Emotional security	Enough personal work and boundary-setting have been done to create inner sense of power, peace and security. I only enter into relationships and situations that feel safe and nourishing for me.	Relying on others to provide emotionally secure situations, manipulating them to do so when necessary. Feeling like a victim when another emotionally unsafe situation huts me. Failing to release past traumas held in mind and body. Displacement of feelings onto additions or escapism.
Self-expression	Speaking my truth with conviction when necessary, being silent when appropriate. Committed to a lifelong programme of improving my understanding the difference. Artistic expression. Movement, eg dance.	Truths go unsaid and cause me frustration and obsessive thoughts. Other people are not always sure who I am or what I want. I am sometimes exploited or manipulated by others.

Wonder & mystery	When I encounter grace, divinity, oneness or things that are ineffable, I do not deny them or try to reduce them to rational concepts. I make space for wonder and mystery in my life, in whatever way seems most truthful and real to me.	I dismiss or deny any experience where I am given transcendental insight. I meet this need in ways that others tell me is ok: religion; spiritual workshops; drugs; fantastical escapism; buying trinkets and cultural appropriation.
Physical touch	I understand that this is a fundamental physical need and I seek our situations that are appropriate and safe in order to meet it.	I am willing to compromise my safety or dignity in order to receive the touch that my body needs.
Play	I find moments where it is appropriate to shed my self-restraint and throw myself bodily and emotionally into delight and silly, free expression.	I only play in ways that are endorsed by others: structured games; sports and events that meet some measure of this need.

Rest	I celebrate and protect my need for rest. I acknowledge that it isn't failure. I develop skills and techniques for high-quality resting.	I either deny that I should need rest at all, or I only rest in ways that others reassure me are ok. I am often tired and depleted.
Love	Recognition that love is not an emotion: it is a return to our most natural, most aware and most real state. Sharing this experience with others in ways that are mutually-understood, balanced and conscious.	Calling other things love, such as: sexual need; affirmation; emotional safety; excitement; somebody who makes me feel like a child again, freeing me from adult responsibilities. Urgently manipulating others to provide for these needs, generally failing to meet an actual need for love. As the need for love goes unmet, so the urgency increases.

Beyond this list of common needs are your unique needs. For some people, change and adventure are deeply held needs: for these people, if things stay the same for a very long time it becomes frustrating and stifling. For others, their core needs include being connected deeply and ever more deeply with the people they care about. For some people, order and things making sense are crucial to their peace of mind, while for others true fulfilment is found in the artistic exploration of beautiful chaos.

Understanding your personal needs is a responsibility for everyone who hopes to be a conscious, empowered adult who acts as a positive force in the world. Ways of beginning or deepening your journey of exploration into your needs might include:

- Take personality tests and read thoroughly about the results you get, noticing what needs are implied in the answers. I particularly recommend the Myers-Briggs test for the depth of answers you can find once you know your 'type'.
- Ask friends and family what they think you've always searched for to be happy and healthy.
- Take time to reflect on the big choices you've made in your life. What fundamental needs were you trying to meet?

This is going to take time. In the beginning, we can name the obvious needs that often make themselves known to us but others, the more subtle or complicated ones, can be tricky to track down and understand. If you find yourself reading the list above and some items make you uncomfortable or they just seem plain wrong or irrelevant to you, that's a place to start your investigation. You may well spend the rest of your life continuing to find deeper understanding of your fundamental needs, and that's ok.

Accepting what we find

Along the way, we're going to be confronted with needs that aren't necessarily what we wanted to find. If I think of myself as a strong and independent person, for example, and I find that I really need the love and affirmation of another person, that can be difficult.

Equally there are those needs that come from the shadow aspects of ourselves. 'Shadow' was a term coined by Carl Jung to describe the parts of people and of society that are considered bad, immoral, shameful and unwanted. The parts that people reject or find disgusting or unacceptable. If I am a good person, so the story of our culture goes, I will not want or need anything that is harmful, selfish, petty, venomous, reckless, destructive, vengeful, cruel or predatory. I will only want and need things that are wholesome, good, virtuous, creative, light, beautiful and full of grace and decency.

Humans aren't like that. We simply aren't perfect. Often, we're not even very nice. Shadow is where we actively want or pursue things that are considered unacceptable, even by ourselves. Those who have readily and un-critically absorbed the cultural stories of our society will follow its teachings: they will strive to be good, upstanding, moral people and they will often ensure that people notice how good and upstanding and moral they are. This is the most basic and unevolved form of ethics, as we'll explore in Principle 4. To be honest and true with ourselves, to attain a real sense of self-knowledge and wholeness, we must accept that we are flawed, and sometimes petty, and sometimes we crave things that aren't pleasant.

We'll look more deeply at this in Principle 5, but suffice to say that there are things lurking within us that we might not like. As a rule of thumb, you can be sure something is from the shadow-realm if it's something you would generally be ashamed to admit publicly, because you know people would find it distasteful or wrong.

As we encounter things within us that are either in contrast to the way we want to be, or see ourselves, or want others to see us; or if they seem unacceptable and unwanted…what do we do with them?

At the end of the day, we need what we need, from the virtuous and noble to the shameful and selfish. Some needs can shift and evolve over time, and this can be an important aspect of personal development. These are needs that are the result of unresolved psycho-spiritual wounds. If you encounter a need that makes you uncomfortable or that makes you feel ashamed, such as the need to bully people or the need to manipulate others, then you can explore the underlying needs behind this. Perhaps it results from a trauma or bad lesson from your childhood, and perhaps it's simply a common thing in your world and you've never reflected on it before. With time and with exploration and compassionate, non-judgemental enquiry you can come to focus on the underlying need and learn a healthy way to meet this so that the surface need is resolved and loses its hold on you.

We remain responsible for the actions that arise from our needs. This is the heart of Principle 1. Even when you are driven to do something by a deep need, it is still your choice to take action. If a need that we carry is applying pressure on us to cause harm to somebody else, that harm remains our responsibility. At times like that, we might have to find a less direct, less effective way to meet this need, or else admit to ourselves that this need cannot be resolved, and live with the consequences of that, consciously managing the resulting ways that our need changes to try to be met.

Some needs are more complex or evolved than others. As young children, our needs are pretty simple, and they tend to remain with us into adulthood. Some needs will be dignified or mature while others might be silly or ridiculous. Be open to what you find.

Counselling can help you become more aware of the needs you carry and their influences on your life. If you're concerned that you are carrying powerful, unconscious needs, or if you've met needs that frighten you or which seem uncontrollable, counselling is something you might want to consider.

What tends to lead to mental ill-health, torment and erratic and unexpected behaviour is when we deny what we need entirely. We might find something within ourselves that doesn't feel ok and we don't want. In response, we suppress it and pretend that it isn't something inside of us. That need will now operate outside of conscious awareness. It won't go away, it'll find another way to be met. By suppressing and denying our intrinsic needs, we try to shift the responsibility for our actions away from our conscious, adult selves and into a semi-conscious "oh I don't know why I did that" state. This is not being honest with ourselves, and it will prevent us from attaining the mastery necessary to reach our most deeply held goals.

As ever, this exploration and acceptance of fundamental needs requires compassionate non-judgement. We are exploring a poorly understood world, and we must equip ourselves with a gentle curiosity to know and understand.

Coming into awareness of our needs is a fundamental step in our journey to awakening and awareness. Accepting what we find, from the obvious to the esoteric, to the silly or ridiculous to even the unwanted or shameful, is part of that journey.

Responsibility for meeting our own needs

Ensuring that you get the things that you need in order to thrive and flourish is a basic part of self-care. It's also a caring and responsible way to treat those we care about. We'll look at boundaries more in Principle 11.

It's rare, however, to find people who truly understand what they need in order to be fulfilled, and who fully assume responsibility for meeting these needs. What's more common is for people to have a poor understanding of what they really need, or to avoid the question entirely, instead using behaviour that *almost* meet their needs or which seemed to meet their needs at an earlier time in their lives. Equally, we meet people who have some understanding about what they need, but they expect and demand that other people meet those needs, and they complain that it isn't fair when their needs are not met.

Complaining without awareness or purpose is one of the most pointless things we can do. It's also, ultimately, toxic to our wellbeing and mental health. The brain likes to use often-repeated pathways, so it will be better at things you regularly do. Complaining tends to be a statement of victimhood. A complaint includes the belief that somebody else is meant to do something, and they've failed to do it, and it's unfair. It will tend to also include the belief that I am a victim in this situation, and I am powerless to change things. In this way, a complaint is the adult version of the baby screaming: it includes no intention to solve a problem, it is simply declares to the world that something is wrong.

As we discussed in Principle 1, a victim mindset is almost always a choice. Conscious adults who seek to escape the patterns of the past learn to avoiding unconscious complaining.

Karla McLaren talks about Conscious Complaining and I'd like to just introduce the idea here. If it appeals to you, I recommend you dive into her work.

For all the problems that go with it, there can be something satisfying and cathartic about complaining. When we share our gripes and frustrations we offload pent-up emotions. We also often bond with people over complaints as we empathise with their struggles and find empathy and understanding of our own. When done in a non-toxic way, complaining can move from a statement of victimhood to a sharing of experiences and adversity. How do we tell the difference? A great deal of this book is about welcoming unconscious, misunderstood and vilified parts of ourselves into conscious awareness. Complaining can be made in an ally in the same way.

Conscious Complaining is done by agreement between two people. We agree to take five minutes each to gripe and bitch and moan and complain. We recognise that it isn't going to achieve anything practical, but we want to vent, and we want to be heard and understood. Being witnessed is a powerful thing. At the end of our five minutes we stop, pack away our grievances and return to our adult responsibility of taking affirmative, positive action to get our needs met. We spend five minutes listening to the other person complain. It can feel great, it can be fun, and it brings us all the benefits of complaining without its poisonous effects on our thoughts.

As we come into greater awareness of the things we need to feel happy, healthy and whole, so we can gain a better understanding of the ways we are compelled to act to get our needs met. Some of my needs are going to be met simply and quickly: a need for exercise is met by going for a walk or going to a fitness class. That's self-contained, it doesn't require anything from anybody else. But my need for love, for connection, for belonging and acceptance all depend on the participation of other people.

The things we're seeking on this journey will include relationship, friendship and some form of belonging. We're going to need other empowered adults around us in order for this to work. Just as I am free and I have the power to choose, so I must support that behaviour in others. We will build the connections we want by respecting and expecting adulthood from the people that we want to connect with.

When I need something from somebody, I state my request clearly. By doing this, I demonstrate and strengthen my adult identity, and I ensure a fair balance of power between myself and the other person.

I absolutely avoid:

- Manipulating somebody into responding to my needs
- Threatening or coercing somebody, either directly or indirectly, to meet my needs
- Using passive-aggressive language or techniques to imply that they are free to choose, but with a sub-text of reprisal or backlash if they don't do what I want

As an empowered adult, nobody else ever becomes responsible for your needs. If you need something from somebody, you ask them clearly if they will help you. If they say no, then you remain responsible for how to deal with your need from that point.

In all relationships, this can begin by feeling like a clumsy way to communicate. Thankfully, it doesn't tend to stay that way as regular practice develops this skill. Stating our needs clearly and requesting somebody's participation to meet that need can begin with bulky statements like, "I need some attention and validation. I would like you to pay me attention and say nice things to me" but when people know each other well and there is trust and understanding, it can become as simple as "I'm feeling a bit low. Can I have a hug and a few nice words?"

The important thing is that we don't explicitly or implicitly transfer the responsibility for meeting our needs onto other people.

Are there exceptions? Of course. If I'm ill, or injured, or incapacitated in some other way, there are going to be times when I'll unconsciously become a bit infantile and crave that somebody look after me. When we're only beginning to learn these skills in noticing, knowing and meeting our emotional and spiritual needs, we're bound to make mistakes. When we notice we've "acted out" one of our needs without noticing, we acknowledge this, forgive ourselves for the mistake and do our best to learn this need and what it wants from us. We learn, grow and become more conscious over time. In this way, we become more able to trust our own reactions, we become a more dependable friend, ally or lover and we gain an ever-increasing capacity to make new and more empowering choices in our lives.

The aspect of the Deep Coaching attitude that's expressed in Principle 2 includes:

1. I am committed to understanding what I need to thrive and flourish in my life
2. I accept what I find with compassionate non-judgement
3. I am responsible for meeting the needs that I find, and for any of my words, choices or actions that result from my needs
4. I can ask for anything from anybody, but I do not allow

myself to unconsciously transfer responsibility for my needs to another person

The affirmation

"I understand and accept my own needs, and I take responsibility for meeting them"

Counter-affirmations

We will not always be surrounded by others who seek to understand and meet their own needs in an empowered, conscious, adult way. Our culture does not support the growth and development of true adults. When we forget the truths behind this Principle, we might say:

- It's your job to make me happy
- I can't be ok without you
- I don't know what will make me happy
- If you don't do this for me, I'll act ok but find a way to hurt you later
- It's your fault I got angry/upset/sad

3.AUTHENTICITY

"I take care not to solve adult problems with childhood answers"

"I am grateful for the solutions that have taken me this far in my life, even when I choose not to use them any more"

The third Principle has two halves. Both are focused on letting go of things that no longer serve us and getting really clear on the nature of our empowered adult identity.

3 a) I take care not to solve adult problems with childhood answers

Big children

Can you remember the moment that you became an adult? You might be able to think of moments that were defining for you, that made it clear that you'd grown up. Maybe going to University, or the first time you reached an adult landmark: driving a car; losing your virginity; having a baby; getting a well-paid job. But when did you fully step from childhood into adulthood?

Most of us never do.

In many other cultures, there is a moment when a child dies and an adult is born. It's witnessed by the community, or by elders that maintain that rites of the society. It's certainly not private.

For a period of your life you would have been allowed to be wholly a child. You'd have had few responsibilities put on you, you would have played and been part of a structured, tribal world so that you absorbed the rules, morals and myths that guide the tribe. You would have been very clear on your part in that culture. Then the day of your initiation into adulthood would have arrived. For girls, this might be dictated by the onset of puberty and your first period. For boys, it would be dictated by reaching a certain age or some other clear sign. You would have entered into a rite of initiation, and you would have known that your life is about to radically change. Often arduous and painful, your initiation would have seen the psychological death of your childhood identity. You would have emerged as an adult, wholly and completely. Not everybody would have physically survived the rite, but if you did your psyche would have shifted fundamentally.

Ask people from another culture and it's very likely that they could tell you the exact moment they became an adult. This kind of adult would have a psychological strength and clarity that would be almost incomprehensible to a lot of modern-day adults.

Our culture has no real equivalent. There are no universally shared myths and rites to facilitate the passage from one state to another like this, and there are few elders with the understanding and the authority to guide us. We left behind such things as our populations grew, and we became farmers and then city-dwellers and the kind of rigid cultural structures necessary to have initiation rituals of that kind became irrelevant to us.

To be clear, I absolutely do not advocate a return to the past. I'll explore this more in Part 3 of this book. Here, I'm simply explaining how we got to the point where there is no clear distinction between childhood and adulthood.

The result of this blending of child-time and adult-time is that we exist as both child and adult. We carry an inner-child who has the same needs and impulses that we had when we were very young. These jostle and compete with our adult needs and intentions. We live in a culture of big children, and each of us step from a child-attitude to an adult-attitude dozens or hundreds of times every day, until we begin doing the work necessary to reach a true and complete adult state and put the child in its proper place. This sliding between child and adult is a hallmark of our culture, and it undermines and sabotages our attempts to reach our full power and potential, both individually and collectively.

Self-Parenting

I'm suggesting, then, that inside you is a child-identity. This inner child is still operating with the level of awareness that you had as a child. Its exact age might not be the same for everyone, but to begin with it's worth assuming that your inner child is about five years old. If you can remember being five, or if you've spent time around five-year-olds, then you can begin to develop an awareness for how this part of you feels. It might be curious, or playful, or it might be fearful, or shy. Certainly, it'll be easily overwhelmed and easily paralyzed by the expectations and demands of your now adult life. But I am suggesting that without working to meet this inner child, you regularly put the child in a position where it's expected to make decisions for you.

This might happen in moments of stress or anxiety, or it might be that in certain situations you're used to abdicating adult responsibility for a while. It might happen when you're having fun and playing, or it might happen when you're around certain people. At these times, whatever they are for you, your inner child will be in charge.

Even when it's not in charge, your inner child will exert an influence on you. It still has the same needs, desires and expectations as a child, and when it's not cared for properly it'll subtly affect your decisions and feelings to try to coerce you into doing the things it feels it needs.

The inner child is baffled by your adult life. None of the things it expects are there, so it'll try to organise your life to recreate the life it expects. Where have your parents, the people who used to keep you safe, gone? Where are all the things that a young child needs and wants? There are a lot of reasons we act erratically, for example our unmet needs that we discussed in Principle 2, but a big part of our crazy behaviour is down to the influence of our inner child. We do all sorts of things to comfort it, to reassure it, to excite and please it, to meet its infantile needs without realising that's what we're doing.

The answer to this is a modern practice called Self-Parenting. We devote time to meeting and listening to the child-presence within us. We learn to distinguish its voice from the adult voice. When we feel something, or think something, or long for something, we begin to notice whether this is our adult self or the inner child. An excellent book, simply called *Self Parenting* by John Pollard, exists to help you learn to do this. You'll be guided through the first steps of distinguishing your childhood impulses from your adult impulses.

My coaching work often involves the next step, which is learning to actively nurture the child. Once you're able to hear what it wants, you can begin to have a relationship with it. A lot of the things the child wants and needs are due to the absence of a parent figure. You're grown up now, there's nobody around to parent you. Even if you spend time with your actual parents or guardians, it's never going to be the same because you're not a child any more. Some adults devote a lot of their energy to recreating their relationships with their parents, often in intimate relationships, because the inner child cries out for a parent.

Even if the inner child is not directly working to rebuild a parent/child relationship in your adult life, it will often bring anxiety and fear into your life. It simply doesn't know how to handle all the things you've learned to handle. A five-year-old doesn't understand and can't appreciate how to do things like working, paying bills, meeting expectations or making empowered adult choices. You can begin to calm its fears by, internally, taking its hand and learning to be its parent. Speak to it as you would a frightened child. Begin to play with it. Forge a relationship with it. This little boy or girl inside you has been waiting for a parent for so long, and we sabotage our adult competence every time we put this need onto another person, so instead we choose to actively parent our inner child ourselves. Over time you can develop your parenting skills, finding what works to make your inner child feel safe and calm. The more you can soothe and reassure your inner child yourself, the less its needs will bleed into your own and affect the choices you're making as an empowered adult.

Another excellent book about adulthood is called *How to be an Adult*, by David Richo. This small book will further help you to understand what 'adult' means, how we understand and strengthen your adult identity and release things from your early life that have affected the way you've developed as an adult. It's a very dense, immensely valuable little book.

Adult answers to adult problems

The aim of all this work and learning about the nature of adulthood is to fully move your choices into the adult realm. You're going to face a lot of challenges as an adult. As we will go on to explore, challenge is a good thing. A life that lacks challenge, risk, adventure and fear is a life that's stagnating. We are at our best when we're pushing ourselves, learning, growing and being stretched by life. If we hand over responsibility for finding answers to our adult problems to our inner child, we will make bad choices.

Once again we are talking about bringing things into conscious control, but this time in a very specific way. We looked at needs as a whole in Principle 2. The choices we make because of the fears and needs of our inner child are so influential and so commonplace in the modern world that we look at them separately here. There are business leaders, religious leaders and political leaders around the world who are dominated by the needs of their frightened inner children. If we want to reach our full potential and escape from things that have always held us back, a relationship with the inner child is vital. It must be the empowered, conscious adult who is making the choices.

Bring compassionate non-judgement to this Principle. As we learn to notice the voice of our inner child, we might discover that it was their needs and behaviour that ruined past relationships, sabotaged business ventures or stopped us being a great parent to our real children. If you notice these things, mourn the things that you have lost or spoiled before you knew the truth, but seek to forgive yourself as you work. We are interested in the future here, in how you can be if you let go of the things that have always held you back. Resolve to make all your choices from your adult-identity, and work to soothe the inner child by getting to know them and parenting them.

3 b) I am grateful for the solutions that have taken me this far in my life, even when I choose not to use them any more

Old ways die hard

You're a really skilled person. Think about all the things you can do effortlessly, and all the other things you can do when you really try. You've survived your whole life up until this moment, overcoming challenges, enduring hard times, having friendships and relationships, providing for yourself and maybe for others. You've developed skills, knowledge, competence and patterns of doing things. Having done something over and over, you can do it without even thinking. This is a survival skill – if we had to rethink how to do something every time we did it, we'd take forever to do even the simplest things. You can watch young children figuring out how to do things for the first time and see how slowly and clumsily they complete simple tasks and you can watch the same in elderly people or those with dementia as the knowledge to make a cup of tea or have a simple conversation fades from memory.

We develop solutions to all sorts of challenges, from simple practical tasks to very complicated challenges like relationships and our careers. We have often-repeated, memorized ways that we talk to people, or respond to questions like "how are you", or the way we behave when we meet new people. We expect certain things from friendships and romantic relationships based on our past experience and based on lessons we were taught by our parents, our upbringing and the stories of our culture. We pick up ideas about how things are meant to be from books, movies and TV and we apply these ideas to our lives, further reinforcing our patterns of behaviour. The way we act in all sorts of situations isn't spontaneous or intentional, but rather the repetition of old conversations, experiences, expectations and lessons. We carry a complex web of behaviour patterns with us and we make use of them without thinking about it or realising what we're doing. This is a big part of the self-image that we discussed in Part 1: the ideas we have about who we are. It says, "I am the kind of person who acts like this".

As long as this is working for us, it's fine. The problem is, most solutions to complex problems tend to have a finite lifespan. Our needs change as we grow, so we will want different things from our relationships, friendships and conversations. As we get more skilled and experienced at work, we need to change perspective and adapt the way we respond to all kinds of situations. The way that we regard ourselves will change over time and our self-esteem will grow or diminish. We'll enter different phases of life, or pass milestones where people expect different things from us. Life does not stand still, but if we cling to out-dated ways of doing things, we'll become increasingly dissatisfied. All sorts of aspects of our lives will become less relevant, less fulfilling and bring us less joy.

So far I've talked about pretty obvious examples. If you've developed a skill in adult life and used it over and over then you're likely to keep using that skill because you know it well. This can be overturned quickly and unexpectedly. For example, technology can evolve suddenly, and people who have used older technology can feel left behind, needing to re-train or adapt to new approaches.

You have been developing skills and patterns of thought, feeling and behaviour your whole life. When you were growing up, your parents will have needed things from you. They probably didn't have the personal awareness or emotional competence that you are developing right now. This tends to result in parents expecting or demanding unreasonable things from children who aren't ready to provide what they need. One common theme, for instance, is parents with low self-esteem or confidence, who seek constant reassurance or help from their young children. The child isn't emotionally ready to have such expectations put on them, but they're not given a choice. They don't have a lifetime of experience to be able to wonder if the parent should be acting like this. It's all they know, so they adapt and start rescuing and reassuring their parent. These children grow up with a pattern of behaviour of helping those around them, without noticing what they're doing. They're not supporting people in a conscious and adult way, they're re-enacting an unconscious, deeply-implanted belief that they need to save people in order to be a good person. That's what they learned from their parents. As a child they learned that they *must* act to rescue people, otherwise the world will fall apart. People like this might go into healing professions, but even if they don't, they structure their lives, from work to friendships and relationships to their hobbies, in a way that makes them the rescuer. They'll be attracted to people who exhibit the same needs that their parents did, so that they can continue to fulfil the same role and, by doing so, feel a sense of self-worth. They will tend to rescue people at work and perhaps even undermine their own wellbeing in their compulsion to rescue.

This is just an example, but it's one of several common patterns in our culture. It's an example of a very old solution to a challenge, adopted by a child who couldn't know any better, which creeps into adult decision-making. Without personal development work, we don't tend to know about these patterns and without this awareness, there's no way we can change them.

What stops us letting go?

Why would we keep doing thing in outdated ways if they're no longer making us happy? If my child reaches an age where she wants to have rich and engaging conversations with me, for instance, why would I continue to treat her like an infant? If I achieve a promotion at work, and I end up managing my peers, why would I continue to relate to them in old ways? When change enters our lives, even in a dramatic way, and our old patterns and choices are exposed as being outdated and unhelpful, why would we continue to try using our old patterns of behaviour?

The reason is self-image. As we discussed in Part 1, we tend to fight to protect our ideas about who we are. We find enormous reassurance in our knowledge and identity, and we tend to fear the idea of letting go of our competence even when we're very clear that we need to do so.

The fear is not-knowing. Who am I, if I don't do these things and act this way? The fear is of the vulnerability of being without our comfortable, well-known routines. Depending on how attached you are to your patterns, the fear can be pretty overwhelming: you might need some support from a coach or counsellor to understand your patterns and be guided through letting them go. However, there is one tremendous ally in letting go of old patterns.

When you know about an old problem-solving pattern that you want to let go of, but you encounter internal resistance or fear to change, you're stuck between two opposing forces. One force is calling you to grow, break free and let go of old ways. The other force is pushing you to stay safe and stay the way you are. Being squashed in the middle leaves a lot of people feeling paralysed. Most clients who I have worked with over the years are experiencing this paralysis on some level. Many people will be stuck in between these two opposing forces for years of their lives, and it can be a demoralizing or exhausting place to be. "I know this doesn't work anymore, I know I should do something different, but I don't know what or how."

What we need is a third option, a sideways step that gets us out of paralysis between the desire to change and the fear of change. Something that can give us a new way to approach change. The best third option I know is gratitude.

Gratitude and gratitude

There is, perhaps, no background mental and emotional state that's more healthy, helpful and real than gratitude. We have an awful lot to be grateful for, even in the most difficult situations, and gratitude can be a hugely transformative experience. But let me quickly cover the *kind* of gratitude I'm talking about here.

Some people can experience gratitude as a disempowering emotion. It can be easy to experience gratitude as a power-dynamic. If I am grateful for something, it can imply that somebody or something has provided for me. They've done something for me, and in feeling grateful I'm saying that they have more power than I do. People who have power over others can use the idea of gratitude to establish dominance. 'You should be grateful for that.' How often have you heard parents reminding their children to say, "thank you"?

It's easy to get angry with this kind of gratitude. I have suggested gratitude as an idea to some of my clients and they've reacted with 'why should I be grateful?' This anger or resentment is a defence mechanism that some people develop against the abusive misuse of power. It could be a parent, or a boss at work, or a partner, or the government. At some time, something with power over you has implied that you should be grateful.

This kind of gratitude exists in a power-exchange where you are the one without power. It begins in early life, when the adults have all the power and you have none. It can continue into adult life. But it's an undeveloped and unhelpful idea of gratitude that can mask the adult, helpful form of gratitude.

Adult gratitude is simply a mental and emotional acknowledgement of a blessing. It is the feeling of gladness for the realisation that you have something of great worth to you. If I am grateful for a delicious meal, for instance, I am simply bringing an appreciation for a positive, pleasant and nourishing experience.

Have you ever tried to list all the things you feel grateful for? It can be an enlightening experience, and it's something I continue to do regularly. We live in an incredibly privileged time, so even if it's difficult to begin with and even if you're in a dark and frustrating chapter of your life, the list can quickly grow.

By bringing your attention to gratitude on a regular basis, you'll quickly gain a number of benefits. One is that you can counteract any annoyances or frustrations in your day by appreciating the bigger picture. This can be calming and help you find perspective, allowing you to make better decisions. Another benefit is that you open a channel for happiness to enter your life more often as you appreciate the good things that you have. It can improve relationships as you notice things that you may have taken for granted. It can be restful, energizing and restorative, bringing you clarity and respite when you're tired or overwhelmed.

Adult gratitude is also not a barrier to working to improve things. I have worked with visionary business leaders who were disruptive and catalysing their industry to create new products or new opportunities. Being grateful helped them stay connected, aware and responsive to the needs of their colleagues and employees, and it helped them create sustainable solutions to problems by appreciating where they came from. It helped them stay energised and creative by bringing them happiness and gladness, even on a difficult day. It also helped them remember that their work was happening in a broader context, and to stay conscious to the effects they were having in the lives of people within and without their business.

I have worked with activists and campaigners of all kind who are working, every day, to make the world a better place. They fight actively every day to overturn outdated systems and structures, or to establish better ways of doing things. It can be a draining way of life, and so these kinds of people have a big need for gratitude. They must learn to bring focus to appreciation on a regular basis to all their blessings, even while they fight against things that might be terribly wrong or unjust. As we'll go on to explore, rage and gratitude do not cancel one another out.

Gratitude, in an adult sense, means bringing your attention to all the small and big things in your life that are blessings. It means admitting when it's right and proper that you acknowledge and express gratitude for something. It's an internal state, this isn't something you necessarily have to vocalise or share with others. It could be something massive and obvious like the birth of your child, or it could be something mundane and everyday like a beautiful view, the sharing of laughter, a safe home or the act of breathing.

We do everything for a good reason

An important assumption that I make in my coaching work is that we never do anything without a reason. Everything is choice. It's either our active, conscious, intentional choice or it's the choice by an unconscious or unnoticed part of us. Even when we offer our choice to somebody else to make, that's an active choice on our part.

A further extension of this idea is that we do everything *for a good reason*. Even when we do things that are foolish, or unhelpful, or strange, or which seem to sabotage our conscious goals, some part of us was trying to do something helpful and positive. It may be, however, that the part of us that's making this choice is outdated and doesn't understand that it's being unhelpful. This is often the case with old problem-solving patterns.

When we establish a pattern of behaviour, thought or emotion at some point in our lives, we do so for good reasons. It's the best solution we have at that time to the problems that we have at that time. Ultimately, the deeply embedded patterns are about safety. At some point in our lives we didn't feel safe, either physically or emotionally, so we developed a solution that made us feel safer. But as our lives change and the types of problem we face change, our solutions become less and less helpful. We need to let them go and learn new approaches.

A lot of clients who have come to me over the years have said 'I know I do this thing, and I tell myself how stupid it is, but I just keep doing it'.

There's a reason this kind of approach often fails. Some part of you believes that it's still the best way to solve this problem. It believes it's keeping you safe. In effect, you're fighting yourself. If the part of you that still wants to use this solution isn't very strong, you'll quickly change your behaviour. But if you spent a long time using an old solution, and if it was strongly or deeply embedded by an intense emotion, it will fight back. It will find ways of being able to do what it feels it must do in order to keep you safe, and it can be creative and devious in finding ways to circumvent your conscious awareness.

This is partly why it is so important to return all your choices to the centre of your awareness. You must, over time, bring all choices into conscious awareness.

The parts of you that are maintaining old patterns of behaviour and old solutions to your problems, however, may not want to be brought into the light, and even when they are they are not going to be willing to let go of such important things as your safety unless they know you have a better solution.

Gratitude is a very effective way of convincing older aspects of yourself to relinquish control.

Bringing it all together

I have suggested that you're carrying a complex collection of problem-solving patterns, some of which are relevant to your current life and some of which are outdated.

I've suggested that being stuck between desire for change and fear of change often leads to a paralysis that traps people in place, sometimes for years.

I've offered the idea that gratitude can be a transformational attitude to bring to your life.

I've explored the idea that letting go of things is often working against an aspect of yourself that is still trying to keep you safe with old ideas about how life works.

The solution to this is to get to know your old patterns so well that you can relate to them and convince them that you now have the adult competence to be able to make better choices than they can. This is related to the idea of self-parenting. An old pattern, or an old aspect of yourself, will happily let go of control when it understands that you are now in a position to do better than it can.

You convince it to do so with gratitude. You say, internally, to the aspect of yourself that keeps re-enacting an old pattern of behaviour that no longer serves you:

'I acknowledge that you are doing this for good reasons, I am grateful for your hard work over the years to keep me safe, but I can handle this now'.

Gratitude changes the dynamic. If you can express gratitude for something, you validate and acknowledge it. You appreciate it. Once an old aspect of you realises that you get it, that its work has been seen, understood and appreciated, it will be far more willing to let go. By expressing frustration, anger or rage towards it, you can reinforce its understanding that you can't cope, that you need its participation in your decision-making. By thanking it for its work, you are showing calm, rational, adult competence.

Over time, this will allow old patterns to lose their hold on your life until they let go entirely.

The affirmations

"I take care not to solve adult problems with childhood answers"

"I am grateful for the solutions that have taken me this far in my life, even when I choose not to use them any more"

Counter-affirmations

- If I behave like a child, I'll get what I want
- Why should I be grateful? Nobody's done anything for me.
- I can't help it, I'm just like this
- I do stupid things that don't make any sense
- It's normal to be out of control

Deep Joy

4. INTEGRITY

"My choices, words and actions are
aligned with integrity and with my
personal sense of honour"

The attitude at the heart of this book is about bringing all of your power back into your awareness and control, and then giving you a structure to apply it to your life so that you feel fulfilled, satisfied, engaged and alive. We've looked at some of the core understanding that makes this possible, and now we're going to turn our attention to how we begin to manifest it in the world.

A truly conscious, empowered and confident adult is one who has considered their own morality, who understands what is right and wrong, and who consistently makes choices based on this. This isn't something that people tend to do, even those who understand the importance of personal development work. In this chapter we'll look at the reasons it's so important to work out your own morality, how this work can transform your life and how to reclaim the old-fashioned idea of 'honour' to open up new possibilities in your work, your relationships, your creative potential and your life.

The importance of integrity

A big reason that people tend not to touch this topic is that true morality is a deeply misunderstood idea. Some people have old-fashioned images of old people giving outdated sermons about right and wrong, or some other authority figure telling us what to do. Morality can be seen as a burden, an annoying limitation on our freedom. But this way of approaching ethics is essentially a recreation of a parent-child relationship. If we think of ethics like this, we put ourselves back in the child role where we're being guided and instructed by a powerful parent-figure who controls our lives. The approach in this book is all about taking back power.

Perhaps the most important word in Principle 4 is *integrity*. What does this word mean to you?

It's used here in two ways. The first meaning is the idea of *wholeness*. Something with integrity is whole, undivided, well held-together, balanced and strong. The second meaning implies honesty and strong moral principles.

This Principle, then, is about your foundations. It's about ensuring that you have a firm, well-defined source for your choices, words and actions. By doing the personal work to explore, establish and deploy your personal morality, you dramatically reinforce the wholeness of your mind, emotions and spirit. It brings a calmness and focus, a trust in the solid foundations for all that you do and all that you are.

It also brings freedom. Most people inherit a vague sense of right and wrong from their families, friends, partners and culture. Our culture teaches, broadly, that things are wrong if you know you'll be punished for doing them, or if there will be consequences that you don't want. Things are right if there won't be a punishment. For some people, this leaves an unsettled need to understand what's expected of us in any given situation, for fear of getting things wrong and being punished. It tends to encourage us to be 'pleasers', to look for ways to please people around us and to compromise our own integrity to ensure that we're 'getting it right'. We can be encouraged to take ourselves off-centre, or to do things that don't sit comfortably with us, if an individual or group expects us to act that way.

Carrying your own clear sense of right and wrong frees you from this pressure. You do not compromise on your morality, no matter where you are and who you're with. This is your own portable moral compass.

Having a set of values and principles that you stand for is a very effective way to increase your confidence. Principle 4 is another step into full adult consciousness. It's an invitation to reflect deeply on the things that you hold dear, the things you believe, to make some conscious choices about what the impact of your life is going to be. Having these in place gives you an inner authority, an unshakeable foundation to your life, a sense of strength and clarity that will, over time, help you feel more purposeful and confident. You can often spot somebody who has taken time to consider their beliefs and developed their personal sense of honour. They embody their beliefs without ever having to voice them, unlike somebody who is simply drifting from choice to choice with no consistency.

At this point, I suggest that you welcome somebody to join you as you read the rest of this chapter. Think back over your life. Is there somebody, or several people, who you deeply respected? Somebody who embodied integrity, honour, dependability and consistency? Many people I've coached have been able to name somebody like this. Perhaps a parent or another relative. Maybe a teacher or another figure you've learned from. It could be somebody at work or somebody in your community. It could be somebody you spent only a short time with, or somebody you've known your whole life.

If somebody comes to mind, you could mentally invite them to read this chapter with you, to lend their presence to your exploration of your own sense of ethics and honour.

Integrity, trust and consistency

I spent several years of my life intensively studying ethical philosophy. I looked at ideas of right and wrong from the last couple of thousand years and how they've influenced things like law and politics. While it's a fascinating subject, I'm not trying to pack this book full of dry theories and impractical ideas. As ever, I fully encourage you to go and research further if you're intrigued by learning about the history and ideas of ethics, but right now I want to give you practical, functional ideas that you can put into practice.

In the field of ethics, we talk about two kind of approaches. Either we have a series of moral principles that must be enforced at all times, or we look at the outcomes of any given situation and decide on the right course of action based on that. As a coach, I'm all about results.

Chapter 10: Integrity

I want to help every one of my clients reach the outcomes that they want for themselves, and this book is about establishing an attitude that will help you shape your life to bring you the things you want. However, there are big problems with trying to work out the right thing to do in each situation as it arises, and foremost amongst these is inconsistency. If you're trying to figure out the right things to do on-the-fly, as things come up, you'll make different choices based on all sorts of factors, including how you're feeling, the expectations of others, the way you've made choices in the past, the information that's available in the moment, and all sorts of other things that don't really apply to the situation.

To look at this another way, let's consider trust between people. Trust is at the heart of all relationships. Intimate relationships that don't have a strong foundation of trust are stressful, fragile and unlikely to last. Friendships exist between people who have learned to trust one another. Good working relationships are based on trust: ideally because you know you the person is trustworthy, or at the very least because you know they're required to do their job by an employer that you trust. Money exists to create a form of trust between people who are often strangers. The basis for community, connection and culture is trust.

Think back to the person you chose to accompany you through this chapter. You've chosen somebody trustworthy, but how did you know you can trust them? What about them makes them trustworthy, how did they inspire you to trust them?

People who inspire trust in others will build stronger relationships and friendships, be more successful in work and business, build healthy families and will be more likely to have the connections and resources to reach their personal goals.

We build this sense of trust by consistently acting from a consistent set of principles. While they give us a personal foundation, independence and confidence, they also bring us stronger and healthier relationships of all kinds. If you are known to be somebody who will act with integrity and honour, who will be dependable and moral at all times, you will inspire this kind of trust in the people in your life.

Exploring personal values

Our personal ethical integrity is based on our values, so I invite you to begin your exploration here. As ever, make sure you bring your curiosity and your compassionate non-judgement with you. Allow yourself to be curious about learning more about what you really care about.

Values are the building blocks of ethics. They're the simple statements that say we really appreciate certain behaviours or the presence of certain things in our lives. While your values may shift and change across your life, many of them will be constant. Some will arise from core parts of your upbringing, while others may seem to be spontaneous and be baffling and alien to your parents and family.

The question at this point is "what is most important to me?" Some of the answers you think of will be profound, others will be shallow. That's ok. If you start a list of your personal values and it includes both "honesty" and "really nice clothes", that's fine. The important thing is not to stop on your first attempt, because underneath everything you immediately think of will be deeper answers. *Why* do you value honesty? It is because you want to know where you stand with people? Is that because you really value a sense of safety and clarity? Maybe it is, maybe it isn't, for you. *Why* do you like nice clothes? Do you really appreciate sensation, beauty, or wealth? Do you want to identify with a group of people who dress like that? Are you looking for a tribe who share common values with you?

These are the kinds of questions that will lead you to your personal values. Begin listing things that you really care about, that steer your choices and goals, and then begin digging into each one for the underpinning values that make them up. One exercise I offer my clients who are trying to understand what they believe and what they stand for, is to give them a long list of over a hundred values and ask them to whittle it down to just a few. You can find lists like this online. This might be helpful in trying to find your own core values.

You will know if a value has strong resonance for you if you have a strong emotional response to it, whether that emotion is excitement, pride, enthusiasm, regret, anger or shame.

You may discover values that you don't want, or that don't sit well with you. If you're very competitive or ambitious, for instance, you may find some values waiting beneath your choices that may not be compatible with the person you want to be. You might also find values that consistently drive your choices which aren't yours. If you had a very demanding parent, or if you spend a lot of time with somebody with a strong personality, you may have taken on their values. You will need to decide if you want these. This book is about returning all choice and power to the centre, to your conscious control. You can't do this if you're living somebody else's ethics. If you find somebody else's values under your longings and choices, and they sit well with you and feel good and valuable, then you can consciously choose to make them yours. Stop relying on somebody else to bring this principle into your life: consciously adopt it yourself.

It may take time to construct your list of values. You will need to watch yourself in different kinds of situations. On one day, or in one kind of situation, you might strongly feel that something is a core part of you, while on another day you might reject it. To begin with, be curious. If your values and priorities change a lot, that's an interesting thing to notice. Add this information to your list. Try not to judge yourself. As your list grows and your awareness of your values grows, you'll reach a point where you will need to choose which of these things is most important to you. Which are your deepest core values, and which are things you'll need to put aside?

Exploring personal ethics

Once you have a set of values that resonate strongly for you, which you know are important to you, you can codify them into a set of ethical principles. The process goes something like this...

1. Think what kind of choices are going to lead to the best result. In this situation, 'best' means your vision for your future, where your values are protected, enshrined or demonstrated. This might include the choices you make that directly lead towards your goals, but it'll also include the choices you make in indirect support of them. The way you choose to treat people. The choices you make that affect that things around you, knowing that you are part of a community, a family, a circle of friends and a wider world. Think about the choices you will make, consistently, that will lead to not only the life you've created in your vision, but also to you being the person you most want to be. Consult, in your imagination and in reality, with people who embody those values and principles that you admire. What do they do, what choices do they consistently make, which make them into good people?
   Consider things like:
   - How you treat yourself
   - How you treat people you care about
   - How you treat those who are vulnerable, needy or less privileged than you
   - How you treat those who have far more than you
   - How you behave when you're working
   - How you behave when you're feeling good about

yourself

- What behaviour you choose when you're feeling low, or angry, or resentful
- Where and on what do you spend money? (the effects of our spending are usually the greatest power we have to affect the world at large)
- How you contribute to your family, friends, community and to the world

2. Now consider whether these are the right choices for you to enact at all times, in all places, and in all situations. You might stop and re-evaluate your choices from time to time, but you don't want to be doing this very often as it'll erode your foundations and your ability to inspire trust. You are looking for things you can believe in, stand for and demonstrate over the coming years, no matter what situation you're in. If you value honesty, for example, one of your ethical principles might be to speak with honesty and request it from others. This would be something you do in all situations, even ones that are difficult. If you want to be a great manager or leader at work, and you've worked out ethical principles to allow you to do this, make sure you can apply them equally at home or with your friends.

3. Steps 1 and 2 will give you the core principles of your ethics. They flow from your values, which flow from your personal needs, desires, ambitions and heart-felt impulses. For this reason, when you realise your personal ethical principles, they will feel like a manifestation of your deepest and truest self.

4. Put your ethics into action. Accept the limitations and the clarity that they bring you. This may take time, you may find it easy to hold to your principles in some situations but difficult in others. Bring your compassionate and non-judgemental attitude with you here too. This will take time. When you realise you've slipped, reconnect with the values

and feelings that underpin your choice to adopt this principle and put it into action again. If you need to have difficult conversations with friends, family or colleagues so that they understand what you're doing, make time to do this. The important thing is to learn, over time, to put your ethics at the heart of your decision-making.

Gateways of choice

Personal honour is the capacity to consistently demonstrate ethical principles through your choices. In that sense, honour is a kind of mental and spiritual fitness. The more often, and the more consistently, you act from a single set of principles, the more deeply held will be your sense of honour. This may start off being difficult or clunky. Give it time. It'll get easier and feel more natural.

A mentally, emotionally and spiritually mature adult is somebody whose choices pass through a number of gateways before they're finally made. When a choice arrives, rather than going with an immediate impulse, an adult reflects. One gateway is your vision. Does this choice bring you closer or further away from your vision? If a choice arrives, even a very tempting one, and it's clearly going to take you off-course and set you back from attaining your vision, a gateway closes in the mind. This isn't really a choice at all. When the gateway was open, it was a choice. But now that you've reflected on your vision, and found that this choice isn't compatible with it, you immediately close this mental gateway. You close it off, shut it down, remove it as a possibility. Your vision is the second gateway that any choice should pass through.

But the first gateway is honour. If you're presented with a choice that isn't compatible with your personal set of ethical principles, the gateway closes. It isn't an option. The choice doesn't even reach the second gateway of your vision. Since you've done the work to establish your core values, which arise out of your deepest feelings and beliefs, your ethical principles will be part of your vision, so you aren't going to lose out. In order to grow your integrity and build this inner sense of honour, you must get used to closing the gateway on choices that violate your personal ethical principles.

This can be hard. A business opportunity or a new relationship might come along that's exciting and tempting. All you need to do is lie about something to make it happen. If honesty is one of your ethical principles, the gateway to this option closes. This firmness of stance is the bedrock to your confidence and sureness about yourself, so allow it to grow into something strong and formidable. Become known as somebody who is flexible and imaginative about all sorts of things…but unbending when it comes to the things you most deeply believe. One of the ways that our confidence grows, as we'll explore in Principle 7, is by putting yourself into challenging and difficult situations. Each time you stick to your ethical principles in a difficult situation when you're tempted, challenged or even mocked for the strength of your beliefs, you will strengthen your inner sense of honour and your confidence will grow.

Honour and disgrace

I've mentioned the idea of toxic shame in this book, and in the next Principle I will dig into this in much more detail, but there is a healthy kind of shame.

Our culture is not, generally, made up of adults who have reflected deeply on their choices and made an empowering commitment to unlock their own potential. This is something you're doing, and it sets you apart. There have been other times and other cultures that promoted and supported people to do the kind of work that you're doing, to be initiated into their own adulthood and to discover their own personal honour and integrity. For example, Native American tribes or the Samurai of feudal Japan. While these were real people whose motivations and dedication would have varied, we know that the ideals in those cultures encouraged them not to blindly follow the prejudices and expectations of others. They developed their own personal principles, they returned their personal power to the centre and they had the mental, emotional and spiritual awareness to be able to make conscious choices that were independent of everyone around them. Such people are capable of anything, but as we've explored, such people naturally develop a sense of right and wrong to underpin their conscious self-image. Having awakened a powerful freedom to choose, they restrict their choice to things that align with their values, giving each choice greater significance and ensuring it's aligned in the direction that the person wants to be going in their lives.

As you become one of these people, it may be useful to think about a balance of honour and shame within yourself. This is an internal process. Others may contribute to it, but it's up to you to manage it.

When you act in a way that's aligned with your principles, which themselves flow out of the things you value most, you gain honour. You have a sense of rightness, of self-assuredness, you consciously acknowledge that the choices you're making are good.

When you act in ways that violate your own ethical principles, which don't sit well with you, which break your sense of integrity with the wholeness of who you are, or which aren't having effects in the world that you can be proud of, then you gain shame. There is a right and appropriate time for shame, and it's when when we act unethically. For instance, when somebody does something that they know will cause harm for no good reason, whether they choose to acknowledge it in that moment or not, it's only right that they should feel ashamed of their choice.

Toxic shame is a cultural straight-jacket that we'll explore in the next Principle. It's rooted in the idea that there's something intrinsically wrong with us, and it's the constant and unspoken fear that if the people we love really saw us for who we are, without our masks and our pretence at goodness and competence, nobody would really love or accept us. Sadly, this is a common belief. I have met only a handful of people in my life who didn't carry this on some level, and that was only true because they'd done extensive personal development work to understand and heal this culturally-enforced wound.

Toxic shame is the idea that you aren't good enough.

To distinguish this kind of shame from the feeling you have when you violated your own values and ethics, I sometimes use the word 'disgrace'. This means, literally, a lack of grace. You've noticed that your choices are lacking in grace. This is a good thing. It's something we feel in our heart and our guts. It's an emotional messenger that exists to tell us we have something to do. We have done something wrong and we need to take action to put it right. This feeling of shame or disgrace is an important companion to anyone seeking to become a resolved and empowered adult. Don't ignore it, suppress it or reject it. It's a wise messenger from your body, your emotions and your spirit to pay more attention to the choices you're making.

The affirmation

"My choices, words and actions are aligned with integrity and with my personal sense of honour"

Counter-affirmations

- I can do anything I want, as long as it feels good
- You can't tell me what to do
- Why should I?
- I don't really like doing things like this, but I'll do it just this once
- I'll become whoever you need me to be
- I'll do whatever makes you happy
- I'm too shy to act consistently
- I like to just go along with things

Chapter 10: Integrity

Deep Joy

5.LIBERATION

"At this time, we are a broken people"

We've looked at some of the important foundations for an empowered, conscious life. So far, we've mostly looked at your life as a solitary thing. Most personal development books, YouTube videos and coaching courses do this. Personal development tends to be divided into the personal and, separately, into the social (like how to succeed at work or how to make friends). This helps you develop skills separately, but the two are so intimately intertwined that there's always something missing if you study one in isolation. We are not islands. We exist in relationship to lots of people and every choice we make is within the context of a time, a place, a society and a culture. In this chapter we'll begin to look at context. What subtle pressures and influences smother our freedom to choose and drown out our happiness, without us even being aware of them? What effect does this have on us, on our relationships and on the future of our world?

Humans are natural storytellers. If you ask a friend about a difficult day at work, or a scary thing that happened on their morning commute, or the last time they visited their family, they'll naturally turn it into a story. They'll give it a beginning, middle and end and they'll naturally use metaphors and characters to bring the story alive. Storytelling is a powerful bonding ritual. By telling stories instead of just listing facts, we create an emotional bond with our listeners, and we engage the emotional centres of our brains instead of just relying on the logical part, improving recall and helping make sense of the things that happen to us. We take our listeners on a journey through the events of our lives, or our ideas or our dreams for the future. They feel what we feel, and share in our lives in an intimate, emotional way. We do this every day, without noticing that we do it.

Stories are used to share information, but they're also used to reinforce the way we see the world, to persuade us to change our point of view, or to manipulate our perspective. Speeches and announcements will often be based around stories that say more than they seem to. For example, Martin Luther King's 'I have a dream' speech was filled with metaphors, references and emotive language that showed millions of people what a better world could look like, while Hitler's passionate rallies told stories that ignited the hatred, prejudice and nationalism of his audience. Newspapers are full of stories, and each story is written to reinforce a certain way of seeing the world.

There are always stories inside our stories. If I tell you a story, I need to know that you'll understand what I'm saying. We speak the same language, so that's a good start. But we also share certain beliefs, we've got certain points of reference in common, we've both grown up in a world with a lot of shared ideas, images and concepts. Maybe we watched the same TV shows as kids, and maybe we've watched the same shows as adults. We can both refer to those and know what we're talking about. We've both been educated, we both know the law pretty well. Maybe we know about famous celebrities and we can refer to those. Maybe we're both into sports. Maybe we both know something about cars or history or fashion. We've got enough common ground that I can refer to these things without saying them directly. I can use metaphors in my stories that you'll understand.

Going deeper than this, we've both been educated in the basic assumptions of our society. We live in a pluralistic, post-modern, complicated world where things are changing rapidly, so this isn't as easy as it once was. If you'd grown up in an indigenous tribal culture, you would have been taught the stories of the tribe, and those stories would have taught you things about the way the world is. Where did we come from? What are men supposed to be like and what are women supposed to be like? How are they meant to treat each other? What's the difference between children and adults? What's the relationship between people and the rest of the world? What things are good, noble, virtuous and heroic, and what things are bad, immoral, cowardly or evil? Who are the heroes from our past and who are our villains? Do we believe in a god or gods, and what do they expect of us?

Most importantly on a personal level, how are you meant to behave so that you'll feel successful, loved and accepted by other people?

If you visited different cultures across human history, you'd get different answers to these fundamental questions. Men might behave in ways you'd find outlandish and women might fulfil roles you wouldn't expect. The way the young are educated and initiated might seem strange or even alarming, as might the way people treat the elderly. All sorts of things, from the way people dress, to the things they believe to be true, to the ways they connect to one another, to their approach to everything from food to sex, might be totally alien to you. To them, it would be normal and obvious, and the way you act and the things you believe would seem bizarre and wrong to them.

We can normalise most things. We can turn almost anything into "just the way things are". Because of this, unless you take the time to notice it, culture is invisible to us. We cannot see the wood for the trees until we take the time to notice it.

In the 21st Century, we are fracturing as a people. During times of plenty this means we are becoming pluralistic and accepting of different points of view. During times of stress, anxiety or want, it means we are being sorted into silos of thought: we are forming antagonistic tribes who see 'the other side' as stupid, wrong, dangerous or deluded. Powerful individuals and institutions are profiting from this division, so it's more important than ever that those of us on a journey of personal awakening and discovery take the time to work out all of the subtle manipulations and pressures that we experience every day through the stories that we're told.

At this time of transformation, we are stuck between old stories and new ones. The older stories tend to be simpler and that makes them persuasive. Men are domineering brutes or over-emotional "new men". Women are fragile waifs or fierce go-getters. Children are annoying, while youth is the most valuable thing in the world. Success is financial wealth.

The new stories are more complicated. Are all the things we used to say about men and women actually oppressive to people who don't feel they fit in one gender or the other? What is success these days? How can we possibly get parenting right, with all the pressures and expectations that are put on parents today? What will make us happy? What can we really be sure of?

From the moment we're born, we're taught the stories behind the stories. These underpinning assumptions, beliefs, expectations and demands are all summed up by one word: culture. A culture is a set of stories that a group of people tell each other about the way the world is, and all the choices and behaviours that those people make based on those stories. Today, the culture we grew up in has spread to dominate the world. One way a culture is expressed is by the clothes we wear. We dress in certain ways to tell other people things about us, and those people know what we're saying because we grew up in the same culture. You will find people wearing jeans and t-shirts in Manhattan, Paris, Beijing, Bangkok, Moscow and Manilla. Regional differences remain, but most of us now live in a worldwide, multi-national, homogenous mono-culture. Indeed, one of the messages of our culture is that success can be measured by how closely we align with this international belief system, and replace our old-fashioned, quaint local customs, traditional clothing or regional accents.

It's now very important to understand the culture that we live in. In many ways it remains a supportive, healthy, nourishing part of our personal lives. It's brought many of us prosperity, security, strong identity and a sense of community. However, even for those of us who are best served by our culture, it's brought us toxic beliefs, divisive sub-cultures, unhealthy pressures and expectations, and limits to our dreams and imaginations. As long as a story works for you, it's invisible. It's only when you start to be oppressed by a story, or marginalised, or somehow hurt or excluded by the story, that it becomes obvious. Most of us go our entire lives without realising that we're basing our beliefs, our expectations of ourselves and our relationships, and our dreams for the future on some made-up stories.

My belief is that our culture causes far more worry and insecurity, confusion and doubt, suffering and death than it causes goodness. The pressures and expectations of our culture mean that we must continue to live in a way that we know causes pain, injustice and inequality for people around the globe and for the natural world. It causes wealth, security, access to healthcare and social mobility to be distributed unevenly: in some countries and places people are rich and safe, in other countries and places they are very poor and live in fear. Our culture has created the impending disaster of climate change, which threatens not just our wellbeing but the survival of our species and many other plants and animals on earth. It is a time of tremendous crisis, but the beliefs and expectations of our culture leave us paralysed. Most of us barely pay attention to the larger needs of the world around us. We don't have time! Our culture keeps us very busy and bombards us with stories and demands.

In this chapter I'll list some common cultural stories that influence us in negative ways, and I'll offer ideas or counter-stories to help you begin figuring out whether or not you want to keep these stories in your own life. What's important, overall, is that you begin noticing how your culture is influencing your thoughts. To begin with, I recommend distancing yourself from these cultural beliefs altogether. Try to spend time with people who believe differently, or try reading different newspapers, unfamiliar books or watching movies from foreign countries or documentaries about things you wouldn't normally consider. Exposure to other points of view helps highlight the assumptions we are making in our own stories. Try to create a gap in your life between yourself and your culture. Then, once you have a clear picture of the underlying assumptions, the 'just the way things are' that's been guiding your life, you can begin to re-enter culture in a healthy and conscious way, only taking on board the things that you want to take on board.

Toxic shame and the Karpman Drama Triangle

The stories of our culture are steeped in shame. Many of us are taught to accept shame about ourselves early in life and it becomes an unconscious weight that we carry for the rest of our lives. This unconscious, shared story of shame is what I've referred to as toxic shame.

What this means is that many of us are carrying a fundamental belief about shame. We hide it deep, but if we were to give it voice it would say something like:

'if people saw me as I really am, if they really knew me, nobody would ever love me'

For some people, this idea is so deeply hidden that at first it sounds bizarre and ridiculous. For others, they live with this belief daily and they're aware of the work they do to keep it hidden. But whether we're conscious of it or not, a great many of us are carrying this story. It was never ours. It has no basis in reality, although we will often create reasons to justify how strongly we feel that it's true.

It's an inherited story, and its history is long, sad and complicated. It began in early childhood as we listened to our parents, siblings and friends and worked hard to develop ourselves based on their example. If you've been taught this story, you'll continue to reinforce it with other people who secretly feel the same for the rest of your life, until you bring it to conscious awareness and take steps to replace it with more constructive, truer, more authentic stories. Until then, we tend to stay mired in the depressing, but very comfortable, belief of being an unworthy and unlovable person. Most of us aren't aware we carry these ideas until we're challenged by something that triggers our most deep insecurities. At those moment, we suddenly realise that we're wearing carefully crafted masks of acceptability in an attempt to please others, to be accepted, to reassure ourselves and to encourage the love and acceptance that we all instinctively need.

The psychologist Stephen Karpman has developed a model for the three main masks we wear. These masks are a response to the pervasive cultural shame that we each carry. We can't bear the idea of being seen as we truly are, so we wear masks, and the Karpman Drama Triangle is made up of the three masks that we wear most often.

The Drama Triangle is a game that many of us are playing with one another. In this game, we choose to play one of three characters for a while, often in response to somebody else who's wearing another mask. We will tend to play different characters at different times, but we'll tend to identify more strongly with one than with others. This most familiar mask becomes our go-to place for all social relationships, and understanding it is important to understanding why our friendships, relationships and parenting turn out the way they do.

Wearing these masks is a choice. It's usually a choice we make unconsciously to hide our true and authentic selves which we've been taught are shameful. But as we've already explored in this book, unconscious choices can be made conscious. That is how we gain power over them.

The three positions in the Karpman Drama Triangle are:

1. The Victim

    (the archetypal infant)

    The Victim knows that they are unable to help themselves or save themselves. Helplessness and hopelessness are the core feelings for the Victim. They exist in a needing state, waiting for somebody to save them. They will tend to twist opportunities into failures, create self-fulfilling prophesies of failure and collapse and will tell people how hopeless things are.

    The Victim is the operator for the other two characters – they need a Victim to function, so if you tend to identify with the Victim role, you'll attract the others to you who will both try to push you deeper into a Victim mentality.

2. The Rescuer

    (the archetypal mother)

    The Rescuer character gains their self-esteem from helping others. If they aren't helping, they are failing. If they are helping, they get great satisfaction and pride from it. This causes them to constantly look for people to help, and to be dependent on the act of helping for their mental wellbeing. You could imagine a fussy mum who's constantly trying to help but is overbearing and smothering. If you identify most strongly with the Rescuer, you'll find yourself consoling people, reassuring them, wanting to support them and be kind to them. Unfortunately, the Rescuer also creates victims in their urgency to feel useful and worthwhile. If a Rescuer finds there is nobody to rescue, they will tend to exaggerate the needs of somebody to try to push them into feeling like a victim. They might say "oh you don't look well, are you *sure* you're feeling ok?" or try to stir up a fight or breakup so they can step in to rescue the Victim.

3. The Persecutor
   (the archetypal father)

   The Persecutor character feels constantly under attack. If you tend to identify with the Persecutor character, you'll often feel like you're simply trying to do your best and be a good person, but people are constantly criticising you, undermining you or draining your energy. People make life so much harder for the Persecutor than it should be. Sometimes this will be true, but it'll also be heavily inflated by the Persecutor's expectations and point of view. Comments will be twisted into attacks or complaints. The Persecutor will also manipulate people around them to fulfil their expectations: they'll subtly invite people to make demands or they'll set up unnecessary conflict to reinforce their belief that people are trying to make their lives hard. In response to this, Persecutors tend towards aggression, bullying and violent outbursts. From their point of view, they're just them trying to defend themselves against everyone else. From an outside perspective, it's mean-spirited hostility.

This simple model sums up so many of our interactions. There's a complex interplay between the characters. You might feel low one day, and a Rescuer may pounce on you and try to save you and validate themselves, but they'll push too hard and knock you into a Persecutor role, which will cause them to feel overwhelmed and bullied so they'll adopt the Victim position. Most of us have a favourite character that we choose to embody most often, and because we've seen ourselves occupy this position so often we can come to believe that this is our true identity.

If you'd like to know more about these characters and how they interact in families, at work, in relationships and friendships and how they appear in parenting, I'd encourage you to research and explore the Karpman Drama Triangle.

The important thing to realise is these characters or masks are just another set of choices we can make.

As mentioned elsewhere in this book, I strongly recommend Brené Brown's research and advice about cultural shame and the role of personal vulnerability in overcoming yours. We cannot overcome toxic shame from within the thinking that created it, we have to make new, more authentic choices about how we're going to show up in the world and let down the masks that keep us safe but trapped. The solution here is vulnerability: the courage and awareness to let down our defences and be seen the way we really are.

This can be hard if you've spent your life wearing the masks that you think will bring you success and love, and it will be hard if you're really good at playing the games of the Karpman Drama Triangle. Two of Brené Brown's talks on TED are a great way to sample her work, or I recommend her book: *Daring Greatly* to begin identifying the masks you wear and learning to lower them to let the world see who you truly are. *Daring Greatly* also deals with the "Vulnerability Hangover", which is the sudden feeling of being overwhelmed we can experience when we begin to let people see us. It's a beautiful little book with a lot of practical advice, so if you're ready to begin delving into your own relationship with toxic shame and how to shake off its shackles, I suggest you dive in.

Deep Joy

Unhelpful and toxic stories at the heart of our culture

Happiness is something you receive

What if you didn't need anyone or anything to make you happy? What if you could source your own happiness right here, right now, without anybody else's help and without having to earn it or have it given to you? Actually, that's the true nature of happiness…

What's the story and how is it told?

Other people teach us the story of needing to inherit happiness. Our parents often believed it, as did our friends at school. Our culture teaches it through books, movies and TV shows. Once you have 'the thing', we're taught, you'll be happy. You just need to earn the thing.

'The thing' might be money; once you're rich, you'll be happy.

It might be success in business; once you've made it, you'll be happy.

It might be marriage and children.

It might be the approval of your friends and family.

It might be goals set by your religion.

It might be fame.

It might be travel to exotic places; once you get there, you'll be happy.

It might be owning something really expensive: a house, boat or expensive car.

But whatever the thing is, *it* is the thing that will bring you happiness. This cultural story says that happiness is something you receive. It comes from outside. It's something you might be blessed with, if you're good enough, or lucky enough, or ruthless enough or if you behave in the right way. If you do everything right, happiness will be given to you.

Chapter 11: Liberation

This unspoken assumption is part of so many of our stories. You can find it in movies about princesses who are happy when they find their prince charming. You can find it in the adoration of the rich and famous; we obsessively follow their lives because they have what we want: a route to happiness. You can find it in fathers who work themselves into the ground and mothers who smother and fuss over their children; their wellbeing is caught up in being the best worker or the best parent they can be. You can see it in the cultural story, embedded in so many movies and TV shows, that it doesn't matter if we do miserable work, because that's normal; we should live for the weekends and holidays and for retirement, when we can be happy because we're free of work.

There is some truth here, of course. The moment your child is born, or the moment you get a big promotion, or the moment you check your bank balance and see a lot of big numbers may well make you very, very happy. But like all feelings, happiness is meant to flow. Emotions pop up to tell us something, to deliver a message, to bring us into the moment and connect with what's really going on. If some fundamental need is met in an extravagant and overwhelming way, then you're likely to respond with happiness. Or, you may not. I have known business owners who worked for decades for that big win, and when it arrived and they achieved everything they'd dreamed of, they felt nothing.

The point is that we're taught that happiness is something we are handed by something or somebody else. A situation will make us happy, owning something will make us happy, being with the right person or getting the right help or being in the right place will make us happy.

Happiness will come. Some of us flow into happiness more easily than others, but no matter how easily happiness arrives in your life, it will flow on again. This too shall pass. No matter how much you love your kids, you won't always be happy around them. No matter how much money you have, you won't always be happy no matter how rich you become. No matter how much you travel, or how much your friends tell you you're a great person, or how often you fall in love, or how often you have lovely experiences or sensations, happiness will come and then it'll flow on again. Nothing outside of you will bring you eternal happiness. Happiness just doesn't work like that. Just like sadness, anger or fear, it flows into our lives, fills us for as long as well need it, and then flows on.

For many people, this leads to a lifetime of chasing. You might feel that you're *meant* to be happy. We can feel a pressure and an expectation to be happy. Also, happiness feels good. We remember happy times from our past and we can fall into the trap of imagining that every moment can be like that if only we find the things that bring us happiness. Happiness can become an addiction, and ideal, a state we desperately long for. In a life that isn't very satisfying, happiness becomes the golden thing that we chase, and the things we imagine make us happy become our dreams. If you fall for the gilded happiness dream, you will end up arranging your whole life around this single priority: stuff it full of as many things that bring you happiness as possible. Happiness becomes the goal of being, and when we're not happy we're looking forward to our next happy moment.

Numerous studies have shown that people are singularly bad at predicting what will make them happy. This is just part of unconscious, unreflected human nature. As a rule, people don't take the time to reflect on what makes them, personally, individually, happy. We inherit our ideas about happiness in obvious and subtle ways, and then we carry them through our lives, believing them to be our own. We are living somebody else's story, and the story almost always involves finding things outside yourself which will bring you the precious state of happiness.

This unconscious, pressured search for outside things that will make us happy isn't the same as consciously working towards a goal. You've begun, or perhaps already completed, a vision for the future you want, and you've begun to bring it alive with lots of living ideas so that you know what it's going to be like when you get there. I'm sure you were pretty happy in aspects of your vision, but you've taken time to flesh out these ideas so they aren't just vague goals that you've inherited from others. If you're reading this section and you think that maybe your vision is just an idea of happiness that somebody else has sold you, then go back and check it out. Ensure it aligns with your core values. Make sure it's what you want, and make sure there's more to it than a need to remain in a peak experience of happiness for as long as possible.

A lot of people live like this. It's a normal, everyday misconception, and it causes a lot of our personal and collective problems. It can make us compromise on our values and beliefs, it can ruin precious friendships and relationships and it can make life a fragile and difficult experience if we're reliant on external things to give us something we believe we should have. As a society, it drives us to be destructive. Most importantly, for long as our happiness is tied up in the accumulation of belongings and wealth, to the exclusion of *how* or *where* these things are made, we become parasites on the world, sucking all the riches and precious belongings to our little corner of the globe and causing tremendous damage as we do.

The stories of our culture are steeped in the things that will make us happy, if only we work hard enough and behave well enough.

An alternative story

Happiness of the moment is a beautiful thing. Some event happens, or we remember to realise something, and we're filled with happiness. That's great.

Healthy, adult emotions come as a full package: you have all of them or you have none of them. That's just how feelings work. Happiness is a proper response to certain situations. It isn't a sustainable way to live.

What if we could replace the search for peak moments and rushes of happiness, which leave us dependent on outside things to trigger the feeling in us, with something more sustainable and autonomous?

What I recommend to my coaching clients is this: seek a simple, calm sense of gladness. An appreciation of the little things. A delight in the day-to-day blessings that we each receive.

This isn't meant to be *instead* of ambition, drive and determination to excel. I strongly encourage you to keep those things alive, to push yourself to excel and reach the dream you've created for yourself. But if you're so focused on the end result that you don't appreciate the small blessings of the now, there's a good chance that you'll arrive at the big goal but fail to appreciate that as well. Appreciation, like so many things, is a kind of training. It's a skill that we can strengthen and nourish over time.

By taking the time, every day, as often as possible, to notice little things that you feel a simple gladness for having in your life, your skill in appreciation grows. The peak moments become even better, and the gaps in between (which will make up most of your life, after all) become filled with good feelings. This kind of subtle, background happiness opens a channel for more intense feelings of joy and wonder to flow into your life.

This state is sustainable and doesn't depend on other people or things providing for your happiness.

What can we do about it?

At all times, we can find appreciative for simple things. Here's a short list of some things you might notice and find gratitude and gladness for:

Breathing

Natural beauty – a tree, the sunlight reflecting off water, the shape of the clouds

Opportunities that lie ahead

Friends and family

A child's laughter

Technological marvels

The movement of the body when it feels good

A kind word and an act of kindness

To live in peace and security, not in war or poverty

Physical touch and closeness

Delicious food or drink, nice sensations

A warm and cosy bed

Pride in having done something well

Adopt an appreciation of simple things as a practice in your life. To begin with, this might need to be a structured thing: keep an appreciation journal or arrange to talk to a friend about simple things you are glad for on a schedule you've both agreed.

Foster the phrase "I am happy with what I have" and say it often.

Allow simple appreciation to creep into all aspects of your life. Try to notice more things as you go about your days: we tend to go onto autopilot easily. Look out for little things that can bring a little wonder and joy into your life, for even the shortest time.

Foster an understanding that life is not about choosing some nice-feeling states and trying to avoid others. Life is about experience, realness, authenticity and empowered action and choice. This means welcoming the full range of emotions, as each will be appropriate and important for a situation or experience.

At the same time, try to look out for cultural stories of chasing happiness and the idea that happiness is something you receive from somewhere else, and notice if they're part of a sales pitch or some other form of manipulation. Try to distance yourself from these stories. Bring yourself back to your vision and where the vision. Where your is in conflict with something that somebody else thinks you should do, prioritise your vision.

Be passive, follow. Victim mindset.

What's the story and how is it told?

In this story, life is a straight line. You are born. For a while, your parents care for you. Then you go to school, maybe university afterwards, and then you work. Companies and the government have made jobs and you just have to pick a job that you are qualified for, that you can do relatively well, that pays well enough and which has enough benefits. You work quite hard, but only as hard as anyone else does. You live for the weekends and holidays, where you don't have to work anymore. The 9 to 5 story dominates your life. The joy of Fridays and the crushing disappointment of Mondays is a constant companion.

This story is everywhere. Dozens of TV shows are based on just following people through their 9 to 5. Comedy sketches are based on the Friday feeling. People have pre-prepared answers to the polite "how are you?" based around which day of the week it is.

Millions of people don't live this story, and find it a bit weird, alien and sad. Some are people lucky enough to have landed a job that's actually satisfying and fulfilling for them. Other are entrepreneurs, radicals and free-thinkers. We'll look at them in a moment. But when you're inside the story, it's hard to see out. The job pays the money that keeps you alive, and we can develop an infantile sense of dependence on this source of nourishment. We cling to our so-so jobs. We might talk about breaking free, but our whole sense of safety and identity is bound up with the job we do: the routine it gives us, the self-esteem we get from doing it well and, perversely, we get reassurance from boredom, drudgery, monotony, repetition. It's known. It's the comfort zone. We can share all the stories about work with our friends and families. We share the known joys and pains and we get a sense of bonding and identity from this.

Work is just an example of this story, though. The story itself is: follow. Stay asleep. Don't feel too much, don't notice too much. Be original and eccentric if you like, but within certain limits. Make sure everything is kept safe for you and for the people around you. Be the cattle pressed up against other cattle: if you act up there will be a stampede and then what will happen? We don't know, so we walk the well-trodden path.

A lot of people like to imagine that we're being controlled and directed by powerful people. We are certainly being manipulated, but we don't need anybody in power to teach us the story of passivity. We do that to ourselves willingly. We exchange our freedom, individuality, potential and wildness for security, validation and anaesthesia.

We console ourselves by complaining. Complaining can be cathartic, but it's also a practice of powerlessness. Every time we complain, we demonstrate that we are dependent, passive and trapped within a lifestyle that we've just said we don't like. We tell stories about the bits of our lives we hate (thus reinforcing them) and then we demonstrate our inability to escape. This approach to struggle is a guaranteed way to reinforce a victim-mindset, and the presence of victims will tend to encourage other people to adopt Persecutor or Rescuer mindsets. Many workplaces are dominated by the Karpman Drama Triangle.

Any idea of personal freedom in this situation is an illusion. We don't choose: we are given limited options and we're generally directed which to choose. We are living at a time when the control and manipulation of people is subtle and sophisticated. We can choose something else at any moment, but it's so much easier not to. Don't choose. Follow. Be like other people. Have heroes and role models who are remote, fantastical, carefully marketed versions of real humanity. Never have principles or ethics: they're annoying and they alienate you from others. Do as your told and choose the easy belief that there's no other way to be, choose to believe that you're trapped and there's no way out.

That is the default state of the industrialised human. It has its benefits. It helps us easily identify with others and it lets us carry on with lifestyles which, while not satisfying and prosperous, are at least safe and predictable. But the personal cost is enormous. Dreams go unrealised. Relationships are surface and only satisfying in the most shallow sense. You have no real control over your future, your earning, your lifestyle or your effects in the world. Things will happen to you randomly and then other things will take their place. It'll be a rough, malnourished life which, as you near death, will seem utterly wasted and pointless.

This book is about showing you a wild, free, powerful way to be. Once you see outside the story of powerless passivity, and once you begin to feel what it's like to live as a wild human, the idea of the mainstream way of life is terrible. People don't naturally live in this stifled way. Each time our culture met another culture that lived in a wild, passionate and free way, it has seen a threat to the passive control that we all exert on one another. Those people have been supressed, generally with violence.

The cost to vulnerable people and to the planet is even higher. Life itself is threatened by our industrial, domesticated mindset.

An alternative story

The alternative story is the one told throughout this book: it is the move from domesticated victimhood to active, conscious choice. It is the reclamation of all the wild power that we are born with. It takes sustained effort to be passive because it isn't our natural way. We are born to grow, explore, connect, to feel present and alive. This whole book is one long lesson in being free, powerful, vulnerable, messy, real and alive.

In this state, complaining, following and victimhood don't feel good. They feel sad, lacking, empty, petty and dissatisfying.

What can we do about it?

The journey away from passivity, domestication and victimhood is the journey of this book. It is about self-awakening, noticing and accepting that everything is choice. It is returning responsibility and tremendous power to your choices. It is breathing mindfully, consciously into each moment with gladness for the true shape of what we find. It's committing to a lifelong programme of determination and curiosity, embracing the idea that you will always be learning, growing and developing.

When people complain, don't play along. When you notice people following along, notice what conscious choices you're making. Let other people keep their victimhood. Stay conscious of what's really going on and strive for your own goals, your own consciousness and your own empowerment.

Men are supposed to be emotionless thugs

What's the story and how is it told?

"What are men supposed to be like?" is one of the questions
that every culture has to answer with its stories. The culture that's
dominant today is based on older beliefs from Europe and the Middle
East. This book doesn't include enough pages to properly explore how
our culture came to be the way it is, but for many centuries, Judaeo-
Christian values underpinned a lot of things that people believed. The
Torah and Bible, and later the Quran, give clear stories about the place
of men and women, and for a long time there were institutions like
the Churches to enforce these stories, to retell them on Sundays, to
shame those who departed from the story and to congratulate those
who conformed.

It wasn't always like this. The belief that a certain narrow definition
of successful men should dominate the world is called Patriarchy, and
it's relatively recent in our history that this idea was born. Stories of
the brutal caveman tribes where the strongest men ruled by tyranny
are mostly just myths made up by men living in a patriarchal world.
There's plenty of historical evidence for matriarchal (women-led)
cultures, or those where multiple genders were equally held in high
esteem. For centuries, women and men have been straight-jacketed by
a patriarchal model that was driven and justified by religion. "Here's
the model of what it is to be a good woman, and here is what it means
to be a good man. Conform to this model and you'll be celebrated as
successful. You will be accepted." But as our certainties about God
faded and our societies became more educated and more mobile,
women began to question why their lot was so poor compared to
the men. Men had the power, the wealth, the opportunities for

advancement, the vote, and most of the stories about good and great people were about men. Men could choose their own path and their own identity. Women were left to be home-makers; obedient, subservient, legally disempowered and relegated to a role that squashed their individuality, their ambition and their ability to grow into whatever they wanted to be.

So they broke the story. Feminism has been through many 'waves', beginning with a struggle for basic legal rights and for the vote, then questioning and protesting against fundamental assumptions about the weakness of their gender and the objectification of women, working for pay equality and a long push to root out hidden patriarchal beliefs in our laws and customs. Breaking and recreating cultural stories isn't a pretty and quiet process, so feminism had plenty of firebrands and powerful activists whose protests and demonstrations were reviled by society until, eventually, they weren't. As the philosophy Artur Schopenhauer said, "All truth passes through three stages: First, it is ridiculed; Second, it is violently opposed; and Third, it is accepted as self-evident." So it was, and continues to be, with gender protest.

Along the way, women learned to engage in personal development and became open to personal growth and evolution. Today you can find women's circles in most major towns and cities. Formal movements like the Red Tent celebrate the unique experience of being a woman. Women are more likely to ask for help, to engage in therapy, to ask for and take advice. Our culture now contains a growing collection of stories about resourceful, strong women who have the ability to learn, change and choose their own destiny. Stories of wild, free, empowered women. Female characters in books and movies who are healthy, strong role models for young women and women returning to their true power.

Men, meanwhile, are in crisis. Our culture doesn't know what to do with men, and we've fractured into several conflicting stories about the place of men. These cultural stories are meant to tell boys and men how to be successful, how to prosper and thrive within our extended tribe, how to find acceptance and, ultimately, love. Without a clear story about this, many men are left with uncertainty, doubt, shame and frustration. Men weren't oppressed the same way as women, and they haven't developed a tradition of protest against stories that don't serve them. They are often set up as the benefactors and persecutors by certain kinds of feminism. This story goes that men were privileged and women were crushed. Feminism came to power because of anger at injustice, and it had the momentum and truth to grow into a self-sustaining movement. Men have no such righteous calling to form a movement, and so they languish without a clear story of success.

Some men react to this by returning to very old ideas about manhood, resurrecting the darkest aspects of patriarchy and becoming bitter and violent towards women. Others adopt a friendly and inoffensive model for masculinity, one that a lot of their friends are using, the 'bloke' model. Cheerful, robust, jokey, a bit thuggish. A down side of this model is that it's inherently shallow. It doesn't allow for any deep introspection or personal growth, and prevents men from making meaningful emotional development, asking for help or reflecting on vital life questions. Another competing story for male identity is the soft man, the 'new man', the sensitive man. He tends to be lacking in fire or direction, but he's harmless to those around him and he finds a measure of acceptance.

The biggest killer of men under 45 in the UK is suicide. There are over 6,000 suicides in the UK each year, and nearly 75 per cent of those are men.

These deaths are entirely preventable. They're the result of the crisis in identity that men experience. This crisis feels like failure, it feels like being lost and angry and confused and utterly powerless and alone, unable to do anything about the feelings. Straight-jacketed by conflicting cultural stories, with no clear direction and a strong imperative to never ask for help (most models of manhood agree that this is always failure), men silently implode. Some are saved by relationships, strong role models who share healthier stories, by falling into a satisfying niche or else they experience healing crises that finally driven them to ask for the help they need. The rest suffer, and some of those end their lives in misery.

Because of the fragility of their identities, men have become easy to manipulate. Beauty products, cosmetic surgery, gym memberships and expensive clothes make use of men's insecurities to sell them products. Men can be coerced easily to do things if their fears about not being 'manly' enough are triggered. Many men will go to great lengths to prove their manhood. They buy things they may not want, take part in things they don't enjoy, have sex with people they have been taught to find attractive and avoid things that they deeply long for, in order to prove to themselves and to the world that they are good men.

Newspapers, TV shows, movies, books, beauty products, health and fitness services, cars and motorbikes, holidays, music, homes and pornography all tell stories to men that reassure them about their identity. They act as balms to a masculinity in profound crisis, and for many men they work, at least for a time. But underneath all the competing, prescriptive stories for strength and solidity, stoicism and independence, force and single-mindedness, shallow sex and abuse, addiction and dependence, heightened sensitivity and pseudo-femininity, ambition and drive, niche-interest and geekery…men languish, their true potential and capacity of individual expression forgotten.

The story says there are a lot of things a man cannot choose without anxiety that he is not a real man. A man cannot choose artistic expression, or to be emotionally vulnerable, or to be a primary care-giver and stay-at-home parent. There are so many things a man cannot be without judgement, blame, ridicule or the gnawing feeling of failure.

The challenge for men is escaping the shadows of the past. Our culture is filled with conflicting, messy stories about heroic and villainous men, each with directions to become a successful man. Almost every one of these stories contains expectations that are violent, severely limiting or dependent on toxic shame. Most involve the subjugation of women, or of people of lower classes or other cultures, or the suppression of the man's own potential to learn, feel and grow. Other stories are reactions against these toxic narratives. Men can feel they should be more effeminate, or that they should deny gender altogether. Men who seek to escape the older stories that straight-jacket their authenticity will sometimes end up in such a complex muddle of stories and expectations that they just stop saying anything. Better to be a genderless, inoffensive neutral being who accepts that it's a failure.

One story, for instance, is that a man should be rich, powerful, highly competitive, have a big house and a posh car for his wife and kids and generally accrue wealth and show it off. That's a story that's obviously competing for a every man's attention. In order for any man to meet the obligations of this story and bask in its rewards, his clothes being cleaned, his home and car kept clean, his roads, pavements and workplace kept ordered and safe, his food brought from around the world with the lowest possible overheads, the fabric for his clothes grown using toxic pesticides, the fuel for his car kept flowing with wars and lies…and that's before we start thinking about the kind of work that he does and effects it has on the wellbeing of others. The story will probably also require him to deny his own feelings and needs and will require his relationships to be shallow and unsatisfying. His wife and children will become part of his success, so they also need to behave themselves and not be too vulnerable or authentic. For a man who is intent on being conscious, empowered, deeply connected, to be a positive influence in the world and to operate from strong foundations of honour, this kind of story leaves a lot to be desired.

Any cultural story which offers guidance to men but denies essential truths about their personal needs and their authentic selves is unhealthy. New stories are emerging. Men and women of vision are, slowly, laying the foundations for a new masculinity which is inspiring, empowering, which allow a man his full range of abilities and potential, which removes the straight jackets from his imagination, his wonder and his emotions.

An alternative story

Mens development movements are in their infancy, and they may never explode in the way that feminism has. Perhaps this has something to do with the discomfort men in our culture can often feel at the idea of sharing, coming together, being vulnerable and being part of a tribe with other men. Perhaps the cultural stories of having to work hard, alone, and prove yourself are simply too deeply ingrained to expect a public outburst of healthy masculine identity. Or perhaps human males have a biological imperative to see themselves thriving in their own way, or an inescapable sense of competition and suspicion of other men. It's difficult to be sure whether this is nature or nurture, and it doesn't really matter. The point here is that if you want to start discovering a healthy, authentic male identity then you're going to need to go looking for it.

There are some classic books about this. You could do worse than beginning your search with Robert Bly's *Iron John* or David Deida's *The Way of the Superior Man*. I'll talk a bit about the latter here.

David Deida's core work is about how to reach an empowered, authentic, spiritually satisfying masculinity. It's a book about passion, purpose, sex and fulfilment. He suggests that men of our time are operating in one of three positions:

THE FIRST MAN – this is the archetypal 50s man. He's hard working, he's tough, he does it all alone. He's closed-off from his emotions. He's likely to be violent and struggling internally but he easily gains social approval. He probably uses alcohol or drugs to cope with the void where his emotions are meant to be.

THE SECOND MAN – this is the 'new man' of the 80s and 90s. He's sensitive, caring, emotional. He holds his woman and cries with her. He's also subservient, directionless and lacks inspiration or grit.

THE THIRD MAN – this man has abandoned the stories of our culture and is focused on a single goal: his life's purpose. He has worked hard to find the thing he was born to do, and it is his top priority. His life is ordered behind this purpose and it shines in everything he says and does. It's inspiring for him and it's inspiring for others. He's dedicated, determined, but spiritually aware and emotionally competent. Deida makes a strong case for the idea that this kind of man is deeply exciting to women.

Another great book that I sometimes recommend to my clients is *King, Warrior, Magician, Lover* by Robert Moore and Douglas Gillette. This book doesn't tell a story as much as provide building blocks for writing your own story. Archetypes are ideas shared by a people. They're common characters that appear in our stories wearing different faces. According to Moore and Gillette, the four core archetypes of manhood are the King (who controls the inner landscape and ensures everything is aligned), the Warrior (whose passion and direction give a man a sense of fire and strength), the Magician (a character steeped in imagination, creativity and mystery who lets a man access his subtler gifts) and the Lover (which brings a man sensuality, enjoyment and desire). This book also explores how each archetype has a shadow aspect and how this manifests in men whose childhood was lacking or those who aren't living conscious lives.

What can we do about it?

If you're a man, and if you feel like you need to work on the story of manhood that you're using as the model for your life, remember that this is your story. Irrespective of gender, a great life is an outpouring of authenticity. Whatever you naturally, honestly are, is right for you.

You might want to return to the values exercises in the previous chapter and see whether you're talking about your values or if you've been trying to live up to the expectations of your father or an ideal of manhood that you've inherited.

Allow this process to take time, and let your heart be your guide. Stop, often, and breathe into your heart and ask whether you are making authentic choices based on the person you are. Are you chasing somebody else's expectations for you? Are you being manipulated? If you notice that these things are happening, gently return to what your heart calls you to do. Use your sense of honour to guide your steps in a determined, authentic way.

Everything is choice. I invite you to choose to deeply explore your masculinity and choose to express it authentically. What are the core archetypes in the story of your life? What is the story that you are authoring in this moment? Are you proud of it, and do you feel pleased and satisfied and fulfilled by it? What story about the man you are would better serve you?

If you feel like this is an area of your journey that needs extra attention, I invite you to dive into men's development work. You can find groups online and there are a number of good books. My only caution is this: in a bid to rescue themselves from the confusion and insecurity that a lack of shared story brings, some men cling to the stories of the past and offer them as a way forward. They will offer to save you by helping you become the toughest manly man there is; or else they'll help you give up your fire and become a soft new man. Be cautious of any book, group or product that sells an easy answer. If they want you to become a man of the old kind, it might be seductive and feel appealing, but it'll also cost you your personal authenticity and individual expression.

The control of wild women

As a man, I needed help to write this section. I consulted and interviewed a lot of women, and I'm deeply grateful to everyone who helped me properly understand the challenges women face at this time.

Some families are progressive and offer supportive, inspiring environments for girls and young women to fully understand themselves, to explore their needs and wishes and to be prepared for the hostility that much of the world will aim at them. Many other young women grow up in families or places that are still steeped in shockingly hostile messages about what a woman is and what she should be. These messages become part of "just the way things are", and women can internalise and believe things that are toxic or hostile towards women almost as easily as men can.

Since the days of suffrage and the beginning of the emancipation of women, we've come a long way as a society. However, a range of deeply ingrained toxic stories still exist, and various forces in the world even want to return to days when women were subservient to men. Many women and men have fought for respect and equality for women, but they also have introduced new pressures and expectations for women to be successful in every possible way, all at once. Today it's difficult for a woman to feel successful without one group or another commenting on her failures. There's also been a striking re-emergence of hate speech against women online. A particular group of men feel that it's acceptable and amusing to say the most vicious, violent things to women while they hide behind the anonymity of the computer screen.

I have been lucky enough to work alongside and learn from a range of courageous, visionary women who have worked hard to free themselves of the limiting beliefs they were indoctrinated with as children. These women were my friends, peers, partners and, later, my coaching clients and the women I interviewed for this book. Every woman's journey is different, but there have been a lot of common feelings and ideas amongst those women who now look back on their lives and wish they knew earlier what they know now. This book is a call to awareness and awakening, a guidebook to freeing yourself from "just the way things are" and recovering your natural, wild consciousness and power. The challenges for women in this journey are different to those faced by men. The journey for women seems to be a journey away from shame and persecution, a letting go of expectation and demands, an accepting of a wild, flowing form of formidable strength. The stories of our culture seem to be designed to rob women of this incredible power and insight, and almost every woman who I spoke to about their own awakening and self-discovery has been angry that they needed to find freedom later in life, that they ever had to lock away their potency because the world attacked them for being who they really were.

This part of the book, then, is offered in the hope that fewer and fewer women will believe these stories or devote their time and energy to meeting the impossible, painful expectations of this broken culture that fears what they might become. Following the feedback and advice I've received, I've also been able to recommend some books about this subject. If you read the stories below and feel that you could benefit from a deeper understanding of the problem, and the solutions that other women have found, then I encourage you to dive into these books. This section is short and only designed to offer ideas and clearly state some ingrained cultural stories. Other books dedicated to this topic are far more eloquent and will offer you real solutions if you're looking for them.

(the words below in italics were written by women I interviewed for this book. I am hugely grateful to those women who took the time to lend me their thoughts and perspective)

What toxic cultural stories exist for women at this time?

A woman's value is how attractive she is and how much she pleases men

"The idea that women need to have a particular body shape has had a huge impact on my life. My mother used to always talk about her weight and be critical of anyone who put weight on - including her own sisters.

I was bulimic as a young woman and constantly worried about putting on weight in case I was no longer attractive. This idea has been so engrained that even now I exercise regularly and diet regularly, so I don't put on the dreaded middle aged spread.

This is reinforced by media all the time - even the attention it pays to what female politicians wear is undermining the gravity any woman can have at the same level as men."

"Women are expected not to 'let themselves go'. So on top of being the perfect mother and wife, the perfect employee or business owner, have the perfect home that is neat and tidy ALL the time, women are expected to always look perfect too. The perfect hair, complexion, clothes, shape and of course size. mostly this pressure leaves any woman feeling inadequate regardless of how brilliant or clever she is, or how fit and healthy or how much of a good mum she is."

A cultural story is something that you're given when you're young and something that's reinforced throughout your life. You'll absorb it through entertainment, magazines, the opinions of people you meet, and you'll make it stronger by teaching it to others in your words, choices and actions. Most people do this unconsciously, without the self-awareness to recognise that they're sustaining something that they haven't properly reflected on. Where it's a toxic story, this means that people can cause harm to themselves and others without noticing, believing that they're doing good things. This book is all about coming to full awareness of yourself, of the moment, of the reality of what's going on around you, so that you have the power and the freedom to make choices that are empowering and nourishing for you.

This particular cultural story is easily mixed up with flattery and self-esteem. So many women have internalised the idea that their value and worth is bound up with how much she excites and pleases men. We encourage our little girls to look pretty. They grow up with images of women who are beautiful, and their beauty is commented on a lot and it obviously brings them value and worth. Villains are ugly.

Many women put huge effort into looking good. Leaving home without perfect hair or makeup would be hard, uncomfortable, even shameful. Even if they're not consciously doing it to please men, why is it important to conform to certain ideas of beauty? Why is it so nice to be told you look nice?

There's a clear hierarchy of looks. Some appearances are worth more than others. Big breasts are better than small ones. Certain face shapes are considered more appealing. Blondes have more fun. Following the latest fashions can get you respect, attention and value in certain circles.

Each sub-culture has its own standards. In some places, high heels or low-cut tops are a status symbol. In others it's about obvious wealth with the right accessories. In some places, piercings and dyed hair demonstrate to the world that you've made the right effort with your appearance. The consistent things is that women are expected to look a certain way in order to prove that they've made an effort, that they've earned worthiness through their beauty. A woman who hasn't, or can't, or is too old, disappears, or becomes a cautionary sad tale for others, or perhaps becomes a figure for mockery and ridicule. She hasn't matched up to the correct standards. She has failed and has lost value as a person.

Fighting against this story, like all the stories in this section, is exhausting. It can bring you face-to-face with anxiety, shame, rejection, frustration and rage. It means finding your own inner value, your own self-worth independent of all the stories you were told when you were growing up. It means doing inner work to unlock your potential, and this is part of the reason that women are often so much further ahead of men in personal development: in order to escape from the toxic expectations of our culture, they're forced to do personal work earlier than men are.

Most men reinforce this story all the time because they don't see a problem. They don't experience the same pressures and expectations. A man's value comes from other places – his appearance and how well he can please women is a long way down the scale of social approval. So, blinded to the pressures a woman experiences to be pretty and pleasing, he tries to be friendly and complimentary, flattering women about their appearance, talking calmly and openly about comparing women for their attractiveness. He thinks this is normal and ok.

Women who have deeply absorbed this story and never really challenged it, will tend to chase the approval of men, gaining self-esteem and reassurance when a man pays her attention, compliments her, or rewards her in some way. This is often a re-creation of the girl-father dynamic of early life. A lot of girls are shown that this is the way to get approval, attention and love. Be a good girl for daddy, be pretty, be giggly, be charming, be pleasant. Dad responds well. When a girl does this at school, it works with boys too. It sets up a belief structure that this is a normal, healthy and effective way to earn approval and love.

As women begin to realise all the opportunities they've missed because they were chasing approval and acceptance by being attractive and pleasant, anger is a pretty natural response, and fury can become a way of life.

What lies beyond this? I'll discuss this more below.

Be ashamed of your body and your cycle.

"I learned about menstruation at school when I was 10 in a very matter of fact way. Aside from much giggling from other girls, it didn't seem like anything to be celebrated. Indeed, my mother told me I could not use her bathroom whilst I was on my period because she didn't want me to bleed over everything. I know that other women have suffered far worse indignities and still this seems to be the general opinion, menstrual cycle issues are to be suffered and hidden. It's been a wonderfully liberating experience even just to be thinking about my menstrual cycle differently. It's still difficult for me to talk with confidence about it with others but simply not judging my period as bad or dreading it is a huge step for me. Learning about my cycle and tracking different patterns has been very useful in many ways. Instead of feeling that my mood might be hijacked by changing emotions, it's easier for me now to understand when and why I will feel a bit more sensitive. I can choose not to make important decisions or have difficult conversations until a different part of my cycle. That feels empowering rather than my previous assumption that sometimes I am incapable of making a decision and must therefore be weak"

"It's time for women to stop being embarrassed and ashamed about their bodies, and in particular their cycle. We have become disconnected from our natural rhythms. We have been taught to hide this part of our womanhood like a shameful, dirty secret. But the truth is that this cycle is part of our nurturing power. When we reconnect with it, we reconnect with our power as women, as creators."

Our culture was set up to benefit straight, white men. In a traditional model, these men are meant to provide for everyone else. The woman and the kids are at home, the man is out there making the money and providing for the family. As the people creating the culture and the economy, and feeling they were due a reward for being providers, men created a culture that works for them more than it works for women. Things have changed a lot since then, but so many of our cultural stories remain the same. Society tends to treat men far better than it treats women, and the reason men can feel so shocked and upset when their world-views are challenged is because they are used to being in such a privileged position. That's a very quick summary of a hugely complex situation, but it's a good starting place.

Men are relatively consistent, hormonally. They can often experience spikes in testosterone, but this makes a man feel sexual and aggressive. In a male-centric culture, these things are often seen as normal and cool. Movies show violence to be exciting and impressive. Male sexuality is pandered to far more than female.

So, what does this culture make of women's monthly hormonal changes and the physical experience of menstruation?

Hormonal changes, and the changes in emotion and behaviour, are often seen as humiliating, shameful, useless and ridiculous. It's so easy to mock PMT and out-of-control, stupid, angry women who are victims of their period.

The physical changes a woman experiences, especially her bleed itself, is generally seen as something that should be hidden. It's a shameful, dirty and disgusting thing. How many times do you hear women, especially women who want the respect of men, talking openly about their cycle or their bleed?

And yet, half of the populations experiences this every month. It's crazy that this be a marginalised, shadow topic. Why isn't it normal to talk about it?

Once it becomes normalised, all sorts of interesting things can happen. Women talk to me about the amazing awakenings they've had when they've connected lovingly with their cycle and their period. They talk about the wild power that exists within their bodies when they stop regarding them with shame and, instead, regard them with curiosity and kindness.

Movements are beginning to spring up that support women to explore and understand these things. At the forefront of this movement is the writer and activist Alexandra Pope. I've had the privilege of spending time with Alexandra, and I've read the booked she has co-written, called *Wild Power*. I cannot recommend this book strongly enough for any women who would like to drop the ingrained, toxic stories of our culture. The book focuses on the menstrual cycle, but it also talks about the broader cycles in a woman's life: about aging and passing through phases of life. It also offers men advice about how to support and connect with their partners in a way that honours her experience.

I cannot recommend this book highly enough.

You should judge, criticise and attack other women

"It's automatic to judge other women. We are constantly judging other women because we are constantly judging ourselves...There is open bitchiness that seems to be the norm and for me started at an early age. It was always a female telling me, my clothes weren't good enough or my chest too flat or I would never get a boyfriend. How on earth that could be known at 11 years old I don't know but apparently, I was not good enough. When I did get my first boyfriend, my best friend laughed

*for a good 10 minutes and then proceeded to tell her mother that I had ""finally""
got a boyfriend. Of course, I was assured by her that the relationship wouldn't last.
All this judgement and she hadn't even met him.*

*Gossiping behind someone's back also seemed normal. This confused me, different
judgements being spoken when out of earshot. It never felt you were safe from
judgement. There is also a sort of perverse camaraderie found when the list of
judgments seems to be aimed at someone else. If we are in agreement, then we are
not the one in the firing line. We become acceptable by putting others down. When
you are young, you get used to not being acceptable and being publicly ridiculed but
that also becomes the stick by which you measure other women."*

A lot of ideas exist in our culture about how women should be.
Depending on who you talk to and their particular emotional needs
and their personal beliefs, they will expect women to live in to a series
of expectations. This applies to both women and men. Some men
are looking to recreate their early life experience because they haven't
done the personal work to move into conscious adulthood, so when
they meet men they are unconsciously comparing them to their own
mothers (more than this, they're comparing the experience of being
around that woman to the experience of being an infant around
their mother – a situation that can never be replicated but which he
may be seeking to recreate). In other situations, a man might have
unmet emotional needs that he expects a woman to provide for. He
outsources his emotional maturity to women, and he judges women if
they don't make him feel the way he demands that they do.

Women judging one another can be, in our culture, particularly vicious.
Women can be venomous, vindictive and cruel in their judgements
of other women. When we're brave enough, determined enough and
curious enough to do our own personal work, we quickly come to
realise that judgement is the tragic expression of unmet need. People
who understand their own need and take responsibility for meeting

them don't waste their time on judgement.

Many women feel a lot of stress because of all the expectations put upon them, beginning with the fundamental expectation that they will be pleasing for men. When you notice other people judging you for falling short, that can be upsetting and stressful. But where you've internalised these beliefs as your own, where you've been taught by your parents that you should be all sorts of things that don't feel good for you, then things become much harder. You might believe that you need to look pretty in order to be a good person. You might believe that you need to be totally dependable, always giving and never ask for anything for yourself. You might feel that you're supposed to be a fiery campaigner for women's rights even when you feel exhausted and you're struggling to even look after yourself.

Until you take the time to explore all of the beliefs about womanhood that you carry, you will have all sorts of emotional needs that pull you in all sorts of directions. You will have unmet needs. In that situation, you are likely to judge and attack others. People who feel shame about who they are and about how they have failed will tend to look around for people who deserve even more shame, who are failing even harder. Attacking them shifts attention from of your own shame.

Our culture provides a lot of language for women and men to attack women for failing to be everything that a woman should be. A confident woman is a bitch. A shy woman is weak or coy. A woman who is confident in her sexuality is a slut. A woman who isn't sexually available is a prude. We have a lot of word to throw at our failing women, and when it brings catharsis from your own sense of shame, it can feel so good to attack them.

Men have their own work to do, to learn not to attack women who fail to meet their emotional needs for sex, power, domination, esteem or reassurance. For women, the journey must begin with tackling their own shame and exploring the toxic stories they've absorbed that put all these expectations and stress onto them.

Women are weak, emotional and crazy

"I see this a lot in the workplace - I work for a council where 70 % of workers are women but only 15% of senior managers are women. Among the men at this level any indication of emotion is considered a weakness and makes a person unsuitable to the senior roles.

Rather than recognising and appreciating a woman's feelings they are often dismissed as either silly feminists or weak. A classic example was a colleague who was made to wait for a man she was meeting with while he talked to a group of other men about football. He was late and made no attempt to apologise. When she raised her view that it was impolite behaviour she was told she was being too sensitive."

"I was constantly told as a child that I was stupid, by my dad and my brothers. Then by my first husband. My second husband never said it, but he thought it. It's a total lack of respect regardless of what a woman achieves!"

The reasons for this kind of belief are just parts of the toxic stories we've already looked at. Thanks to their hormonal cycle, women will tend to feel different on different days of the month. Men who haven't learned about the value of this will tend to just find it confusing and frustrating. When there's a belief that women should be consistently caring, or always be ready to provide for the sexual needs of a man, then her cyclical nature will be labelled as unstable and crazy.

It always comes back to the beliefs we each carry about what women are meant to be like. But what is a woman, what is your experience of womanhood, if you can drop all of these expectations and just explore the reality of your own experience without needing to judge or criticise?

The expectation that you take advantage of everything that feminism has achieved

"Being female is really difficult when it comes to working and having children. you are criticised if you decide to be a stay at home mum and be there for your kids, and criticised if you continue your career and have your kids looked after by others. A woman simply can't win. Succeeding in a career often means women don't have kids or have to make the choice to risk having children when older - maybe risking not being able to conceive at all. Women often have to behave like a man to get anywhere in their workplace, to be taken seriously. Women who do have full time careers often end up being the ones who run the household, do the housework, manage the finances and the kids. It's a juggling act all the time. Women who work feel guilty for leaving their kids - women who don't work feel guilty for not working...... and the poison cherry on top is that it's mostly other women doing the judging and criticising!"

"We're supposed to look magnificent, be zen and hold everything together while having no time to ourselves. The media doesn't help, portraying the ""perfect"" woman as one in a high powered or otherwise successful career, in a happy marriage with at least one child, and always looking somewhat under the age of 40.

I decided not to have children. I'm 34. I don't feel judged as such, but i do feel that i don't fit into the ideal-woman model."

"...if an opportunity is afforded to me and I don't take it, am I missing my potential? Should I not stand up and accept the rights hard fought by those who came before me? Am I letting someone down if I don't? Will I look weak - am I weak if I don't maintain a successful career?"

For everything that feminism has achieved for women, from the vote to the pill and the right to control her own destiny, it has also set up new expectations. Not only do you have the right to choose whether you be a stay-at-home mum or go out to work, you're expected to do both. You're expected to be part of the fight against patriarchy.

This book is a call to power, an invitation to your personal awakening and the unleashing of your potential. Ultimately, I encourage everyone to fight for the things they believe in. This added expectation (that you be an activist for women's rights or defend yourself and your choices from those who are) is not part of this awakening unless you choose for it to be. It's all choice.

I encourage you to engage with modern feminist thought in some way, with determination and curiosity, but to be aware of any shame or unconscious beliefs that might be influencing your choices.

Different standards for men and women

"One of the most toxic stories I've been told is that women should not be assertive. This message came from my father who was threatened by the idea of having a strong opinionated daughter with her own ideas about things. While my brother was considered weak for not having strong opinions.

He branded my desire to be a strong woman standing up for myself as feminist rubbish. He made comments that I would change my ideas about wanting to have a career and children when I had children of my own. He saw my husband as being soft because he ended up staying at home to care for the children when they were young.

In the workplace this was also reinforced when I was told I was too aggressive in the work place when I was asserting myself. I was displaying the exact same behaviour as the men in the workplace.

I struggled with this for feedback as it had a massive impact on the success of my career and really damaged my self-esteem. After doing a lot of personal development work, I have been able to recognise that it wasn't aggression but assertion that they felt threatened by."

"The occasions when my husband has helped me with housework it's clear that the woman's chores are degrading to him, he complains that he is reduced to folding clothes. It is often easier not to ask for help. Things will be completed faster with less complaining.

I don't need to be told that if I earn more money than my husband, its emasculating for him. I can see and feel his resentment. Even if I am outwardly encouraged, the effect of any success I have seems to be a diminishing of his confidence and defensiveness which often results in him listing the things he has accomplished that day. If I listed my own accomplishments in the same way, we'd be here all night. So I say nothing and tell him, thanks very much for doing all that. The exhaustion comes both from having to fulfil multiple roles and keeping everyone happy whilst doing it."

How our culture treats violence against women and rape

"This is deeply embedded that rape and sexual assault is encouraged by how a woman behaves, dresses and her location choice. Even choices about recreation are judged so a woman who chooses to do a particular activity attracts a certain attitude about her personality and her integrity. For example, if a woman chooses to ride a motorbike everyone will consider that she is a certain type of woman sexually, i.e. that she is promiscuous or easy and keen for sex. If a woman says no or acts unwilling then she is considered to be either a lesbian or frigid. Whatever a woman does her sexuality and looks are brought into it no matter how unrelated to the activity.""

"Nothing makes me sadder than this. It's not just a male issue, its' a women's issue too - there are women who have been brainwashed into thinking that it is

ok, somehow acceptable. Look at all those women who voted for the US president despite all the sexist crap he came out with.

The culture of ""she was asking for it"" is still present. This is a culture that is actively promoted - look at some video games. A tough man - which men are supposed to aspire to be - always gets his own way."

"It's about power and violation. The experience of victims brave enough to fight for justice who are treated shockingly, during the trial and outcome. Look at the recent case of the NI rugby players. It made me so sad."

"Thankfully we have a new wave of young women who are so much more sexually liberated. But do they have the confidence in this climate to assert their ideas about what is acceptable and unacceptable behaviour?"

Finding your own, authentic story

I've tried in this section to name some of the massive problems that exist in our culture for women, some of the unhelpful, harmful and toxic stories that uniquely affect women. There are a lot of amazing books out there to help you explore this properly.

Here are three pieces of advice that I've been handed by wise women that I have been lucky enough to know, for any woman who wants to break free from the toxic stories of our culture:

First, get to know your own shame. Our culture wants you to feel ashamed as a woman. You have failed to live up to all of the expectations that everybody has, so you should feel ashamed. So many women that I have met have internalised shame about who they are, the way they behave, the way they look, the things they've done or failed to do. This shame is a heavy burden to carry, so I encourage you to turn to face it and get to know it, exploring with compassionate non-judgement as much as you can. Allow for the possibility that you are a complex, wonderful person who has grown up in a culture that doesn't understand her or the things she needs. Use the techniques in this book for exploring and understanding shame and belief, but particularly focus on the shame that our culture has dumped on you for not being the shallow, pleasant women it expected of you.

Second, become an expert in your own body and its cycles. The amazing book *Wild Power* by Alexandra Pope and Sjanie Hugo Wurlitzer is a fantastic ally here. Understanding, accepting and loving the rich tapestry of experience and wisdom that your body offers through your cycle might be the most liberating experience you can have.

Finally, do not do this alone. Women's circles are becoming increasingly mainstream. Some are deeply spiritual, some are focused heavily on womb wisdom, some are groups of business women and entrepreneurs who meet for mutual support and inspiration. Wherever you are, there will probably be at least a few women's circles happening around you. If you can, find one that's facilitated by an experienced woman who can hold the space and offer you a chance to speak and be heard without judgement. I've heard so many remarkable stories of the healing and release that's come for women when they simply sat with other women and spoke their truth without judgement or criticism. Magic can happen that way, and you can rewrite the pattern of hostility between women into a story of sisterhood and mutual care and support.

Resources for your own journey

Women Who Run With the Wolves: Myths and Stories of the Wild Woman Archetype by Clarissa Pinkola Estés

Men explain things to me and other essays by Rebeca Solnit

We Should All Be Feminists by Chimamanda Ngozi Adichie

The Period Poem by Dominique Christina

Shrill: notes from a loud woman by Lindy West

Traumas don't heal (hurt people, hurt people)

What's the story and how is it told?

I've spent a lot of my life working with trauma: my own or that of my clients. I see the widespread effects of unhealed personal trauma on TV and in newspapers every day. Deeply held hurts that we carry in our minds and our tissues cause us to act in strange and irrational ways, and once that strangeness and irrationality becomes the norm, we stop noticing it. Today, trauma has a huge influence on everything from personal shopping habits, to relationships, to politics.

There are a lot of theories and approaches to injury, healing and trauma and the most helpful approach that I know, from a psycho-spiritual point of view, is offered by psychologist and bodywork therapist Peter Levine. Levine's ideas are at the heart of a lot of modern approaches that try to understand, heal and release the deeply ingrained pain that many of us carry through our lives.

Trauma is the memory of injury. Whether the original cause of the trauma was physical, emotional, mental or spiritual, the load is shared between the four. A profound psychological hurt will manifest in the body. It'll be held in the tissues of the body, or it'll cause patterns of behaviour that weren't there before the injury happened. A lot of people carry pains and soreness in their bodies that aren't the result of any injury they can remember, but if invited to think about mental or emotional hurts they might remember that this pain started just after something really shocking and hurtful happened. Traumas that result from physical injuries will translate into mental and emotional unbalance, such as Post-Traumatic Stress disorders, obsessive behaviours or new beliefs that significantly limit freedom of choice. A sustained lack of spiritual connection and expression causes tension and stress which contribute to trauma. Trauma of any kind causes emotional disconnection to some degree. When we're suffering, when we're holding on to the echoes of past pain, we cannot feel as deeply as we can when we're free of pain. Empathy fades: our ability to feel the emotions of others decreases. Where before we were free to feel, to let emotions flow freely, to hear the messages that our emotions bring us and to connect to others with empathy, now we have emotions that are truncated and cauterised, drawn-in to avoid further hurt.

Trauma then sits and waits to be healed. Until this happens, we are transformed from one type of person (free, creative, expressive and whole) into a more limited version of ourselves. We draw in upon ourselves and try to shield ourselves from further harm. Sometimes the physical manifestations of held trauma look like drawing-in: limbs that won't straighten, hunched shoulders, bowed head. Like any other mammal responding to hurt, we try to make ourselves small and protected.

However, unlike other mammals, we tend to hold on to our traumas. This isn't a natural response in humans, it's a learned response. Physical trauma is shed by things like shaking, crying, restorative breathing, tantruming and screaming. Emotional trauma is shed by sharing, connecting and feeling safely held and deeply witnessed. But how many of us experience this regularly? How many of us would welcome these things to heal the traumas we carry? Instead, in general, we just 'carry on'. The effects of the hurts of our lives just become part of the story of 'just the way things are'.

What happens when you have millions of people holding on to traumas?

For one thing, we hurt each other. Without a conscious ownership of our hurt, we will tend to thrash about in a reckless and unconscious way. Our goals are relief and healing, but without recognising this, we tend to attack people, use people, demonise groups of people, or engage in passive-aggressive behaviour. We're prone to addictions and dependencies on substances, affection, attention, reassurance or stimulation. We can crave and yet reject intimacy and connection.

We also tend to pass the trauma around. Each time we hurt someone, or use them to meet our own needs, or reduce them to a stereotype or a limited version of a real person, we reinforce the thinking caused by our own traumas and we cause hurt in others.

We pass our traumas down through generations. Perhaps a deeply wounded father, whose own father failed him, beats his wife and terrifies his children. Perhaps a woman whose true potential was stolen by a traumatic experience earlier in life teaches her daughter that she needs to be pretty in order to be worthy of love. A parent who finds relief from their secret, hidden hurts through drink, drugs, gambling, abusive intimacy, excessive wealth or the adoration of their peers, teaches their children to do the same. In very early life, a child's parents are their world. A young child has no filters or defences. Throughout childhood, parents are models of how to be a human that a child will mimic. If a parent teaches their child to manifest trauma, either directly (through physical or psychological violence) or indirectly (by passing on beliefs or behaviour patterns that grow out of held traumas) then that hurt is passed on to another generation. This is so-called 'ancestral trauma', and many people today are carrying echoes of profound hurt that was done to their parents or ancestors. I have worked with clients whose limiting beliefs or sabotaging behaviour can be traced back to the trauma brought home by a grandparent who went to war.

Groups of people who are hurting badly will tend to be more

comfortable with violence than people who don't carry traumas. The history of conquest and conflict around the world is the history of traumatised, emotionally cauterised people spreading their hurt to other parts of the world. We have cultural stories of heroic warriors and generals, of the Romans who civilised Europe, of the colonising European powers that dominated most of the world during the 20th Century, and a thousand stories of uncivilised people being dominated and improved by settlers and conquerors. All of this can be seen through the lens of trauma as simply hurt people, hurting people.

We continue to do it, and we continue to normalise it. People who do not carry trauma are unlikely to have any appetite for cruelty, violence, unfairness or exploitation, because they feel that it's wrong and they feel the suffering of others. Today we are so familiar with the effects of unhealed trauma that we live within social structures that normalise and contribute to trauma.

The short version of this story is: I am hurting, because I've been hurt, but I don't know what to do with it, so I inflict hurt on others in a search for peace and security.

An alternative story

The alternative to this narrative is to expose trauma for what it is. People who are comfortable with the regular use of violence are neither monsters nor heroes. They're tragic figures trapped in the effects of their own unhealed pain. Rather than making movies about them, writing headlines about then or shutting them away, we can regard a lot of cruelty, bitterness and prejudice as cries for help by people carrying traumas that they don't recognise or own. They don't deserve our veneration or our hostility: they deserve sympathy and treatment.

We would need to begin unpicking many of the cultural myths and stories that underpin a lot of our assumptions and behaviours. We'd need to rethink how we handle the relationships in our lives.

What can we do about it?

This work begins with the self. Ask yourself: what do I do, regularly, that's my attempt to get relief for traumas that I carry? What hurtful baggage did you inherit from your parents? What shared cultural traumas do you participate in? What personal pain and trauma have you endured, that you continue to carry with you in your mind, your heart, your spirit or, most commonly, your body?

Then decide that you will no longer expect others to carry your traumas for you. We'll look at depending on others to save you (and how not to) in Principle 10.

Ask for the help you need and commit to practices that will heal the traumas in your life.

In an alternative to the mainstream stories about the horror and wonder of manifested trauma, we each become heroes by refusing to pass our trauma on to our children. We heal as much as we can. We contribute towards a better world by not being part of the old story of normalised trauma. We take responsibility, get the help, do the work, and heal the hurts.

There are a lot of forms of support out there for healing trauma. The body holds our greatest traumas, endures the worst of the effects and holds the wisdom for building a new life free of trauma. If you begin to notice the effects of old, deeply held hurts on your thinking, choices or feelings, I invite you to begin experimenting with approaches to physical healing alongside more direct approaches through talking therapies, counselling or coaching.

Effective physical therapies include: traditional physiotherapy, remedial massage, Trauma Release Experience (TRE), facilitated breathwork, shiatsu and Craniosacral Therapy.

The healing of trauma is like everything else in this book: if we take the time to notice what's going on, we explore it with determination and curiosity, and we take whatever logical steps are open to us, including asking for help and getting support. What's important is results, in this case a new sense of freedom and possibility that lies behind the healing of trauma.

We also develop strong and consistent boundaries (Principle 11) so that when somebody acts out their traumas towards us, we see clearly what's going on and we refuse to take it from them, gently handing it back with non-judgemental compassion.

Beyond our personal healing, we regard the consequences of our personal traumas in our lives with determination and curiosity: determination to be a force for healing and consciousness in the world and to keep our choices, words and actions consistent with our personal sense of honour; and curiosity to explore and understand our own traumas and the behaviours they cause with compassion and forgiveness. We become the end-point for trauma, rather than another carrier who passes it on to others. We stop venerating or attacking violent people whose trauma causes them to act in destructive ways, and we approach them with the compassion to support their healing, while working to contain their effects in the world.

We recognise what hurts were passed to us by our parents, by people we've met and by our culture at large, and we make the truly heroic choice to withhold their effects from our children and from all children, human and non-human.

The alternative story says: I am hurting, because I was hurt, but I recognise this, I seek healing and understanding of my hurt so that I can unlock new possibilities for myself. I offer those who don't understand their hurt my compassion and empathy, but I refuse to take on their suffering.

Ideas of success and the myth of progress

What's the story and how is it told?

This toxic story can be difficult to spot sometimes because progress and success sound like such good things. However, the story is not that it would be good to make things better in the world, it's the expectation that progress is always good. Progress for the sake of progress.

Certainly a few hundred years ago, people would have seen the idea of progress very differently. It's a modern obsession for new things, better things, more things to be a virtue. It can manifest in a number of ways...

We might experience pressure to excel in our lives, even if this doesn't serve our own flourishing and happiness. For example, you might want to be a potter, a dancer or a gardener and you might be able to envision a happy, stable and fulfilling life doing something like this, but others might judge you for not wanting a career that's seen as more successful and more impressive. If you've internalised this story, you might beat yourself up for not doing the right thing and you might feel like you're never a proper person unless you meet these kind of expectations.

Some people become compulsive shoppers and hoarders of stuff, putting their wealth and success on public display, because this meets a deep-seated, unconscious need to be seen (and to see themselves) as successful.

Some people abandon happy jobs, relationships or places because of the pressure to do better.

Amplified to a social level, we are obsessed with the notion of progress. It is easily one of the most formidable driving forces in the way we do business, cast votes and run our politics. There must be economic growth. There must be constant improvement. And yet, we live at a time of obvious contraction. The enormous explosion in prosperity and material wealth in the 20th century was the result of a few unique historic situations. Most notably, it was the wealth created by progresses in efficiency during the industrial revolution and by the vast reservoirs of easily accessible energy found in fossil fuels. This energy let us surge ahead in technology and material wealth, revolutionising every aspect of our lives. Huge steps were taken in every decade and people got used to these leaps forwards as being normal. A kind of expectation of 'newer, better, more' seeped into a couple of generations, and these generations are now the ones in power, making the decisions.

Most of the terrible damage wrought on the world was done under the optimism, self-righteousness and relentlessness of the myth of progress. We can progress. We must. Things must get better. Things must grow and improve. We must each have new things, better things, more things. The price is now clear for everyone to see, but we continue to see the effects of this ideology on every level of society.

The myth often trumps compassion and empathy. Homeless people are often blamed for their situation and attacked for interfering with the important story that everything is good and getting better. Unemployed people and people who are different (immigrants, people of other colours or sexual orientation) can easily be attacked by politicians and other leaders because we are all used to the idea that our society, and the people we know, are the best. We know we're the best because we've progressed so far. People from other countries are less than we are, because they don't have our wealth, our technology and our obvious displays of material wealth. If a community stands in the way of a new road, the community must be destroyed in the name of progress. If a peaceful but unproductive society exists where there could be mines and farms, it must be moved on or eliminated. Making excuses for this is so easy because many of us have been raised with the myth of progress. Things are meant to get better all the time.

I am not at all saying that improvement is bad, especially socially. If anything, this book advocates a lot of personal and social developments. But where progress has seeped into our unconscious as the most important thing, as something that must be pursued even where great suffering is caused, even when we know that the short-term luxuries of today will lead to damage and harm for our children, then it's become something toxic. It drives individuals mad with the idea they they're not good enough without a certain kind of job or social position, and it drives our society away from justice and responsible action and towards short-term gain for a terrible cost.

On a personal level, we are successful if we make progress in our lives and unsuccessful if we don't. It isn't ok to find your niche, feel satisfied and live your life there. You must do better, year on year. It's shameful not to make progress.

The final way that progress is shown is in capitalism's need to commodify everything. If you have a strong ideological need to keep growing an economy, you need to keep looking for new markets to exploit. As we become an increasingly efficient culture without much room for physical expansion, more things must be transferred from being freely available to being products that people can buy. In this way, the economy will still be said to expand because people continue to spend money. The cost is purely emotional and relational, and things like feelings and relationships don't have any economic value in themselves. Open spaces become paid spaces. Peace and quiet become retreats and spas. Free water becomes paid water fountains or expensive (and destructive) bottled water. Time with neighbours and community become support groups and other services that you need to pay for. Spending time with friends becomes sitting at home on social media. Shared journeys become taxi rides. Local sports leagues become commercialised.

The myth of progress, which exists in the unconscious mind of almost everyone unless we've done the personal work to identify it and escape it, makes it a shameful act to cling on to any of these free, lovely things. They're cooler, easier, better or more glamorous if they're branded products.

This story is found in our adoration of the rich and powerful. It's told in our history classes, where progress from less sophisticated tribes to more sophisticated societies is taught as triumph. It's told in how ok we are when people lose their homes or livelihoods in the name of progress. It's demonstrated every time our empathy is asleep or shutdown when we hear about injustice but shrug and say to ourselves 'that's just the way things are' or 'yes what a shame, but it had to happen'. It's told every time we imply our superiority to people living in countries that are less technologically or economically developed. It's told in how we prioritise products and wealth over experiences and connections. It's told when we turn the living natural world into resources that we are free to exploit.

Nowhere in the political rhetoric of our times will you find the idea that we've gone too far, exploited too much, that we each consume too much and waste too much. There is a great fear about saying this, because the people making the speeches grew up at the height of the great economic fossil-fuel boom. Instead, we claim a sacred right to better, newer and more. The economy must grow. Wars for resources and all the hurt they cause are justified. We must pass on to our children more stuff than we inherited from our parents.

The story of progress brings huge pressure with it. We must continue, and we must go further, faster, in more luxury and more waste.

An alternative story

There are a number of alternative stories to the myth of progress. Energy reduction combined with the reconnection with community. Spiritual and emotional connection with the wild without denying humanity. Entrepreneurial creativity directed towards real, long-term sustainability. Social media that includes social justice. Personal empowerment with political engagement. The active choice about whether more, better and faster is good for our children and for all children.

It begins by noticing how the pressure to progress pops up in our lives. Ambition is a good thing: it drives us to excel and stretch ourselves into the full manifestation of our gifts. But let your ambitions be for things that meet your deepest needs and will make you truly happy, not ambitions based on the expectation of others that you should make progress. Whoever you are and whatever your personal needs, you will be satisfied by many things that are here and now, and which don't need improving or to be made more exciting or more stimulating.

I invite you to reflect that you don't need more stuff or better stuff in order to be happy. What if we all turned all that drive for economic growth, personal wealth and luxury, into better quality of life, into appreciation of the things we have, into stronger connections, a greater sense of belonging, our own personal development and the nurturing of more happiness in our lives?

If it means getting more stuff, better stuff, more luxury products then ok, but I encourage you to remain aware of the price that you might be paying in all sorts of subtle ways. Be aware, too, of the price that other people and the natural world must pay for you to have things. Be conscious that the effects of your spending will be felt all around the world and compare these effects with your personal values and decision-making process.

How does the myth of progress manifest in your life? How is it manipulating your dreams and your sense of pride or ok-ness with yourself?

What can we do about it?

Be honest, real and authentic in your choices. Don't be led by a cultural story that we MUST make progress, that we MUST have new things. Reflect on what you really need, instead of what you've been told you should need.

There can be enormous joy and satisfaction in being part of the reuse/repurpose/upcycle movement. If this calls to you, dive right in.

But more generally, look for the subtle pressures that exist within cultural stories of progress. What possibilities for genuine flourishing are being shut down by these stories? How are people who don't want to make progress being ridiculed or attacked? What is the true cost of progress, and how are you contributing to it?

Nothing you do matters

What's the story and how is it told?

This story begins whenever somebody thinks or says, "but really, what can I do about that?" It grows when we justify this with stories about how disempowered we are and how small we are in a big world. We reinforce this story, as well, through our complaining: we announce how powerless we are when we complain that nothing ever changes. We declare that we're victims to the powerful. We look at injustice, or bad decisions, or things going wrong, and we shake our heads that the wrong people are in power, or stupid people have been allowed to make bad decisions.

The story goes: corporations and governments run the world. People can't make a difference. I can't make a difference.

It's becoming more and more embedded in our society over the last few decades. People now ridicule the idea that we can ever make a difference. The proud history of protestors and responsible citizens who stood up for what they believed in the 19th and 20th Centuries has been forgotten. Today, people are more likely to roll their eyes at those who protest or who are politically engaged. We've become mired in a story that says, don't worry too much, because there's nothing you can really do.

An alternative story

There are things we can do. Believing that you're disempowered in the face of a big and unchangeable world is not consistent with a conscious life, lived with determination and curiosity, and a commitment to personal growth and consciousness. If we just turn inwards and try to live good lives, ignoring the larger picture, we deceive ourselves. A truly satisfying life that brings deep happiness and peace must involve, to whatever degree you can manage, a contribution to the communities around you. This involvement is often the missing piece in a person's growth and development. Turning a blind eye to the world isn't authentic. As overwhelming as it might be to engage with the bigger stories, you will grow by doing so.

The story that we should be fostering in ourselves and between one another is: we are each powerful beings who can make a difference. The decisions we face are not *if* we get involved, but *how* we are best suited to making a positive difference in the world. There are people in positions of power who are either misguided, or lack decency and a personal sense of honour. How will *you* contribute to the betterment of the world?

What can we do about it?

As much as possible, work to dispel the story that you are disempowered and disenfranchised. You can make a difference.

Whenever a big organisation like a government or a company makes an unjust decision, we can do something. For example, we can:

- Spend our money wisely. The way you spend is probably the most powerful political force you have. Boycotts are an obvious way to make a difference, but even just sustained spending in ways that support the things you value will, over time, make a difference. Big companies are only big because lots of people buy their products. They watch what people buy carefully. The free market can be a force for good if consumers make ethical choices about their spending, because the growth of the market will go wherever the money goes. The price of ethical goods and services will come down, steadily, if the demand for them increases and there's a reason for companies to develop more efficient and cost-effective processes. With sustained ethical shopping, we can change the world.

- Invite journalists to write stories about it, bringing it to a wider audience
- Vote in ways that are consistent with our beliefs, values and sense of honour. We can use the incredible power of our votes and our political involvement to contribute to a better world.
- Take to the streets and protest. Governments take less notice of protests these days because they know that most people don't care. But if more people cared, and if the protests became more widespread and more obvious, governments and companies would be forced to take notice and reverse policy decisions. I urge you to research the history of protest: so many things that we take for granted were not given to us, they were demanded publicly through effective protest. The working week, the vote for all people, fair labour laws and measures to combat institutional racism are just some examples of things won through protest.

The body is a burden. Stress is all in your head.

What's the story and how is it told?

This story says that your body is a simple, lumpen thing. It's a machine that needs the right fuel to keep it working, and sometimes you're going to need to do some maintenance on it. Do exercise. Follow a diet. Do the things that make this body thing work properly. Sometimes the body hurts or aches or doesn't move properly. As you get older, the body begins to break down.

The story says that you need to buy products that you smear onto the body, making it more appealing. It says you must spend time in the sun to brown the body, to be sexier and get validation through people finding you attractive. It says you should feel ashamed if your body isn't a certain shape, a certain size, with certain proportions. This story gives a voice to the narcissistic and the insecure, who happened to be born into bodies that conformed to a cultural norm of beauty (this in itself can be a prison for freedom and authentic expression).

But what the story is most strongly reinforcing is: stay in your head. Be trapped in your mind. Look for stimulation and excitement for the mind and ignore everything else. The body is just an organic machine that moves around the only thing of any value (the mind). Of the senses, this story strongly emphasises sight and sound – senses that happen in the head and bypass the rest of the self.

If the body complains, or acts strangely, or doesn't do what we want, then it's an annoyance. We have to stop focusing on worthwhile things like computer screens, TV screens, magazines and music and briefly focus on this confusing mass of cells that lives underneath the eyes.

The story puts the body in the same category as the car: remote; mechanical; expensive; sometimes fun; often necessary; but most certainly not part of your vital, conscious self. It's just a thing.

An alternative story

Accessing another story isn't hard, but the volume of our culture's obsession with the mind will tend to drown out any bodily discoveries you make unless you remain focused and conscious. Our culture does not want you to discover your body.

In the alternate story, the body is wise. The body is smart. The body is remarkable. The body is alive, and is part of your every conscious moment. The dividing line between mind and body is not a line at all, but a mysterious melding of realities. Thoughts are affected by the workings of the body. Emotions are physically felt. Spiritual moments resonate powerfully through the body.

In this alternative story, the body is a friend. It's an exciting, infinitely interesting companion on your journey through life. It has things to show you and teach you, and it needs your attention and involvement.

Its value is in its participation in your life, in the richness it brings to your experiences. By feeling all of the sensations in a single breath, each moment is given far more depth than the mind alone can bring you. Chewing a single mouthful of food slowly and purposefully, mindfully, brings a world of experience. Shifting your awareness to your body as you exercise, for example doing yoga or hard physical training, you can come to appreciate all the subtle things it's doing to keep you healthy and well. Growing this relationship will, over time, reduce the injuries you suffer and help you recover from illness. You will naturally eat better as you want to give the body what it needs and you get the feedback from its improved health on your thinking and feeling.

Life opens up into something quite different if you live this story instead of the mainstream one.

A lot of pressures to *be* something, physically, disappear. Beauty becomes more about embodiment and realness, rather than conforming to a stereotype or model. As you move more and celebrate the natural freedom and wonder of your body, to whatever extent you can, and as you watch your body change and adapt to the joyful movements you're enjoying with it, you will become more beautiful. A joyful relationship with the body becomes an extraordinary natural beauty that no amount of makeup or muscle-toning can equal.

Health becomes a pleasure rather than a burden.

Ageing becomes discovering.

Sex is remarkably enhanced as you become aware of a much greater range of sensation, and as you add the body's richness of experience to the voyeuristic demands of the mind.

Confidence grows as you know your body is just right, just enough as it is. Its companionship can also reassure you in difficult moments. Breathe into the body and feel its solidity and presence and it'll strengthen you in difficult times.

Illness, too, will change if you develop this kind of loving relationship with the body. Illness is never going to be *nice*, but it becomes a journey that you undertake with your companion rather than something that's holding you back from the mind-led priorities of the world.

What can we do about it?

Replacing the toxic stories our culture tells about bodies is hard work, like all of these projects of re-telling, but it pays off. Be determined and be curious.

Bring your curiosity to bear on your body. Ask your toes what they have to tell you. Try to talk to your organs. Engage in a yoga practice. Experiment with different breathing. Pay attention to what your body is telling you at any moment. Quietly tell it that you love it, that you're glad it's with you.

Be determined with your practice. Don't let a day go by without doing something that brings you into the body, whether that's some intense exercise, a yoga routine, or just making some time for some deep, relaxing breathing. Feel what's going on inside you as you breathe, as you eat, as you stretch, as you sit, while you're walking, while you're making love.

Be aware of the way that your mind regards your body. Do you see your body as a thing of beauty that's doing its best for you, or do you see it as a hassle, a burden, an annoyance, or even an object of shame and revulsion? Do you think your body is meant to be different?

Lovingly, gently, and with determination over a long period of time, correct yourself every time you find yourself thinking badly of your body. Write yourself affirmations about loving and cherishing your friend, the body. Over time let the beliefs about shame and failure be replaced with a pride for the uniqueness and wonder of the body you've been given. No other body is like it. Give it what it needs and develop a relationship with it. Don't speak or think about your body any differently than you would a friend or child that you love dearly.

And hug often. The body loves to touch other bodies. Hug your friends. Cuddle your lovers. If you're brave enough, hug strangers. Let the body relax a little into each hug and feel the reassurance that comes from simple touch.

Becoming embodied in a real, vital sense is another step towards freedom and empowerment. It's a powerful way to meet your wild self. You will only have this one body, so take care about which story you choose tell about it.

You're meant to figure it all out yourself

What's the story and how is it told?

Not everybody lives with this story, but it comes to dominate the lives of those who do. It's particularly common among men.

This story tells us that only personal achievements matter. If you did it alone, if you knew everything you had to know and succeeded on your own, then that's good. If you needed to ask for help, or if anybody was involved at any time, you've failed. It's humiliating and shameful to ask for help. You should know it all, be able to do it all, be impressive, alone.

The cultural story of 'cool' is responsible for a lot of the reinforcement of this story. The word 'cool' rose to prominence in the 20th Century. A cool person is never seen to make effort. They just exude confidence and competence, completing things without showing any effort.

'Cool' is a straight-jacket.

Other ways this story is told are the archetype of the 'self-made man' and the ruthless business woman.

We live more solitary lives than ever before. Loneliness is a big problem in our culture – it does us a lot of harm. But it's normal, when you're used to living alone or doing a lot of things for yourself, to default to this. I'm a big believer in developing pride in your achievements, but we can sometimes use pride as a defence mechanism. If we've become used to doing everything alone, we can stop ever reaching out or asking for help because doing so would remind us how alone we usually are. We become rigid in our independence, proud of our loneliness, defended against rejection or disappointment by never becoming dependent on other people for anything.

Our culture tells this story in subtle ways. The commodification of community leaves us more independent and more alone. 'Cool' is a persistent narrative, leaving us trying to seem more relaxed and competent than we feel, unable to visibly struggle or show real vulnerability that might lead to connection and sharing. If we had lessons in early life from parents or school that enshrined the importance of doing it by yourself, this can be difficult to shake.

An alternative story

It's increasingly clear that really successful people ask for help all the time. They invest heavily in their own development, both in terms of skills and competence, and in their personal development. They read books, get therapy, go on courses and seminars. They reinvest a lot of their earnings into increasing their own personal value: as a leader, as an employee, as an entrepreneur, as a partner and lover, as a parent, as a friend.

For anyone who's been taught the self-made story, or who takes the story of 'cool' very literally, it requires a mental shift to leave this behind. The story of 'going it alone' is only of value when there's no other option. It's useful when resources are scarce, or you're in the wilderness, or there is no help around. But much more often, it's just a hinderance.

What can we do about it?

The key is results-focused thinking. What's the result that you want from any given situation? Ok, now that you're clear on that, what is the most efficient and effective way to reach that conclusion, within the limitations of what's available to you and your own sense of personal honour? Often, it'll include asking for help, or being taught new skills, or sharing a burden with someone. Even if it doesn't seem that way at the beginning, you should be flexible about your methods, but stubborn about the results you want. If, half way through your journey towards your goal, you realise that somebody else is doing much better, learn from them. Watch them, learn what makes them successful, and start incorporating this into your approach. Maybe ask them directly for help, or if this isn't appropriate or possible, just study them and learn.

Sex and shame

What's the story and how is it told?

This is a story about pain and trauma, which are things we've explored several times already in this book. We each carry the pain of psycho-spiritual wounding, and we each find ways to express that pain. Many of us want catharsis and relief. We want to show it to others and be seen and understood. We want to escape it. We want to make it go away.

There have been a lot of investigations into our sexual fantasies and desires. From careful scientific studies to magazine questionnaires, we love to know what turns us on, and we're always curious about what turns other people on. Am I normal? The fun of reading about weird stuff that excited some people, or the reassurance that we're not alone in being so strange.

Chapter 11: Liberation

Unsurprisingly, taboos always fill the top slots in these studies.

Fantasies about rape are common for women. BDSM is virtually mainstream today, with the *50 Shades of Grey* series amongst the best-selling books of all time with over 150 million copies bought worldwide. For those of us whose pain manifests in particular ways, we fantasise about being tied up or doing the tying, which is exciting because we lose or steal freedom: the victim is trapped and unable to escape. Perhaps we fantasise about spanking, teasing, humiliation, violence and violation. These things occupy intense, visceral, primal parts of our sexual needs.

Sex is a shortcut to primitive parts of the human person. Naked, breathing deeply, vulnerable with another human being in a way that we've rarely been since we were infants, sex takes us to unique psycho-spiritual places. Things that would be hidden or inaccessible to us elsewhere in our lives become needs, desires or compulsions when we move into the realm of sexuality.

Sexuality is such an intense and unique expression of self that it crosses a lot of internal boundaries. Consciousness touches unconscious. Needs that are carefully contained break loose and demand to be met. Wounds become manifested. Shame, which I've said suffuses and defines our culture, can take centre-stage, and sexuality can transmute the experience of shame from one of disgust, distaste, discomfort and loathing into excitement, curiosity, need and catharsis. In the intense crucible of sex, unexpected things merge. Pain can become pleasure. Revulsion can become fascination. Shame can become craving.

For many people, sex is the only place where they have permission to put down the burden of shame that our culture puts on them. By allowing intensity and excitement to overwhelm control, they can break free from the limitations of their daily lives.

Sex is racing heartbeats, physical overwhelm, rushing hormones, touch and pleasure driven by need. But in a shame-based culture, it takes on other aspects. On one hand, some things become exciting because they're not allowed. It's breaking rules, breaking boundaries, doing shameful things, and transmuting that shame into excitement and intensity; and it's catharsis from shame, replacing the expectations of society with glorification in the simplicity of the moment. On the other hand, it's the expectation that we each be physically beautiful, perform perfectly, have no more or less emotion than is proper and behave correctly in every way. Shame pulls us in different directions in our sexuality. It gives us new kinds of excitement as our masks slip and our daily shame is transmuted in a quest for atonement and catharsis, but at the same time we are straight-jacketed by shame for not being perfect in the way that TV or pornographic sex are.

Stories about shame and sex weave through our culture in complex ways, but they tend to put burdens and expectations on us to be something, do things in certain ways, and not to talk about sex. They tell men to be promiscuous and emotionless about sex, and they tell women to be sex-dolls whose value is in the sexual pleasure they bring men. We must choose labels to define our sexual interests: straight or gay, kinky or vanilla. These are some examples of a wide array of culture stories which intertwine shame and sex, and few of them are empowering to the individual.

In my experience, it's pretty unusual to find somebody who doesn't bring shame into their sexuality. People either feel ashamed of their bodies, their needs, their desires or their sexuality histories; or else they feed off the shame they feel about other aspects of their lives and use the crucible of sex to lay aside this burden for a while and indulge in fetishes and kinks that make shame into something pleasurable. Far more people than you might imagine are paralysed by shame when it comes to sex. They either don't (or can't) have sex, can't reach orgasm, are scathing or avoidant of sex, meet blocks or unexpected discomfort during sex, or can be afraid of being vulnerable during sex, so they mask this with promiscuity, obsessions with performance or turn sex into a mind-led, pornographic experience.

To be clear: I'm not saying anything of this with judgement. Sex is part of self-image. We have sex in the way that we feel best expresses us. In some ways, we meet our true selves in our sexual needs and expression. But sex is such an intense, highly-valued experience that our culture does strange things with it. I'm inviting you to choose the way you interact with your sexuality.

An alternative story

If sex is place where we meet all sorts of aspect of ourselves, and if sex is important to us, then an alternative to the confusing, convoluted, shame-ridden stories of mainstream culture is to embrace your unique form of sexual identity. You can learn things about yourself through sex than you can't learn from anything else, because aspects of you will be revealed through sex that you can hide, mask or ignore elsewhere.

In any alternative, empowering story about sex, curiosity and compassionate non-judgement is essential. Sex is a tender spot. Learning about sex should be done gently, playfully and with an open mind. Begin identifying all the ways that shame creeps into your sex. You feel ashamed of things you do or have done? Are you ashamed of what you want? Are you ashamed of how you look or act?

I invite you to gently explore the idea that you can be proud of your own sexual identity. Reject labels and expectations. Pleasure is ok. Intimacy and vulnerability are beautiful things. Explore your physical, mental, emotional and spiritual connections to sex. What might it mean, for example, for you to be wholly emotionally open with your partner? What might it be like to bring a spiritual connection with your lover, even with the world itself, into your love-making?

What can we do about it?

Shame, like everything else, is a choice. How would your sex be different if you didn't bring shame to it? How could you express yourself, enjoy yourself, learn about yourself and meet yourself differently through sex if you weren't bringing shame to it?

Own your desires. They're ok. You can fantasise about anything you want and get a thrill from any thought that pleases you. Only your actions are limited by your personal sense of honour. Even if some aspect of your sexuality turns out to be the thrill that comes from taboo, own that. Allow sexual confidence to be part of the way you think, feel, move, breathe and touch.

Be curious about where things come from. Learn about yourself. Where it feels right, ask for help. There are therapists who specialise in sex, and there are books, courses and podcasts.

Watch how shame about sex is used to manipulate you. Notice the subtle pressures in advertising, products, intimate relationships and conversations with friends. If somebody uses shame about sex to pressure you into anything or to imply that you should be something that you don't want to be, don't take this on board. Gently but firmly refuse to let their expectations or needs define you. Introduce new, strong boundaries that protect your own sexual identity.

The great denial of death

What's the story and how is it told?

This story is simple: death isn't ok. This applies to both metaphorical deaths and our personal, final, absolute death. Death is not ok: it's shut away, kept out of view, not talked about, denied and rejected. Huge amounts of money are invested into researching ways to prevent it, and most of the money spent on our medical care is spent in our last weeks or months to make sure our endings are quiet, painless, normal and private. On the surface, this seems natural and good: we want our parents or older relatives to be comfortable, and many of us fear the pain and loss of dignity at the end of life at least as much as we fear the death of self.

We have the opportunity to learn and grow through metaphorical deaths all the time. Everything that has a beginning has an end, and often new things can't be birthed until something old has been allowed to die. Personal crises are often the consequence of holding on to old things for too long, for not allowing old relationships, old realities and old versions of self-image to die. Equally, suicidal urges aren't always what they seem: sometimes they're a yearning for a part of the self to die, to let go of things that no longer serve us, interpreted as urges to end the whole self.

But it's the denial of the final death that causes us the most problems. For people who have been diagnosed with terminal illness, there is often a tremendous pressure to 'carry on'. There's a lot of shame associated with the idea of making death visible or letting illness be seen, and a lot of congratulations that are meted out to those who manage to hide their terror and suffering behind a mask of normality. This makes the ending of many people's lives a lonely time. They aren't allowed to be dying, because that would be unacceptable. They must be ok, fine, carrying on as best they can, until they suddenly disappear. We'll remember them as having 'gone away', 'finally lost the battle with cancer'. We'll remember their lives and their absence. But there is often a lot of pressure to ignore that somebody was ever in the process of dying.

We are all dying. We know this, but we tend to know it on an intellectual level, if we ever reflect on it at all.

I've had the honour of spending a little time with Stephen Jenkinson, a Canadian author, psychotherapist, theologian and teacher who proudly goes by the title 'The Angel of Death'. Jenkinson has spent time with thousands of dying people and has some important things to tell us about death and dying. I can't recommend his book, *Die Wise*, highly enough. It's one of those books we could all do with reading.

> *"The actual, observable truth of it, if you go by people's behavior when the time comes, is that everyone knows that everyone else is going to die. Generally, in my experience of the thing, the dismay of learning that your best friend or your beloved partner will die is dwarfed severely by the bolt from the blue shock of learning that you too will die. There is nothing in what I have seen working in the death trade for years that persuades me for five minutes that everyone knows they are going to die. You simply cannot tell that we know we're going to die from how we live. What is it called in training modules designed for physicians, the first discussion of diagnosis and prognosis with terminally ill patients? It is called "Breaking Bad News." Why is it news? It is not news because it is so sudden: Most people receiving that diagnosis have had symptoms and suspicions for a period of time before the consult. It is news because prior to its broadcast, it wasn't a known thing. For most of us, our death is not a known thing."*

> \- Stephen Jenkinson, Die Wise

There are some great and timeless fears that wait for us when we confront the reality of our own personal death. A lot of things stop being important or relevant. Priorities shift and realign. We begin to ask ourselves questions about the meaning of life, about what we're here to do, about whether we've lived well and fully.

These are the kinds of deeply uncomfortable questions that women and men have been asking since the beginning. Our current culture does not support people to ask these questions, or to search for the meaning they contain, but many people will search eventually. For many people, the last weeks or months of their lives will be their first opportunity to ask the deeper questions, to reflect on meaning and fulfilment. There's a fantasy that dying people are gifted with superior or supernatural knowledge by the proximity of their death. According to Stephen Jenkinson and all of the dying he has witnessed, they aren't. While there are famous quotes or inspiring memes by people who are dying and found profound things to share with us, there are profound things said by a lot of people. Death doesn't bring you any more information than the fact that you are soon to cease to be you. You will have no more resources to answer deep and eternal questions then than you do now, and you will have run out of time to explore them or to bring their answers into your life.

Death represents an unspoken, unspeakable horror that is carefully and consistently avoided in our culture. We do this to ourselves and one another out of care, and out of total unfamiliarity with the topic. Nobody wants to be reminded of their mortality. Better to carry on, live life 'to the full' and deny the undeniable reality of our endings for as long as we can.

Thus, life has no real value to us. Experience does, and certainly things, money and resources do, but life itself is cheap. We participate in systems of death every day. Many of our cultural heroes were killers. Everything that we do and love can be put off for another day, because we pretend that we have an unlimited number of days. There's no need to take risks or do the things that are frightening and necessary: I'll do them another day, or later in my life. We are happy to buy things that cause pollution and suffering because we don't have a personal sense of what death really is. It's my view that we're a cavorting, confused culture of children who cause terrible harm with our lack of reflection and consciousness.

This is the price of the denial of death. There's a loss of realness and significance to our moments and we avoid deep and piercing reflections on the great questions as we stumble through life without thought for the consequences of our choices. We are too busy for all that, and there's no real need for it anyway.

An alternative story

What is a conscious adult response to all of this? How does a person who has full conscious awareness of their power, their wounding and their needs respond to the idea of death?

Certainly, the answer isn't denial.

In my experience, death can be a powerful ally. Being aware that all relationships and situations in your life are fragile and finite helps you to be more attentive to them, to remember to be appreciative and glad of them in real time, as they're happening. Being conscious of the fact that all things will pass can help you enjoy good things and endure suffering more easily. Knowing that all things will die, whether they're precious and welcome or difficult and unwelcome, brings an edge of significance to the moments of our lives.

"I shall pass this way but once; any good that I can do or any kindness I can show to any human being, let me do it now. Let me not defer nor neglect it, for I shall not pass this way again."

- Etienne De Grellet

You do not have an unlimited number of days ahead. They will end, you will cease, and this life will be over. Do you want your final moments to be cast in terror, confusion and regret, or would you like to begin the reflection on your mortality now? This is entirely your choice and you may well choose that the mainstream story of our culture offers you a lot of value in its soothing approach to death. Like everything else, this is about choice. But I've sat with too many people who are dying, or who have had a health scare, and who profoundly regret the transient, flippant way they regarded their days. They tell me that life is short and precious.

The alternative story, then, is to live in awareness of your death, to carry the idea and feeling of endings with you, to make death something you know, personally. To draw strength and motivation from it, to let it make things more real and significant in your life, and to work out your own response to the fact that your death is inevitable, unavoidable and inexorably drawing closer.

What can we do about it?

What will you do with this extraordinary gift of life?

I invite you to consider this question. This whole book, really, is an invitation to elevate your life from a series of disconnected moments to a life aligned with significance and conscious choice. To discover who you are through a commitment to lifelong learning and growth. To apply what you find to the moments of your life. To allow the reality of death to be a companion on this journey and make it a subject for personal enquiry alongside all the others.

Steven Jenkinson calls us to make death public. He says, "the worst thing you can do is approach death as a rookie", because that's a sure way to find bafflement and terror waiting for you. If you want to make death a companion in your life, I encourage you to have those difficult conversations about endings. When you notice somebody uncomfortable and shying away from the whole subject of death, wonder why and notice whether you do the same thing. Bring your curiosity and compassionate non-judgement to the question of how we, personally and collectively, regard death, how we push one other to deny it, and why we do this to ourselves and to each other. Be conscious of the 'death is not ok' story and, if you want, choose something else.

A broken people

When I say 'a people', I mean it in the old sense. A people is a group brought together through shared history, shared intention, shared myths and stories. It's a group bonded by connection, need and alignment.

Our stories have broken us. In this chapter I've given you a handful of examples of the most common, most pernicious stories that mess us up and cause us to forget our true needs, potentials and ambitions.

I hope I've been able to show that this is only true as long as we keep tearing ourselves apart with all these unhelpful and toxic stories. Our stories were designed to serve another time and another set of needs. Some have been manipulated or warped in order to meet the needs and greed of people in power. Every story can be challenged and, over time, replaced by something more authentic, more real and more nourishing.

For the moment, these are the stories that our culture teaches to each generation. Each person in the culture is doing good if they live those stories and if they pass them on to others. In the eyes of this culture, it is good and noble and right for a person to teach each one of these stories to their children, to shame others for failing to live up to the stories, and to feel shame if they find themselves failing, as they surely will.

We live with this reality every day. It drives our choices. For some of us, those choices are where to spend our money, how to speak to our children, what to do with our time. For others, it is the setting of national and international policy, deciding on educational programmes for millions of children, executive decisions that will see waterways poisoned, mountains levelled, or species destroyed. The harm that the human race is doing to our home planet is the result of the same cultural stories that hurt us on a personal basis.

We each live, separated from one another by our shame, trying to reinforce the stories of our culture even as they hurt us, hurt our children and systematically poison our homes. We're left unhappy, unsupported, desperately chasing success, salvation or redemption. We have few bonds with a community. We judge and feel judged by others.

At this time, we are a broken people. As a species with so much power, our hurtful stories now cause terrible harm. Our bonds to one another are broken and our trust and empathy for one another is limited.

It doesn't have to be this way. It could be very, very different if we each do the work, step out of the grip of shame and make better, empowered choices for ourselves, for our children and for the world.

What would this look like?

What would it take to restore a people?

How far can personal growth, awareness and empowerment really go without engaging with the bigger picture?

What part might you play in the reimaging of the great stories of our culture?

We'll look at this more in Part 3 of this book.

Chapter 11: Liberation

Deep Joy

6.WILDERNESS

"The land remembers who I am"

Deep Joy

This book is about an attitude. It's about empowerment through awakening and through developing a sense of consciousness and ownerships of your whole self. It's about becoming the author of your life: choosing your destiny and working hard to make it real. Beyond this, it's about understanding. Every piece of information we have gives us more power, more options, more possibilities. Knowing yourself intimately on mental, emotional, physical and spiritual levels gives you a tremendous power. Knowing the cultural context that you move through gives you another level of freedom and possibility.

In this chapter we will look at the most forgotten influence on your power and freedom, one that's missing from almost every personal development book you might read: the vital relationship between your wild self and the rest of the natural world.

Most of us live our lives in sterile cubes made of stone, steel, timber and glass. Sometimes we visit a tamed part of nature, or we watch a documentary. It's nice, it's fascinating, often it's beautiful and wondrous. Sometimes it's not, it's boring or mundane. We're aware of the damage that's being done by the way humans treat non-humans. On some level, we have an emotional response to this. But it's a distant response. It's the same feelings we have to the suffering of people in a famine or earthquake that we see on the news: we feel bad for them, but then we carry on with our lives.

Some of us want to get closer to nature. We spend more time outdoors, we go to places in the world that are famous for their superb natural wonder. Some of us swim in wild places and get ourselves lost in woods. Some of us hug trees.

Most of us don't, and even if we like the idea of more time spent outdoors, who has the time for all that? We have jobs to do, and most of us are canny urbane beings. Our priorities are work, home, family, friends, getting enough sleep, looking forward to Friday or the next holiday, getting a good takeaway. Being realistic, the natural world is like the horizon or the light we read by: we know it's there, but we only notice it now and then.

What's missing from all of this? We can choose nature, or not. We can go for a walk in the park or the countryside, or not. We can feel wracked with guilt about the dwindling numbers of fish in the sea, or islands of plastic in the middle of the oceans, or the burning of rainforests to feed hungry, picky humans, or the extermination of whole species…or not. It's all optional. It's all something we choose.

Nature is, essentially, entertainment. We switch it on when we want, and we switch it off again when we go back to the real priorities in life.

While our world is dismantled and turned into raw resources by bulldozers and explosives and the strategic decisions of men in suits, we carry on. As reports of the gathering storm of climate change and the impending danger to our children seep into our awareness, we go to work and normalise the way things are. Who has the time for all that?

There is a missing piece in all this.

Historically-speaking, humans have been on a journey away from the natural world for about ten thousand years, which isn't very long in terms of our history. Humans have been around for something like 200,000 years, after all, so for 95% of our time on this earth we lived as hunter-gatherers. At this point, the stories of progress in our culture will step in and imply that these people were primitive victims of their situations, weren't very bright, and the development of the world into its current state was inevitable and a very good thing indeed. Look how much better things are now! I'm not saying things aren't, in some ways, better. But this question is far more complicated than simply: things were bad, now they're good. Progress for its own sake is often very harmful. There is so much more going on here than just things being improved by the coming of civilisation.

To lend a little balance to inform your conscious adult choice, I invite you to consider whether civilisation is, in fact, a source of terrible suffering and harm for both humans and to the non-human world.

Even after we started basic agriculture, we were still intimately tied to the natural world. It's very recent indeed that a single, homogenised culture that's totally divorced from nature has come to dominate the world. Today, even those who spend their lives campaigning for the rights of nature and try to protect the forests and oceans of the world with things like the ecocide laws, only see nature as a passive and dead thing.

For almost all of our history, we knew something else to be true. Over the past centuries, science has replaced religion and mysticism as our primary source of information about the world. The world has become steadily more sterile and lifeless. There are simple physical laws at work, certain chemical reactions, certain biological relationships. There you go, that's the world.

But this is *information*, not knowledge, and it's a long way from wisdom. We've lost something precious in our quest for knowing: we've lost relating. Along with the truths that science has taught us, we've also swallowed a cultural shift which has nothing, actually, to do with scientific learning. We've surrendered genuine, personal connection with the wild. We've forgotten mystery and wonder. We've rendered the world into cold, dead facts instead of something that's alive, dynamic, conscious and wise.

This is the lost part of the puzzle. All of the things that science teaches us are fact-based and verifiable, but we've come to believe that only facts are true. The missing piece of the puzzle, the thing that lets us carry on as normal while the world dies and becomes steadily unsuitable for human habitation, is that the world is alive. This isn't a one-way relationship. Wild beauty is not entertainment. The belief that it's a nice thing to visit, but that we can turn it off when we're done, is based on the assumption that it isn't alive. But the world is alive, and it holds a piece of our soul.

People who spend time in nature feel better

There are many, many studies that show that time in nature has positive effects on people, from behaviour in young people to adults suffering from trauma or burn-out. Time in the wild has been proven to help people suffering from depression. A meta-analysis in 2010 called *The current status of urban-rural differences in psychiatric disorders* (Acta Psychiatr Scand. 2010 Feb;121(2):84-93) showed that people in urban environments are 20% more likely to develop anxiety disorders and almost 40% more likely to develop mood disorders. It's good for us to be in nature.

While the scientific basis for the benefits of time in nature is still being understood, governments and developers are taking notice, and policies are shifting towards adding more nature-connection into our lives. This is a big move away from city development in the 20th Century, when the only considerations were how efficiently we could live our lives in a brick-and-concrete world.

A Japanese practice called Shinrin-yoku is beginning to spread around the world. This 'forest therapy' is, at its root, simply spending time quietly in nature. Healing comes to us. It's not something we do, or something somebody teaches us, it is the healing qualities of nature itself. According to Shinrin-yoku.org, the proven benefits of this therapy include:

- Boosted immune system functioning, with an increase in the count of the body's Natural Killer (NK) cells.

- Reduced blood pressure
- Reduced stress
- Improved mood
- Increased ability to focus, even in children with ADHD
- Accelerated recovery from surgery or illness
- Increased energy level
- Improved sleep

For many of us, nature is a nice idea but it doesn't rank highly in our priorities. If you need an excuse or a rationalisation to begin building your own connection with the natural world, there is plenty of evidence that human health is improved by time in woods, fields, moorland, mountains or by the sea.

A living world

This Principle says: The world remembers who I am. It doesn't say: The world helps me remember. And not: Nature is an important thing. It is the living land that's doing the remembering.

Nature isn't always a nice thing. It isn't entertainment. Spend time out in a storm without a shelter to go home to, or in a biting cold wind, or afraid of predators, and you'll quickly realise that nature isn't nice. It can be terrifying. It can be miserable. It can be hard work. It can be tedious.

But this is the world that our species evolved to live in. Our minds, emotions, bodies and spirits were formed to thrive in the midst of the wild. Everything we do now to compensate for the stifling, numbing routines of our civilised world are pale echoes of the intense, visceral lessons that the natural world has to teach us. It is a patient, relentless teacher and some of its lessons might be so intense that they would threaten your very life.

A night spent in the wild, beneath an awe-inspiring canopy of stars, amid woods that shake and rattle and groan, amid the calls of animals harsh and clear, with no door to lock, no entertainment to numb the senses, without the confines and reassurances of our people…this take us to a place we have often forgotten. We feel our hearts, we are compelled to be in the moment by the demands of our senses, we hear the whispers and the shouts of the many voices in the wild and we find ourselves returning to that which is most precious to us. For some of us it comes quickly, in only minutes or hours spent away from domesticated concrete and asphalt. For others it will take days. The senses will sharpen. Minutes and seconds will seem less important than sunrise and sunset. The mind and spirit unpack from their regimented, domesticated shapes into something alien and wild and free.

Today, we recapture these lessons in safer forms. Personal development is, in effect, a modern successor for the teachings of the wild world, and of the traditional elders who would have reinforced its lessons. Shamans have become course leaders. Storms, floods, droughts and freezing winters have been replaced by invitations to take risks, to try new things, to travel, to practice extreme sports, to seek out thrills. But I'm sure you can appreciate that so much of the depth of these lessons, the subtle understandings that come out of learning from nature herself, have been lost in our safer forms.

Now, we have the culture we have. It brings us so many benefits, so many things we can be honestly grateful for, but still a wilderness exists within each of us. The memory of endless forests, of hunting proud wild animals, of knowing a place so well that we could easily find food in its undergrowth, rivers and marshes. A part of us cries out to run bare-footed through the wild, to return to tribe, to live in fear and mysterious wonder of the terrible power of the earth-mother.

When we reconnect with this part of ourselves, and when we welcome the lessons of nature again in an unfiltered way, we touch on a kind of healing that we must all, eventually, endure: a terrible and a bottomless grief.

Grieving for the death of the world

I have not yet met anybody who has discovered their wild centre, who has not also touched a terrible grief. While nature is something remote, theoretical and distant to us, while it remains a nice place to visit at the weekend, we can shield ourselves from the personal consequences of what humans have done to the non-human world. When we begin to remember the earth as our mother, when we begin to realise that all these quaint-sounding words of indigenous people were meant *literally*, that the earth is really and truly alive, then we witness the suffering of a living person, one who we are bound to as tightly as to a human mother. Our spirits and the spirit of the world are linked like an umbilical to an unborn baby: that's the sensation that people talk about when they remember this aspect of self. The suffering of the mother becomes the suffering of the infant.

We looked at grief in the last Principle. Grief has a unique power to bring us into the present moment and make us appreciate things more fully and more intensely, to notice and wonder at the interconnected significance of things. It's about breaking and awakening. Grief at the death of a loved one is an experience that can change your whole life, if you let it and don't struggle to get back to 'just the way things are'. Grief at the death of the world can be, for many of us, simply overwhelming. I've seen tear-streaked faces of people beginning to realise how hurt they are by the wounding of the world. I've seen eyes haunted by the realisation of grief that is simply too big to be understood or processed.

This might be weird and alien to you. You might not have a clue what I'm talking about, and if you don't then all of this might seem a bit outlandish and make-believe. I can only tell you that I've seen this too often to believe that it's just the personal issues of a few people. I've come to believe that this trauma and this grief is within all of us. If you feel a resonance with this idea, a lot of personal choices to remain busy, to avoid too much time in nature, to be constantly distracted by entertainment, by personal dramas and by little obsessions, all begin to make sense. Our cultural stories about progress and affirmation through wealth and success become reassurances to protect us from the emotional fallout of our collective actions.

If the idea of personal trauma caused by the suffering of the world doesn't make much sense to you, you can skip the rest of this chapter. It may be something that'll make more sense to you in time, or it may not. Your own personal truth is what matters, your own authentic experience, and there is no expectation or judgement in this book for what feels right for you.

If this touches something in you, if you've begun to meet this level of your personal work or if, perhaps, it stirs some longing or need in you, then I can only urge you to lean gently into it. Grief at the death of the world is an overwhelming experience, beyond the capacity of the human person to handle on their own.

I know of two routes to help you transmute the trauma that we each feel at the suffering of our spiritual mother.

The first is to find training, courses or therapy that can help you to make sense of what you're feeling. The most famous of these is *The Work That Reconnects*, created by Joanna Macy. This work is held in books (for example, *Coming Back to Life*), but mostly it's delivered through workshops and courses. These are a great place to start, so I invite you to research and connect with this material. It'll help give you tools and processes to deal with this level of personal awakening.

You can also look for eco-psychologists or other professionals who help people to process the hurt when they realise that the suffering of the world is their own suffering. Reach out to these, if you feel like it's right for you.

The second route is to draw together with other people who feel similarly, and just spend time with them. Share the grief through proximity. There might be groups or meetups near you where you can do this. If there aren't, consider setting one up yourself. There may be other people around who feel the way you feel. You don't need to feel like you have all the answers, you don't need to have clever things to say to them, but it's good to have the chance to say things if you want to. The important thing is just to be with other people who are shaken in the way that you're shaken.

There are so many aspects of ourselves that would be nourished and healed by the rediscovery of community. We've lost so many skills for this task, and we have so little dependence on one another (instead, depending on commodities, systems, processes and services) that there isn't much obvious incentive to re-learn how to share our lives with others who aren't our close friends or lovers. But as I believe that we benefit on many levels from an extended community of like-minded people, linked by their desire to understand themselves and the world and be part of something good. If you feel called to take faltering steps back into a relationship with your own inner wildness, and the wildness of the land, then having people of common purpose around is really helpful. Our culture does not want you to do this. It wants you to behave, be normal, conform, comply and consume. It's helpful to have people around you who join you in saying, no.

So many people meet this level of psycho-spiritual wounding and become paralysed or overwhelmed by it. That's ok, for a while. But the world does not need more people who sit in trauma and let it destroy their creativity. At this time, what we most need is people of personal power, awareness and consciousness who hold an awareness of the consequences that this society brings in the world, and who act with

personal honour and integrity with a determination not to contribute
to further suffering. If you feel called to active campaign work, you
can do this. But we can all, in small ways, refuse to be part of the
slide towards ecological and spiritual ruin. You don't have to take on
responsibility for saving the whole world. But you are called to take a
stand for what you believe and what you know to be true. The world
requests and expects this of you.

We live at an unprecedented time in history. The world is not the
quiet, plodding humdrum of 'just the way things are'. This is a time
when personal choices matter more than ever before. When you
make your choices, realise the true significance that an empowered,
conscious adult can have in the world. I invite you to draw self-esteem
and pride from knowing you are a force for good in the world.

We are the ones we have been waiting for.

Things no human can teach you

There are a lot of great books about reconnecting with the wild. *Wild*
by Jay Griffiths is one. *Swim Wild* by Jack Hudson is another. I am
grateful to you for taking the time to read this book and allow me to
share with you the truths I have learned over the past 20 years. I hope
that you find things in the book that will be profound and helpful for
you.

However, no book, teacher or human companion can restore to you
the piece of yourself you have lost by becoming alienated from the
wild. I have talked in this book about the nature of domesticated
humanity – how we have shut down a lot of ourselves in order to
behave well around one another. I have encouraged you to rediscover
your inner wildness. You can do much of this yourself. With curiosity
and determination you can awaken your inner wildness and recover
that alert sense of power and freedom that you've lost. There are
things, though, that cannot be learned alone. Healing that no doctor,

spiritual guide or therapist can bring you. There are mental, emotional, physical and spiritual parts of us that will only be restored and made whole by a return to time in the wild.

Where is the wilderness that calls to you? Is it the deep woods, the sea, the mountains, the moors, a particular river or lake? I particularly encourage you not to look too far away when you're beginning your return to nature. The land of your birth is the best place to start. Perhaps a sacred mountain or a wide tundra somewhere else will be able to teach you something that the river near your childhood home cannot, but I encourage you to start your journey at home.

As often as you can manage it, for as long as possible, begin returning to the wild. Take as little with you as possible. Do not regard this as fun or entertainment, but rather an adventure or quest to recover a part of you that you've lost. Listen. Explore. Stop and be. Breathe deeply.

It may take time, but I encourage you to treat the land as your teacher, mother and healer. Learn your own unique way of listening to her, feeling her breath, dancing with her and letting her restore that which you've lost.

The affirmation

"The land remembers who I am"

Counter-affirmations

Most people do not remember that the natural world is alive, and waiting to resume an ancient relationship with each of us. People who don't feel this call might say...

- It's boring outside
- Staring at that view and daydreaming is self-indulgent
- I don't care about the rainforests, or whales or whatever
- It's cold out there, let's just watch telly

Deep Joy

7.ADVENTURE

"Peace is only found in the storm - I must engage with risk, adventure and change in order to find peace"

Our exploration together has looked at personal empowerment and the true nature of choice, the conscious meeting and owning of personal needs, adulthood, gratitude and honour. We've looked at how and why we are a 'broken people' and some of the ways that this influences free choice and personal power. We've looked at the idea of inner- and outer-wildness, and how what it calls us to meet in ourselves and in the world. We've used the virtues of determination, curiosity and compassionate non-judgement to navigate these steps.

This has been a very inwards-focused journey so far, with a lot of gentle exploration of complex or subtle ideas.

But an empowered person moves with purpose and with passion. All the awareness and understanding in the world won't bring change and growth in your life without an understanding of risk and adventure.

Adventure is our next focus: taking everything we've learned about choice, power, need and value and turning it into potent action. Building confidence and courage through conscious risk-taking. Moving the idea of adventure to the centre of your life.

Comfort Zone, Risk Zone, Panic Zone

This is one of the most commonly taught psychological models, and it's the bread-and-butter of life coaches everywhere. It's a model about learning, growth and development. It was originally known as the Learning Zone Model, created by Tom Senninger. Over the years, I've adapted the original model a little to meet the needs of my coaching clients.

The model says that all of life can be broken down into three zones. These aren't physical places, but rather parts of your life and how you relate to them.

The Comfort Zone is where we all live. Here, things are familiar, known, understood and relatively predictable. They include home, close friendships, most parts of intimate relationships, daily routine, work, favourite hobbies and TV shows. The Comfort Zone is where you know how everything works. When you get up in the morning and do your routine before work, that's the Comfort Zone. When you meet up with old friends and have the same conversations you always have, that's the Comfort Zone.

Everyone's Comfort Zone is different. For a farmer, her home, fields and the demands of the farm are the Comfort Zone. For the city banker, perhaps a high-adrenaline day of trading and working for demanding shareholders is the Comfort Zone. For a stay-at-home mum, the Comfort Zone might be the home, the children, the trips to the shops, inviting friends round for tea.

The Comfort Zone is not necessarily a nice place, it's simply familiar. For a wife with an abusive husband, the fear of the home is part of the Comfort Zone. For a man living beyond his means, the desperate juggle of money from one card to another, the slow increase of debt, is the Comfort Zone.

Our culture, with its priorities of conformity, progress and security, teaches that the Comfort Zone is the goal. To have a predictable, safe home with a predictable, safe life is a thing to aspire to.

The problem is that the human person did not evolve in a predictable and safe world. Our minds, hearts, bodies and spirits do not thrive in security. We each carry a vital, passionate wildness, free from the domesticated story of our broken culture, and this wildness isn't nourished by being safe and comfortable. The Comfort Zone should be a place we return to for rest and peace. We thrive on adventure, and that's found in the Risk Zone.

Whenever you leave the familiar and the secure, in any way, whenever you feel out of your depth, nervous or insecure, whenever there's a risk of getting things wrong, whenever you need to learn something new to overcome a challenge…you're in the Risk Zone. The Risk Zone is where all learning happens. You can't learn anything at all in the Comfort Zone, because you know it all. All you're doing is replaying predictable and secure realities.

If you go to a new class, or move in a new circle of friends, you're in the Risk Zone.

If you travel to a new place, perhaps a new home or an exotic culture, you're in the Risk Zone.

If you can ever say to yourself, "I have no idea what I'm doing" but you carry on anyway, you're in the Risk Zone.

The Risk Zone is where you meet entirely new ideas and where you risk failure, disappointment and embarrassment. In the Risk Zone you'll be surprised, delighted, shocked, have your mind opened and your heart filled. Things might go really wrong and you'll have to deal with that, and they can go wrong publicly and humiliatingly. Even if things go right, you will be changed by the experience.

That's the point. The person you are now, the whole shape of your life, your 'just the way things are' is actually a work in progress. You are not the finished product. You can grow and learn and develop and whatever direction you want, developing new skills and abilities, reshaping your life into something that truly nourishes and excites you. To get any of that, you will need to engage with risk, and become somebody who embraces risk by default.

The Panic Zone isn't something we'll explore in this book, except to say that you can go too far into Risk. Risk should be challenging, engaging, enlivening and developmental. When you go too far, you've gone into Panic. In the Panic Zone you either learn very quickly indeed, or you fail utterly and get seriously hurt by the experience. It doesn't make for sustained learning. It's the equivalent of jumping into the deep end of the pool when you're learning to swim: you either learn to swim within about a minute, or you drown. The Panic Zone exists in the model as a warning to those who think that more and more Risk can only be a good thing. You can go too far.

There's one further aspect to this model. It isn't static. A person with an active Risk life, who engages with change and learning often, has a big Comfort Zone. It grows as you learn new things. Those things become familiar and known, so the circle of the Comfort Zone expands to include them. You can recognise someone with a big, fat Comfort Zone when you meet someone with a lot of skills, a lot of confidence and a lot of experiences and stories to tell.

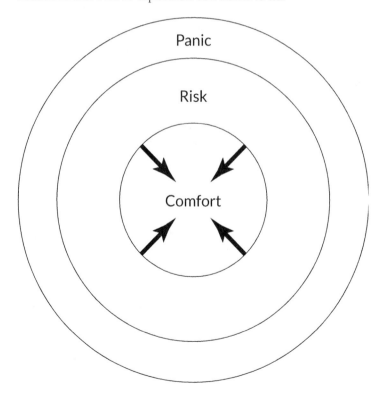

But the Comfort Zone is constantly shrinking. That's just a part of the human experience. The human brain has evolved to store the most important information first, to aid survival in difficult situations. Things that haven't been used for a while are shunted into less-used parts of the mind. Emotionally, things that were comfortable a while ago become uncomfortable and eventually frightening and unnerving if you don't do them for long enough. The longer the wait, the more intimidating they seem. The Comfort Zone contracts, so something that was easy now seems difficult and things that used to be manageable become frightening. The longer we go without brave adventures into our personal risk zones, the more intimidating things become. We end up locked within a little bubble of safety, and doing anything new seems almost unbearable. A lot of my clients had ended up here, and we've engaged in a steady programme of taking steps deeper into risk, combined with personal work to understand the limiting beliefs that had kept them choosing to stay within the confines of the comfort zone.

The classic example of this is elderly people who are frightened of teenagers. They were teenagers once. They were probably reckless and loud and disrespectful. But it's been a long time and they haven't had much experience of teenagers for years, so now, loud and rebellious kids seem scary. The elderly end up frightened to leave their homes.

In less extreme ways, this is happening to all of us, all the time. Unused skills atrophy; unvisited places become unappealing and then frightening; challenges that we used to relish become things we doubt we can do anymore; people we haven't seen in a long time become people we avoid.

The size of the Comfort Zone is a good indicator of confidence. It's the sign of a brave life. If your Comfort Zone is big (if there are lots of places, people, situations and skills that you feel confident about) then you've demonstrated your courage often. That is how confidence grows. If you don't feel competent and secure in many places, with many people or about many of your skills, then perhaps you need to stretch out into Risk more often.

Risk, then, is good for us. We learn new things, we grow as a person, and we hold back the contraction of the Comfort Zone, keeping our confidence high.

We'll look more at learning to handle Risk in Principle 8.

A life of adventure

A conscious life is an active life. In the moments when you're most alive, you're actively exploring new possibilities, experimenting, learning and generally making conscious choices in your life. I call this 'leaning into life', like a hunting dog straining at the leash, eager to dash forwards or the hawk scanning the ground for prey, ready to stoop and dive. This is where your wild nature comes to the fore. The price of being asleep, being domesticated and being safe is that moments merge into one another. Opportunities are lost. Life slides by. Normal is good enough. Every now and then you will notice that days, months or years have gone by and nothing's changed, that your life remains so-so.

The ideal place for humans, for our mental, emotional, physical and spiritual health, is on the edge between Comfort and Risk. My coaching clients often find me asking them, "where is your edge right now?" They know I'm asking where Comfort and Risk meet for them right now. It's important to focus your attention in good places, and you should know where your Comfort Zone ends, where your Risk Zone begins and what your next adventures into Risk will be. Where are you next going to stretch, grow, learn and lean into life?

We do need time in the Comfort Zone. It's where we come home and enjoy the benefits of everything we've found, created and learned.

But we need to spend time, every day, in the Risk Zone. Learning, challenging ourselves, being out of our depth, succeeding, failing, forgiving ourselves, dusting off and trying something else.

Life as adventure means staying conscious and stepping into life at every opportunity. It means a keen, wild eye on your surroundings. It means resisting the urge to get bored just because things around you are the way they've always been. It means consciously bringing a *second naivety* to everything, looking with fresh eyes at your home, your route to work, your workplace, your career, your prospects and opportunities, your friendships, your parenting and your intimate relationships.

Bring curiosity to every moment. What possibilities exist, now? Where can you surge forwards, explore, take a risk, learn something new, put yourself in a better position? Using the goals and vision that you've set for yourself, how can you re-imagine your journey towards your goals based on new information? Be stubborn about your goals, but flexible about your methods.

Bring tremendous determination to every moment. Be relentless in your awareness, in your willingness to risk, grow and improve. Once you've found a route that works for you, be relentless in its pursuit. When you wake up with heavy limbs and tired eyes, remember your adventure and your wild heart and swing your legs out of bed. On days when you're filled with energy, do all you can to take new steps into adventure.

Carry this phrase with you: **"what would I do, if I were a little bit braver?"**

Ask yourself this every day, about different aspects of your life, and then take action. Prove to yourself that you are a little bit braver. Do the things you didn't think you could.

Fear will be part of this journey. That's normal and ok. We'll look at how to handle the fear in Principle 8.

Life as adventure is living on your edge, always alert, always curious, always determined, except for the times when you consciously choose to go back to Comfort and enjoy its relaxing familiarity. It's ok to make time for this. Rest is a vital part of life. Just don't get too comfy!

Some of the features of an adventurous life might be:

- Be the first person to say hello and shake hands.
- Be the person with the wild stories to tell.
- Follow your curiosity to new places.
- Have that scary conversation with your partner.
- Set yourself daunting physical challenges.
- If you tend towards a certain way of feeling and thinking, challenge yourself to think and feel in another way which better supports your goals.
- Is your self-image compatible with the life you want to create? If not, engage in the adventure of re-imagining yourself.
- Stretch yourself, spiritually.
- Seek true inner stillness, silence and awareness. Adventure is not always loud – but it's always challenging.
- Dare to make that secret dream come true.

This is why we needed to do the work to establish your personal sense of honour. A person who lives life as adventure is capable of anything. Every time you take a risk, whether you succeed or fail, you will grow in confidence and personal power. That's broadly how confidence works. It's the response you have to evidence that you're brave.

Don't let a day go by without doing something, however small, that you would do if you were a little bit braver.

I will never 'get there'.

We'll look at this more in Principle 12, but I invite you to consciously, systematically begin replacing this mind-set:

I just need to hold on through this hard time, through this difficult thing. I can see a better time ahead, when I can relax and be happy again.

With this mind-set:

I embrace the challenge, the adversity and struggle. This is life. I don't try to shield myself from it, I step bravely to meet it, heart and mind open. Perhaps later, I'll be in a quieter time, and I'll fully inhabit that space too. But I don't wait, I love this struggle.

In his book *The Way of the SEAL*, Mark Divine calls this learning to 'embrace the suck'. He uses stories from his time training to be a US Navy SEAL, moments when the training was so hard and so intense that it was almost overwhelming, when he suddenly realised that the people who thrived were those who didn't brace themselves to endure the hard time, they welcomed the hardship. When things sucked, they embraced the suck. A whole chapter of *The Way of the SEAL* is devoted to developing this positive mind-set towards challenge and hardship. It's a great book and I can't recommend it enough.

Let go of the idea that things will be better one day, if only you can endure this moment. Make the future better, actively become the author of your Self and your life, remaining conscious and wild-minded through good times and bad. Give birth to your vision and commemorate the death of your old life. Be awake and conscious throughout your day. Every moment has something to teach you. Every day is a school day.

The most inspiring elders I have known, the ones whose guidance and stories have been really nourishing in my life, didn't really believe in retirement. As much as they were able, in whatever way felt good for them, they remained active and engaged throughout their latter days. The idea of the quiet retirement, when you have 'earned' your chance to stop doing the things you hate, so that you can slowly wither until a quiet and hidden death, is the final insult of a domesticated culture to the potential of the human person. Just when we know the most, have the most wisdom, can guide the younger generations best with advice, inspiration and timeless ideas, we surrender to living out the last chapter of somebody else's story.

I invite you to abandon ideas of retirement and an earned rest. Stay conscious, explore and stretch yourself to the end of your days.

Your journey, your standards

Take care, as you adopt your wild mind-set, that you don't fall into the trap of living somebody else's challenges. As we begin to challenge ourselves, we can look outside for ideas of how to live a life of adventure. We can try to be like our parents, or our friends who do amazing or interesting things, like our idols and those we most respect.

Follow your own heart and engage with the adventures that are right for you.

If the right adventure for you is to become the best parent you can be, you aren't a failure if you don't go on adventure holidays, earn a huge salary or live in a big house. Your adventures and challenges will be different. Learning about parenting. Being with your child through difficult times, when other parents just tell their children to stop acting-up or to be quiet. Structuring your life around your child to be as supportive, inspiring and educational as you can.

If you feel that you have some big healing to do, that your childhood or an event of your life has left a mark of trauma upon you, then your adventure may be into healing. It may be quiet, it may not look like adventure to others. But it will involve risk, bravery and danger for you.

Even if your adventure follows mainstream lines, if your risks and growth bring you wealth and travel and prestige, try to remain detached from society's approval. This is your adventure. Don't walk your path for anyone else, and don't choose your risks based on someone else's expectation, or with the hope of earning someone's approval. Affirmation comes from noticing your own courage, and from sharing moments with peers you respect. If you work to meet somebody's expectations of you, you return to a child mentality and you will lose your wild edge.

In my experience, the hardest thing that humans can do is relationship. It is challenging in every way, stretching our every dimension. I invite you to stay curious about how relationship will enter into your personal adventure, and what you can learn next about how to relate in deeper, fuller, more conscious ways.

Peace is only found in the storm

The fallacy of our culture, told in its stories and backed up by its structures and habits, is that you will be happy, with a background sense of peace, if you avoid stress. This is a total misunderstanding of stress.

Stress is a bodily response to danger. In a healthy, wild animal it's the perfect way to handle dangerous situations. When you're stressed, hormones surge into your blood to prepare you for fight or flight, then after the danger has passed you shed the stress and return to equilibrium. But in a domesticated world, low-grade, background stress is a normal part of life. Annoyances and demands at work. Nagging partners or children. Constant background noise. Physical tension that's never shed.

Chapter 13: Adventure

Animals penned together with a lot of other animals, fed poorly, lacking proper exercise and other things that they need to thrive, will become stressed. Human animals are the same.

As we try to live a calm and stress-free life, we condition ourselves to deal poorly with stress. As time passes without any risk and adventure, the number of things that cause fear and anxiety in our lives multiply…so there are more causes of stress in our lives. Without the wild mind-set, where we constantly seek for adventures and new opportunities, we hold tight to our stress…so we never shed the stress we hold.

A life that contains true peace and inner stillness, also involves a lot of risk and adventure. Like a ship that plies stormy waters, sails straining, water frothing from the bow, crew working urgently to keep the mighty vessel afloat. How much more profound is the stillness and serenity when the ship returns to port and sits quiet and at peace? This is the forgotten secret to a peaceful life. Looking for peace by making your life quiet and safe just leads the human mind to worry and fear. We aren't built to work like that. Peace is the earned reward of the adventurous soul. Whatever personal challenges and risks wait for you, I invite you to dive into them with relish. As you shift your mind and heart to this attitude to risk and change, you will find that peace begins to manifest in your life without effort. You will have recaptured the potential of your wild heart, and your confidence and strength will grow. Your Comfort Zone expands, making more and more things safe and relaxing for you. This is the best and most sustainable way I know to find peace in your life.

The affirmation

"Peace is only found in the storm - I must engage with risk, adventure and change in order to find peace"

Counter-affirmations

If people don't understand that risk and change are essential to human flourishing, they might say…

- I wouldn't do that, think of everything you could lose
- That's not normal, why can't you just be normal?
- I could never do that

Chapter 13: Adventure

Deep Joy

8.COURAGE

"I will never be ready"

This is an extension of Principle 7, but it's a caution against one of the greatest barriers to change, growth and success: waiting to be ready.

So many opportunities, lessons, businesses or relationships never happen because people wait for things to be just right. People can spend years preparing for a challenge, an adventure or a change. 'Eventually', they say, 'I'll be ready for this.' Friends ask them when they're going to do the thing, and they list all the things they need to do before they can take the big step.

It could be a promotion at work. Asking somebody out. Launching a business. Moving house. Having children. Having an important conversation that might end a precious relationship. Going on the ultimate dream holiday.

Years of people's lives go by while they wait to be ready.

The fact is that if you are ready then you're thinking about something you've done before. By 'getting ready', what you mean is that you're rehearsing bits of the adventure so things are less likely to go wrong, so things are a bit less scary.

Somebody living a life of adventure does things they're not ready for all the time.

Overshooting Risk and landing in Panic

Let your heart guide the scale of your risk. Remember the phrase: "What would I do, if I were a little bit braver?". This is not about taking enormous leaps, far beyond fear and into panic. Try not to oscillate between the extremes of Comfort and Panic, either frightened or overwhelmed. This can be a tempting way to begin engaging with risk. It's a common mistake of those new to a life of adventure.

Daily, relatively gentle experiences of Risk, are the goal. Steady, incremental steps that grow your courage. Bigger steps sometimes, which are frightening and enlivening. But be cautious of the temptation to take massive, dramatic Risks. Panic can be tempting place for newcomers to adventure.

How to handle the fear of doing scary, new things

If you're doing new things, you're going to get scared sometimes. If you were ready, it isn't really adventure. If you're not ready, you're going to be out of your depth. That's the point. And that's scary.

As you do this over and over again, every day, in different ways and in different dimensions of your life, your courage and confidence will bloom and you'll find yourself more and more comfortable with risk, change and adventure. But even then, the scale of the challenge will increase. New directions of challenge will pop up in your life to help you become more rounded. There will always be new adventures that you're not ready for.

Handling fear becomes a key skill in building a really satisfying life.

Karla McLaren, whose work on emotional intelligence is so brilliant and so revolutionary, says in *The Language of Emotions* that the function of fear is to aid you in focusing on the moment. Fear calls you to now. Its purpose is to ensure that when something dangerous is happening, your attention is where it should be: right here and right now.

As with all emotions, fear will hang around until its work is done. When you feel frightened of something, that's not the time to avoid moving forwards. It's a time to pay more attention as you move forwards.

Fear is inevitable. It's a companion on your journey. When you're about to do something scary, embrace the fear. Welcome it and thank your fear for the gifts of consciousness and awareness that it brings. Even if your limbs tremble and you feel sick, welcome the feeling in. Fear is not about being paralysed, it's about being conscious. Take your fear with you on your adventure.

For example, if you are going to a meeting, a party or if you're making a presentation, and if this makes you nervous, notice your fear. Be curious about your fear. What, exactly, are you afraid of? What does this tell you? What do you have to learn? What parts of the coming experience are the real challenge for you?

Walk into the room with your head held high and your fear held close. Denying fear will only multiply its effects. If fear is ignored, supressed or denied then your emotional wisdom will give you more fear until you pay attention to the moment. So be conscious, be present, walk and breathe and speak with conscious intention.

When you're done, consciously celebrate your courage. Maybe treat yourself to something or come up with another way to actively celebrate what you've just achieved. Notice that you have done something hard, and remained conscious, and done it to the best of your ability. Review how it went. What did you learn? What gratitude can you find for the challenge, for the learning, for the experience and for the fear itself? Return to the Comfort Zone, thank fear and let it go.

If you struggle to let the fear go, or if the echoes of it continue in your mind, your heart or your body, breathe it out. Take deep breaths, hold them for a moment, and then breathe out long and with purpose. Visualise yourself shedding tension and fear with each outbreath.

Imagine it streaming out of your body in a coloured cloud. What colour is your fear? Continue to breathe out your fears until they begin to subside.

This is the way to manage fear when you embark on a life of adventure, when you're regularly doing things that you're not ready for.

1. Become conscious of your fear. Admit it and accept it.
2. Welcome your fear into your whole person and try to be aware of the lessons it is bringing you. What are you not paying attention to? Where should your attention be?
3. Do the thing, holding your fear close and acting with courage and purpose.
4. Return to Comfort, consciously acknowledging the courage you have just shown.
5. If needed, take the time to shed the echoes of your fear in a conscious, grateful way.

Failure is just information

The fear of failure is one of the most common barriers to risk-taking. Most of us have it, on some level, and it can be really hard to shift your approach to risk and failure. In the mainstream mind-set of this bizarre, domesticated culture, failure feels so horrible because we mix it up with our self-esteem. Failure to achieve something, especially when other people might see our failure, is far more than just not succeeding. We are not kind to others or to ourselves when failure happens. We associate failure with personal value. A person who fails *is* a failure, in a broad way that touches on their worth as a person. A great amount of shame can be heaped on a person who fails, and we do this most aggressively to ourselves.

It's easy to slip into the idea that risks are bad things. After all, a 'vulnerability hangover', as Brené Brown calls it, can be savage. Somebody might laugh. We might be judged harshly for not doing well. But the thing we tend to fear most is our own inner critic and all the things it'll say when we witness our own personal failures.

This is perfectly normal. We were raised in an elaborate network of rules and expectations to keep us all calm and safe. We tend to use shame to control ourselves and other people, and we can easily beat ourselves up if we don't do something well.

For a person with a wild-minded, results-focused approach, the approach to failure is totally different.

As we've explored, all learning and growth happen through risk-taking. Risk is, by its nature, a gamble. You try something new, something you're not quite ready for, and you might succeed, or you might fail. The harder the challenge and the bigger the leap beyond the things you feel ready for, the greater the chance of failure.

Everything you can do now, you had to learn to do. Think about the things you can do effortlessly. Everything from being able to walk, being able to write and do maths, managing and organising your adult life, the skills you have at work, your social skills…you are a highly skilled person, and you had to learn how to do it all.

You will have stumbled and fallen when you learned to walk. You made mistakes with people and at work. Maybe you screwed up your bills and had a scare with money. Maybe you made a mistake that ended a precious relationship. You took the information in your failures and you adapted, you grew, you improved, you got better at things.

Failing, for the wild, empowered person, is just information. I did a thing and it didn't work. Either it was the wrong approach, or I need more practice at it before I can succeed. If other people judge me, it's just a reflection on who they are. If I judge myself, that's an unhelpful, old response. I am engaged in a life of adventure, and I'm going to fail a lot. I can't afford to be mired in self-condemnation.

With this approach, with relentless determination and with gentle, playful curiosity, the wild adult learns and grows. This is the way that all highly successful people approach risk and failure. Failure has nothing to do with shame, and to apply shame to failure is to misunderstand the nature of growth. It's the old domesticated mind-set coming back to haunt you. Once you have slowly, gently, relentlessly grown beyond this approach, you will be free to experiment, take risks, succeed and fail without even touching on the idea of shame.

The affirmation

"I will never be ready"

Counter-affirmations

- Maybe one day, but definitely not any time soon
- I'll get there, but I've got to get all this stuff done first
- I'm not ready

Deep Joy

9.COMPASSION

"I cannot save anybody else.
That's not my job"

Principles 9, 10 and 11 are about relationships. We've looked at creating and uncovering the best very of you, the you that will live the life you dream of, the you that will reach your goals and do wild, brave, amazing things.

Relationships are very complicated things. Making sure there's enough of you and not getting lost in the intensity of relationship. Making sure you don't focus wholly on the other so that you forget about your own needs, is a hard juggling act. Each person brings so much to a relationship. We each bring the expectations, stories and obligations from our upbringing, we bring our own wounds and deep needs, we bring desires and intentions and longings, we bring ideas about where we want to go and what we want to create. We have a unique idea about what will make us happy. And of course, humans aren't static: we're either engaging in adventure and risk, and thus growing; or we're drawing-in on ourselves, avoiding risk and diminishing. The friends and lovers that you meet today aren't going to be the same in the years to come. They will change and you will change.

Relationships, then, are a complex dance. There are a lot of books about how to do relationships, and many of them are really useful if you're struggling to get a hold of this massive topic.

The next three Principles are core truths about human relating. They apply, in different ways, to relationships of all kinds: your relationships with colleagues and partners at work; your relationships with your family; and your romantic and sexual relationships.

Principle 9 is about the nature of compassion.

I show you love by not rescuing you

Sometimes, we just want to be rescued. Things get hard, you feel like you're struggling or drowning, and you just want someone to come along and make things ok.

If you're witnessing a friend or lover in this kind of situation, it's normal and healthy to feel compassion for them. You want them to be ok and if you've got strong empathy skills, you'll feel a measure of their suffering as your own. We've all been in hard places and we all want to reach out to those we love and take away some of their pain.

Doing this isn't always rescuing. If help is consciously asked for, one adult to another, then you get to make a conscious, adult decision about whether you want to give that help or not. That isn't rescuing.

We looked at the Karpman Drama Triangle in Principle 5. People adopt one of the three masks of the Drama Triangle in a response to an environment of shame. Where shame is normal (where most people carry the secret belief that they aren't good enough and aren't worthy of being loved), people hide their authentic selves by adopting a dramatic role and wearing it as a mask. They try to be good at the mask so that others won't notice who they really are and, therefore, might accept and love them.

The Rescuer is one of these roles. The Rescuer gets self-esteem by saving others. Where there isn't anyone to save, the Rescuer will try to push someone into being a Victim.

This Principle is a simple caution against being a Rescuer in this sense. It can seem great and it can feel wonderful. You can get a lot of affirmation and respect from people for being such a great person, but you hold yourself back and you smother the other. What appears to be love and being a good person is a mask for insecurity and, in the worst situations, abuse.

Your own personal growth suffers because you aren't being a whole, authentic self. You're playing a role, through fear of exposure and fear of not being good enough. Rescuing, and the reassurance and affirmation you get through rescuing, can be addictive. You get a feeling of being a good person, and you get feedback from others that you're lovely and supportive and caring. But the longer you pretend to be this two-dimensional rescuing persona, the longer you stall your own growth and authentic expression.

A rescuer needs a victim, and with the best will in the world, if your relationship with someone is based on the Rescuer/Victim dynamic, you're going to squash them. You're going to subtly manipulate them to remain stuck, overwhelmed, unable to cope. You will encourage them to think they can't be ok without you. You will supress their journey and abandon your own.

We protect ourselves and others from getting mired in shame by having the courage to show up and be authentically vulnerable. We'll look at this more in Principle 11.

Asking for help

Life is a messy business. A child who doesn't yet appreciate how complicated and messy life can be, will turn to their parents, who have acted as protectors and providers for as long as they've been alive, and say 'help', or something like it. This generally won't be a specific request. It's a request to be saved from a situation by somebody more competent, more skilled, bigger, stronger and wiser. A child who's scared, overwhelmed, trapped or fed up will cry for their parents to pick them up and make things better. It's a simple, general cry for help.

Adults don't do this. There's nobody around who's dramatically more competent than you anymore. The enormous gulf between infant and parent has shrunk to subtle differences in skill and experience. If you ever put out a general cry for help as an adult, there's a big chance that you're adopting the mask of the Victim.

The adult way of asking for help is to be specific.

'Hey, please will you help me do this thing? I can't do it on my own?'

'Can you teach me how to do this? You know more about it than I do.'

'Will you hug me and cook me dinner? I need some support from a friend right now.'

These are different from a general cry for help or a statement that you can't cope. If you find yourself on the receiving end of a generalised cry for salvation from an adult, resist the urge to step in and rescue. You don't serve that person's highest self by saving them and answering their infantile plea. At the same time, you don't help them by abandoning them and shutting down your compassion.

So, what is your job?
Authentic compassion and holding space

Authentic, adult compassion means paying attention, empathising and being ready to offer help when asked. It's never rescuing. We don't offer help unless there's some kind of request for it. We don't push our ideas about how things should be onto the person who is struggling.

The key skill here is called, in therapeutic circles, 'holding space'. It's creating a place where somebody feels safe to be able to vent, rage, cry, feel anything they need to feel and express anything they need to express. You can do this in the middle of a busy office or in a quiet room. You can do it at home or out in the wild. What you do is:

1. Give somebody your full attention, without judgement or criticism
2. Engage your empathy so you can feel what they're feeling. In this way you're really 'with them' through their experience.

3. Be warm, supportive and positive
4. Only ever offer advice or practical help when you've been asked. If you're not sure, you can ask them "would you like some advice?" They might say no.

This can be deeply unsatisfying, for them and for you. If one of you is used to domesticated-thinking and Victim/Rescuer relationships, you'll be left waiting for that to happen. 'Ok, I've told you all my problems, when are you going to sort them out for me?' and 'I've seen somebody's struggling, when do I get to fix all this for them?'

I encourage you to resist this temptation. For people who aren't doing this personal work and who don't understand the dangers of rescuing, it can seem heartless and weird if somebody doesn't rescue them. You can use some reassuring language around this, be vocal with your empathy and your compassion, but still resist the urge to step in and take over. The important thing is to only own your own feelings, don't voice the other person's feelings for them. A wonderful book about this art is *Nonviolent Communication* by Marshell Rosenberg. It offers a lot of examples of how to keep your language just about you, and not assume somebody else's feelings, to rescue them or steal their agency.

Very young children will need to be rescued regularly, of course. Children, and anyone who's incapable of making a specific, adult request for help, will need you to step in without an invitation. But as a parent, encourage your children towards making specific requests for help when you feel they're ready. It's an important skill to have as an adult.

In this way, we develop a healthier network of friendships and relationships. We stop stealing power and freedom from one another and we model the kind of behaviour that leads to a more empowered, more competent adulthood. When people join us in this behaviour, we know they are capable of more meaningful connections than those who hide behind masks and use domesticated, shame-based solutions to their problems. Two people who meet without the Victim/Rescuer relationship are able to relate to one another in a more adult, more respectful way. They will be able to trust each other in ways they can't trust people who cling to the mainstream approach, and over time they will have the potential to develop a deeper, more nourishing, more supportive, more creative relationship.

The affirmation

"I cannot save anybody else. That's not my job"

Counter-affirmations

Some of us want to follow deeply-ingrained patterns to rescue others. People who draw their self-esteem from this, who don't want to learn proper boundaries, might say:

- It's my job to look after you
- We need each other
- That person's doing so much better now I've helped them, I must be a good person

Deep Joy

10.RESILIENCE

"Nobody else can save me.
I will save myself with fierce self-love."

So far in this book we've focused a lot on the self. How to unlock your power to make good choices and make steady, determined steps towards a truly nourishing, beautiful life. We've looked at being real about your needs, about your responsibilities, about stepping into empowered adulthood, about building healthy and appropriate guidelines to manifest your values in your choices and in the world. We've considered some of the toxic stories that our broken culture pushed on to us and how to begin shaking free from them, and we've looked at how our inner wildness needs to meet the greater wildness of the world. We've looked at how a wild, strong adult approaches risk, adventure and change and how to handle the inevitable setbacks.

One of the most important, core needs that we all carry is the need for love, the need for tender and resilient care in the face of the challenges that this messy life throws at us. In this Principle, we keep looking at healthy boundaries, and we explore how we ensure we get the love and care we need while we keep our healthy boundaries in place.

When we stop playing the shame-based games of our culture, when we step away from domesticated-thinking and begin to rediscover our wild, fierce, curious, determined selves, we assume our full adult potential. An adult who is aware of the power of choice, who takes responsibility for their own needs, who explores and enshrines their own sense of personal honour, who is committed to always learning and growing and living a life of adventure, who explores all the truths in this book, is capable of anything. They aren't bound by limited thinking, by the limiting stories of our culture, by the need to conform in order to avoid the stigma of shame. They can be anything, achieve anything, build the life they want and assume the self-image that supports their needs and desires.

The cost, as I mentioned in Part 1, is innocence. We lose the comforting sensations of childhood, where somebody else knows more than we do and can protect us and rescue us when things are hard. On some level, everybody in the mainstream culture is still harbouring this desire. The bad lessons and stories of our culture are created and maintained by adults who haven't yet learned the skills and awareness that are an essential part of true adulthood. They continue to worship childhood, like a long-lost homeland that they hope, one day, to return to.

We shed this illusion when we adopt our full adulthood. We need to be sure that we will keep meeting our needs once the illusion of salvation by others has been lost. If nobody else is coming to rescue you, you will need to take on that role, and do it well.

This is just another aspect to a life of adventure. The wild-hearted adult is always looking out for new adventures, new risks, new ways to grow and thrive. One of the ways they use this active, passionate approach is the way they love themselves. When you know that you are an independent adult, who can't be rescued because nobody is actually qualified to rescue you in the same way that a parent rescues a child, it's important to ensure that you have the positive regard, care and love that you need.

If you have a network of close friends, or a partner or lover who shows you positive regard, care and love, this might seem pointless. But each of us has a profound, instinctive need for love. If we lack that, we put a burden on others to love us. Giving and receiving love with another person is one of the great delights in life, but if we know that other people are our sole source of love, we become unhealthily dependent on them to love it. We know that without them, our need for love won't be met. This can make relationships complicated and it can make you avoid risks and difficult conversations because you fear to lose the love and positive regard that others give you. Whether love and care are being offered to you by others or not, life become more stable and sustainable if you take the time to develop your own sense of positive self-regard, care and love.

Doing this in a half-hearted way, occasionally remembering to show yourself a bit of compassion, is a good start. But the wild-hearted adult who is engaged in adventure can bring their passion, determination and curiosity to this too. Like a mother lioness guarding her cubs, a conscious adult can bring a fierceness to their self-love.

Self-love isn't always supported or encouraged by the mainstream culture. If somebody truly loves and accepts who they are, they don't need products that make them feel lovable, attractive or appealing. Whole industries would go bankrupt overnight if we all woke up and chose to actively love ourselves. Instead, the mainstream story is that we should love others, but loving ourselves is at best silly and meaningless and, at worst, shamefully self-indulgent. Not everybody has been taught this, but it's a common story. It can be difficult to learn how to love yourself if you've grown up like this.

If you're new to this, or if you want to develop this skill more fully, I invite you to try this…

Begin by identifying who you are loving. Take some deep breaths and follow your intuition to work out where in your body the 'I' that you're going to show love, lives. It's handy to know where this person-that-is-you is located in your body.

It may be that you'll find your inner child as you do this work. Many of us direct love to ourselves through our inner child, because the child's innocence makes loving so much easier. For those of us whose inner children carry wounds, you can also do profound healing work by channelling your self-love through your inner child.

Next, open your heart to this part of yourself, in the same way you would to a dear friend or precious lover who you love deeply. Feel the warmth of your love washing over yourself. Breathe in time with your love and feel how your breaths spread the sensation of love through your body. If it helps, imagine that you are breathing in love and breathing it out to yourself.

I invite you to make this ritual a daily part of your life until it begins to feel natural and until you begin incorporating it into your day without needing to think about it.

If you notice that you have a lot of resistance to loving yourself, or that a rush of critical or cruel self-judgements come into your mind when you try, then this is an important area of growth for you. I encourage you to look for books or online resources to help you understand this, introduce a daily practice of self-love and, if necessary, spend some time with a therapist or coach to overcome your blocks to loving yourself deeply and freely.

A life nourished by self-love

We treat our loved-ones with care. They become precious to us as we open our hearts to them and make them part of our little circles of love and trust. The same is true when you love yourself.

If you actively, fiercely love yourself as you might a child or a lover, you will not allow certain thing to happen. You won't tolerate being treated badly by others. You will want the best for yourself. You will find it easy to give yourself delightful experiences or healthy food, knowing that you're nourishing somebody you love.

Shame becomes much less easy to take on. We become less susceptible to others dumping of shame on us and shame tends to be play less of a role in our decision-making. Our inner-critic, whose role is to protect us by warning us against shameful experiences, finds another voice to balance up the narrative of shame: the voice of our self-love. When you find that shame is playing a big role in your life, or when you're struggling to do something because of the toxic shame that comes with it, remembering your self-love can ease the sensation and leave you more free to act.

Play becomes easier. Adults in our culture struggle a lot with play, mostly due to embarrassment and lack of practice. There's a growing trend towards adults engaging in free-form, restorative play, and a lot of evidence that it's good for our adult wellbeing. *Play* by Stuart Brown is a great resource if you want more play in your adult life.

A person with an active practice of self-love plays freely and gently, welcoming lightness and joy more easily into your life.

All of this is very supportive in a life of challenge and adventure. It's the counter-balance to the relentless determination to explore, create and adopt the full power of your choice.

The affirmation

"Nobody else can save me. I will save myself with fierce self-love."

Counter-affirmations

- When I find the right person, everything will be ok
- I don't want to love myself
- I hate myself

Chapter 16: Resilience

Deep Joy

11.CONNECTION

"I find deep connection when I combine vulnerability with clear boundaries"

This is the last of the Principles that focuses on relationships. Here, we look at two essential elements of any healthy relationship: appropriate vulnerability and healthy boundaries. We've looked at both subjects earlier, but here we're going into more detail. A satisfying life is one where our relationships are balanced, healthy and nourishing. Boundaries and vulnerability are the two elements that make this possible.

Types of boundaries

A boundary is a line between you and the other. It's a limit that you don't cross, and you don't let them cross. It takes awareness to notice when your boundaries are crossed, and deciding on the boundaries that you want to set takes time, effort and understanding. Setting and maintaining clear boundaries is one of the greatest gifts you can give yourself. It's a profound statement of self-care, self-esteem and compassion for yourself. It's also an act of kindness to the people you value in your life. Maintaining good, strong boundaries makes you a dependable, clear, responsible person. People know what they get. It encourages trust, vulnerability, sharing and intimacy.

The emotion of anger is the watchdog of your boundaries. Whenever somebody crosses the limits that you've set, either consciously or unconsciously, your anger will flare up so that you remain safe and whole. That is the purpose of anger, as outlined by *The Language of Emotions* by Karla McLaren.

Whenever you enter into a relationship, of any kind, with somebody, the health of that relationship is dictated by the nature of three types of boundary:

Ethical boundaries

These are the limits you've set by exploring your personal sense of honour. They are the clarity of what is right and what is wrong. By keeping these boundaries strong in all your relationships, you become an inspiring, strong person and you lend integrity and safety to the relationships in your life.

These boundaries also help you stop adopting the toxic stories of our culture. If you know what is right and what is wrong, if you've done the work to bring your conscious awareness to the limits of what's ok and what's not ok for you, the needy manipulations of a broken culture are easier to notice and easier to resist.

Relational boundaries

These are the limits of what's ok and what's not ok between you and another person. These are unique to every relationship and will sometimes change over time. A friend becomes a lover. A work colleague betrays a trust. A partner becomes an ex. You launch a business venture with a friend.

What kind of physical closeness is ok for you?

What level of trust exists between you? How honest are you with one another?

What kind of language do you use with each other?

How often and in what ways do you contact each other?

Where do you sit in each other's hierarchy of importance?

It's ok for you to decide these things. Indeed, it's a tremendous gift to a friend or a lover to have strong, clear boundaries. It's important, though, to be sure they're communicated well. So many relationships disintegrate because one person thought differently than the other person about the boundaries of that relationship. Communicating boundaries can be as simple as clearly demonstrating them, in your words, actions and choices, over time. But if you feel that boundaries aren't clear, or if notice that they're being crossed regularly, then it's ok to speak to the other person and make your boundaries clear.

Maintaining consistent, clear, strong boundaries requires confidence and determination. Most people do not do the work necessary to understand their needs, their ethics and thus, their boundaries. They may cross yours without noticing, they may understand your boundaries and cross them anyway or they may try to manipulate you into abandoning your boundaries to meet their needs. A person who isn't aware of their needs for love, reassurance, acceptance or intimacy is likely to spend a lot of their lives blundering across people's boundaries in their search to get their own needs met. This is another reason why personal development work is so important. If you have done the work to understand yourself, your needs, the power of your choice, your own sense of ethics and your own direction in life, then you will be much better placed to set and respect boundaries.

When boundaries change, it's healthy and helpful if this is done consciously and with communication. If it isn't possible at the time, have the conversation as soon as you can. You can say things directly and precisely or, if you know the person well and you have a shared language for being more subtle about things, you can imply what the new boundaries are. For example, if you've suddenly taken the step from hanging out with an old friend to sleeping with a new lover, and if you want this to become an exclusive relationship, you're going to need to find a way to say that. For some people, saying "let's not see other people, yeah?" is going to be enough. For others, it's going to be a clumsier, long winded explanation of what's ok for you and what you need from this new situation.

The important thing is to communicate. 'I have these boundaries. This is ok for me. This isn't ok for me.' Then keep those boundaries strong. Be sure to correct people if they cross your boundaries. Sometimes, when it seems appropriate, you might thank them for respecting the boundaries you've set.

When it comes to bigger and more complicated situations, like community, where a lot of relationships are all subtly influencing each other, relational boundaries become even more important. A community can be hurt a lot by unclear, uncommunicated or badly maintained boundaries.

Boundaries of identity

The most subtle boundaries are the ones between you and not-you. Where do you end and the other begins? That may sound strange, but a lot of messy relationships are caused by the breakdown of this clarity.

If you barely know someone, the boundary between you and them are clear. Who they are, what they want and need, their dreams and intentions and fears exist over there, and all the things that make up who you are exist over here.

As you get closer to someone, things become less clear. A friend's feelings can easily become your feelings. The needs of a lover become your needs. Your self-image begins to merge with the other. People pass around their needs and feelings, generally without noticing, dumping them on each, stealing them from each other, demanding that the other provides for their unconscious demands. This creates messy, unhealthy dynamics in social groups and between individuals. Whole friendships and relationships can be based on passing feelings back and forth, unconsciously, blurring the lines between 'you' and 'me'.

This creates big problems for people seeking healthy adulthood.

If you easily take on other people's 'stuff' (feelings, needs, dreams, desires, fears, expectations), how can you be sure what's you and what's not you? As you move between friendships and relationships, your own priorities will change – how can you be sure which ones are yours?

Consistency becomes really hard to maintain if the lines between you and the other become too blurred. How will you make consistent choices that build on each other towards a nourishing and successful future? How will you consistently take steps towards empowered adult awareness and away from the use of unconscious, childhood answers? How will you consistently deepen your awareness of your own authentic stories and stop yourself taking on the unhealthy stories of our culture?

Marshall Rosenberg, whose work I've briefly mentioned before, developed an approach to healthy connections, boundaries and communication called *Nonviolent Communication*. He used it successfully in conflict resolution all over the world and it can be a powerful tool in learning to build and maintain healthy relationships at home, at work, with your friends or in any other aspect of your life. I regularly recommend his work to my clients, and they tell me it's enormously helpful in understanding and improving their friendships and relationships.

Rosenberg suggests that a lot of the ways we communicate are subtly violent: they can be manipulative, aggressive and unconsciously needy. In his book, *Nonviolent Communication*, he explores a way of communicating with one another where we listen for the needs that somebody is trying to meet in the things they're saying and the way they're acting.

We all have needs. We've looked at both the obvious and the subtle kinds of needs that we bring to our lives in Principle 2. The things we do, the words we say, the choices we make and the relationships we create are all attempts to meet those needs. As we become more conscious of these priorities in ourselves and in others, we begin to hear what they say differently. An angry outburst, that we might have met before with our own anger or fear, becomes a cry for help. By meeting the cry instead of the anger, we resolve the situation much more gracefully than by meeting the outburst itself. A defensive comment is recognised as a need for love and recognition. A friend who goes home instead of coming out is understood as meeting their own needs for rest and recovery. By perceiving somebody's fundamental needs instead of reacting to the method they're using to meet their need, we communicate with them more effectively and more caringly.

This practice also helps your boundaries. As you notice the needs, demands, expectations and feelings of others, so you can separate out yourself from them. Their anger isn't your anger. Their insecurity isn't yours. Their ideas of success aren't yours. Their aggression, desire, fear or sadness clearly belong to them and not to you.

With a clearer idea of where you and they begin, you will be a better friend or lover. You will naturally defuse difficult situations. You won't feel so burdened by needy friends and you won't get upset by demanding partners. You'll be able to offer caring compassion and you'll be less likely to rescue or persecute somebody.

People who don't do boundaries, who aren't particularly aware of themselves and who aren't committed to unlocking their potential and power may find it a bit strange. But you will be modelling healthy adulthood, and this can be comforting and inspiring for others. You may lose some friends, and some relationships may no longer seem right for you, but those friends, colleagues and partners who remain in your life when you develop strong, clearly communicated boundaries will be more trustworthy, more mature and capable of deeper connection than any you lost along the way.

Boundaries take time to develop, so be patient and compassionate with yourself and be determined to slowly grow them over time. Be curious and inquisitive about your blind spots (that is, the places you tend to let people cross your boundaries). Take the time to work out what your ethical, relational and personal boundaries are. You might want to write them down, to remind yourself of what you're trying to establish in your life. Tell the people you love and trust what you're doing. They can help you to remember that you intend to change your behaviour, and they'll be fore-warned if you start acting differently to the way you used to. Experiment with different ways of expressing your boundaries: do you need to say them directly or can you find more subtle ways to express and enforce your boundaries.

Over time, get better at correcting people when they cross your boundaries. If you're not used to doing this it might be intimidating at first, but use that self-love that you're developing to guide you in taking proper care of yourself. Protecting your boundaries is an act of self-love. It's keeping yourself safe in the same way you would a friend, lover or child that you love very much. Your anger will be a guide to your boundaries being violated, but people who aren't used to setting and maintaining boundaries are sometimes skilled at suppressing their anger. You may find, then, that as your boundaries become stronger and clearer, you actually feel angry more often. Keep your behaviour aligned with your personal sense of honour and try not to worry too much. Try to observe what's going on using your compassionate non-judgement. If your anger does flare up, it will calm as you consciously step in to re-establish your boundaries.

Tolerate no violation of your boundaries. Be firm about this. At first, this conscious process may require a lot of energy from you, but over time you'll internalise your boundaries and your behaviour will adapt so that you automatically correct people (or yourself) when your boundaries are crossed.

Vulnerability: the ultimate expression of personal strength

Vulnerability is the willingness to say to the world: this is who I really am. We live in a culture riddled with shame. Sadly, many people are more comfortable and more familiar with the masks they wear to earn approval than they are with their real, naked, authentic, broken, beautiful selves. In this context, a willingness to be vulnerable is a truly courageous act.

It's a choice that brings transformation. It frees you up to be happier, more present, more real than ever before and it can radically redefine the limits of your potential. It also affects people around you. Some will find it annoying, challenging, distracting or frightening. Others will draw inspiration from your example. Either way, people who stand with authenticity in their lives are forces for change, and if you want change in your life then vulnerability is going to be essential. Both planned and unexpected possibilities open up for you, and if you have a strong and clear vision and a strong sense of longing for the life you want to create, these possibilities will begin to align to bring you towards your vision. Your presence opens up possibilities for people and communities around you, too, as you introduce an element of reality and chaotic potential into the stifled system of our shame-laden culture.

Vulnerability is the way of life for people who want to be real, who want to be strong and confident, who want to live a life of creativity and adventure. Because this, I've discovered, is the natural state of all human beings.

Relationships between people who are brave enough to be vulnerable tend to be more rewarding, more passionate and more nourishing physically, mentally, emotionally and spiritually.

People who choose vulnerable authenticity are weird. We all carry hurts and scars, we all have our particular needs and desires, we've grown up with particular expectations and demands of the world and by now you've done some work to create the vision that you, uniquely, want to create in your life. When we drop the masks and stop trying to please or reassure others, when we stop playing out dramatic roles that make us acceptable to others, when we hold our self-image loosely and are willing to change and grow and surprise ourselves, we aren't going to seem normal any more. We aren't going to live up to somebody's idea of excellence, professionalism, expertise or perfection. We are going to transcend the expectations the others had for us, and even that we had for ourselves.

We're going to live up to our own ideas, our own goals that we've chosen for ourselves. Our choices, words and actions are based on the longings in our own hearts, bound and guided by our sense of right and wrong. We choose things consciously, powerfully, with purpose and integrity. We freely show our feelings and we ask for things in clear, adult ways. We act on what we know to be right, knowing that some people will reject us, judge us, condemn us or mock us.

Our culture does not like vulnerability. It's the opposite of everything we're supposed to be. We are supposed to protect ourselves from failure, disappointment, rejection and hurt by trying to live up to other people's ideas of who we're meant to be. A successful person is one who wears the best mask, somebody who is the best actor in the grand social story. We praise and reward people who do this the best.

A vulnerable person is an outsider in this world. Unpredictable. Eccentric. Willing to say things that make people uncomfortable, because they're true. Willing to show up, even when afraid or insecure, not hiding their fear and insecurity from a judging world.

Masks do not satisfy the human spirit.

Thanks to the great denial of death in our culture, we do not really believe we're going to die. We know, logically, that it's going to happen. But on a personal, emotional level, death is something that happens to other people. It's an idea, a fact. It's something that we suppress and avoid for as long as possible. But when the reality of your own personal death arrives, it often brings with it a need to evaluate the value of your life. At this time, the worth of houses, money, cars, prestige and power tend to seem hollow and pointless. The ultimate death is not the only thing that brings this clarity: every crisis we suffer is a gift and an invitation to put aside other people's priorities.

When the illusions of our culture are suddenly and painfully pierced, by whatever crisis or moment of clarity, the real value of things is revealed. What the human person values when they aren't chasing the approval and reassurance of other mask-wearers, are relationships, connections, contributions and the effects they have in the world. Moments of truth and vulnerability, moments when we meet another person without filters or deception, moments when we shared joy, tragedy, profound growth or wonder with another person. Moments of connection with the wilderness inside or the power of the wild world outside. These are the kinds of things that seem to have real value to people who make the courageous choice of vulnerability.

Brené Brown says that vulnerability is the antidote to toxic shame. Her books are best-sellers and her talks are some of the most viewed online, so she is clearly touching on something that resonates with a lot of people. Each of us carries this toxic shame to a greater or lesser extent, and each of us wears masks and takes on dramatic roles to cope with the shame, pretending to one another that we're fine. You pass people on the street every day who are mired in the belief that if somebody saw them as they truly are, without filters or defences, nobody would love or accept them. You work alongside people who believe this. The most robust people that you know, the people who seem the most fine, the most aggressive bullies, the quietest and most insecure victims, the people you most respect and the people you loathe, the people you love the most, are probably all playing this game to defend their authentic selves from rejection and disappointment.

Daring Greatly, Brené's book that introduces and explores her research and ideas about vulnerability, is a wonderful way to begin grappling with the nature and manifestation of your own shame, the toxic burdens that you've taken on from the world and how to begin making the first brave steps into showing up with vulnerability and realness. Some people find this easy, taking only a few knocks as they step into the light without their masks. Some people find it very hard, and it'll take a long time and a lot of difficult practice to peel away the masks that keep you safe, but smothered.

Take your determination and your curiosity with you. The journey is worth it. We are all called to dump the constricting, false masks of a shameful culture and step into a life of freedom, power and authentic self-expression. If you haven't yet done the work to explore your own vulnerability, a kind of freedom and terrible, wonderful confidence and power are waiting for you to rediscover them. Be determined to get there, even when you stumble. You're going to get things wrong sometimes. Sometimes people are going to mock you or try to push you back into your old behaviours that make them feel safe. Sometimes you're going to doubt that this hard work was a good idea. Stay focused. Your dream for your future will be easier to reach, and far more satisfying and fulfilling, if you get there being your true, vulnerable self than if you achieve it all, only to still be locked within the expectations of a profoundly sick society.

Be curious and playful with this work. This is all building towards having more delight and wonder in your life. All of the truths and realities we've explored so far in this book, some of which might have seemed dark or overwhelming, are just bringing you to the point where you can choose to be you, free of illusions. Let yourself be curious about what it's going to be like when you get there. What might you be like? What choices will you make when you get there?

Deep connection

Clear, consistent boundaries that are communicated clearly will give you a background stability. Clarity about what's ok and what's not ok for you, and where you end and the other begins, brings you a sense of stability and assuredness. Others will begin to respond to your consistency and clarity. People know where they stand with you.

Vulnerability makes you real. You show your feelings. You are honest and clear with people. Your authenticity lends you a uniqueness, an originality, a sense of the wild that we've often completely forgotten. Your lack of filters and masks will bring energy and significance to moments and to relationships. Things feel more real, less rehearsed, more adventurous.

Together, these two profound skills can transform your connections with others.

Intimate relationships can feel more solid, grounded and safe, while also bringing a wealth of authentic experiences that can't happen between people still hiding behind masks. Sex becomes the wild meeting of passionate hearts, authentic and tender.

Friendships are more rewarding, since you can offer a kind of shared experience and a reliability that others can't.

Business relationships become far more creative and dynamic as you can create trust through your clarity and inspire confidence through your vulnerable communication.

All forms of connection will flourish and grow when you're able to show up without masks, and when you are rooted in a strong sense of who you are, what you stand for and what's ok and not ok for you.

Connections, after all, happen between people, so the more real you are, the more willing you are to show yourself, unique talents, wounds, fears, needs and all, the greater potential exists for connection between you and others.

The affirmation

"I find deep connection when I combine vulnerability with clear boundaries"

Counter-affirmations

- I shouldn't let them see this side of me
- I'll do whatever it takes
- If I become what they need, they will love me

Chapter 17: Connection

Deep Joy

12.COMMITMENT

"I will never 'get there'
- my life is a sacred journey"

Deep Joy

This book is about an attitude that you can choose to bring to your life. It's many-layered, complex and conscious, but it's rooted in the true longings of the human spirit. In a supportive, healthy environment, we would all grow into mature adults with fierce, wild hearts, who connect deeply with others and with the natural world, who carry a potent inner confidence that lets us dream great dreams and have the courage, the resilience and the conviction to make them come true. That, I have learned, is the birth right of every human being.

In the slow poisoning of our communities and the warping of our culture into something that constrains us rather than supports us, loneliness and isolation have been the norm. Many of us choose to play the games that bring us security and a simple form of identity rather than stand alone. Thus, adulthood is becoming more rare. We are a society of big children: confused, frustrated, unsatisfied and mired in a belief that we cannot save ourselves. We look outside for salvation: relationships, jobs, money, prestige, sex, travel, drugs or a fixation on peak experiences.

This book is about how you might choose to step aside from this story, if you want to. The mainstream story has tremendous value: it gives us a path, it tells us who to be and what to do, and we will be surrounded by people living the same story. Although we will never truly connect with someone in a wild and free way, we will find networks of friends and lovers who speak our language. We will have work, and if we play the roles that society wants of us well enough, we'll go far in our work.

But we all know that this is illusion. It's a fable, told and re-told by people who choose to believe that they don't know any other way to be. We do know. Our hearts long for wilderness. But in the confusing jumble of this culture and the messy business that is life itself, it can take a long time and a lot of hard work to figure out what impulses are really *you*, and which are somebody else's expectations of you. That is the point of Part 2 of this book.

The truths in Part 2, which you have almost finished, are offered without judgement or expectation. If you choose to step into your full adult power, to assume conscious awareness of all the parts of you and step with courage and trembling into a life of significance, then that's your choice to make. I offer you some guidance for your personal journey and some tools to start making meaningful changes.

The path is yours. The choice to begin, and to continue when the road is darkest, is yours.

We've talked about choosing a life of adventure, where you embrace your wild nature and look at your life with fresh eyes and second naivety every day, looking for new opportunities and bringing yourself consciously into the present moment with gladness and gratitude. We've talked about the bad lesson taught by our culture that hard stuff is something you just hunker down and endure until you can reach the next period of safety and peace. Instead, I've invited you to learn to love the struggle, to feel yourself alive in the hard stuff and to find gratitude and wild joy in the midst of difficulty, uncertainty and even suffering.

We've also talked about building and refining a vision for your ideal future, and aligning it with your values and personal sense of honour. This vision will meet your deepest needs and nourish you physically, mentally, emotionally and spiritually. You will do the work to uncover your needs, to take full conscious responsibility for them and then set yourself on course to make your vision come true. It may take time, there will be setbacks, and you may need to adjust your methods as you learn better ways of reaching your ultimate goal, but you will get there. You bring relentless determination and playful curiosity to bear on making it into a reality.

So, surely, you're going to 'get there', right? This journey will be over. You'll get it, and you can relax and enjoy?

What is a sacred journey?

Something is 'sacred' when it goes beyond common importance. It's the word we use for something that's sacrosanct, holy or touched by something that goes beyond natural significance. It implies something to do with god, or gods, or the oldest myths and traditions of mankind.

You have this one, precious, wild life. When we shift our focus away from playing the games of our culture and start to ask deeper questions about what's really fulfilling, what it means to be human and how we should best act to meet our needs on every level, we will begin to stray out of mundane significance and into the parts of our minds that feel far deeper, older and touched by wonder and awe. When our ancestors beheld the world, they moved in a world of mystery and wonder, of fear and delight.

I have spent a lot of my life studying religions and spiritual traditions from around the world and across time. There is something they contain that's missing from our modern, sceptical, post-modern minds. The idea that world is dead isn't logical. Science is not a culture. The scientific method of experimentation and observing results to create theories, has nothing whatever to say about personal experiences of wonder. It has no more to say about human experiences of awe than does a ruler or a microscope. We've adopted a culture of a dead, mechanical world as a rejection of older religions, but we've confused a scientific approach to learning with a mature way to live. Maturity means accepting the world as it is, and our personal experiences of the world are filled with mystery. Every breath can contain curiosity and feelings of amazement and awe.

When we are fully present in the moments of our lives, choosing our path, committed to deepening our understanding, questioning everything and relentlessly pushing towards our goals, life becomes more than a string of empty moments. When we remember that we are spiritual beings, and we explore this dimension of ourselves alongside the dimensions of body, mind and heart, we begin to be more comfortable with things being 'sacred'. When we accept the reality of personal death, that we have a finite number of heartbeats until we lose this remarkable gift of embodied consciousness, we begin to appreciate things on a deeper level.

Take 'sacred' to mean whatever feels right for you. It might carry you into deep spiritual searching, looking for teachers and travelling to other places in the world to unlock the sacred aspects of your life. It may mean the profound connection that you find with people or a place. It may be the feeling you have when you're working or contributing with consciousness and focus.

Goals, vision and the lifelong journey

Determination and curiosity have no expiry date. A life of adventure isn't something we do for a while and then step back from, resuming the mainstream story of sheltering in safety. We need rest and recovery, so we choose to rest when we need to. We have, after all, a fierce sense of self-love which compels us to care for ourselves.

At the beginning of this book, I invited you to commit to a life-long journey of personal awakening and empowerment. The rest of this book is an exploration of the lifestyle that this commitment becomes. The 12 Principles are some essential core truths that support that commitment. When we live this commitment and step more fully into ourselves, we live in a different way. It's my belief that human flourishing, both personal and collective, both now and for our descendants, is supported by living in this way.

You have a vision, or you have the beginnings of one that you're going to add to and develop over time. One day you're going to have done all of the work and achieved all of the milestones to make that vision a reality, no matter how difficult or distant it might seem right now. If you make that vision so real that you can taste it, and if you commit fully to the journey to get there, you will achieve it.

But we've also talked about not being addicted to peak moments. We've looked at how most of life is mundane, simple, commonplace. We've talked about finding appreciation and gratitude for the simplest things, because each of them is truly a gift if we stop glossing over them in our search for peak experiences, in our pursuit of the cultural story of progress. Every breath is a blessing. Every meal, every conversation, every beautiful sight we see and every nice sensation we receive can be something we actively feel gratitude for.

Ultimately, the journey is at least as important as the destination. The struggles you overcome will be things you can celebrate. The moments of delight and joy that enter your life will nourish you and support you. The authentic connections you make along the way will be the memories that you take with you. Be here, now, and appreciate what is.

When you reach your vision, when you stand in triumph having made this truly joyful and fulfilling life a reality, do you think you'll want to stop? You will have learned to live in a conscious, honourable, determined, curious way. It won't end there.

This Principle is a caution against returning to the cultural illusion that we should endure hard times until we can return to easier ones.

There will always be things to appreciate and be glad of.

There will always be more learning, more growing, more challenges and more adventures to have.

You will always be in connection with others, and you will always have things you can contribute.

Let this journey be the journey of your life.

The affirmation

"I will never 'get there' - my life is a sacred journey"

Counter-affirmations

- Just a few more years, then I can stop
- I know who I am now, I know everything about me
- I'm done with learning

Deep Joy

Part 3

Integration

Deep Joy

The one thing

You've completed Parts 1 and 2 of this book. In Part 1 we looked at the foundations for your journey of personal awakening: why is it so important, what keeps us locked in smaller versions of ourselves and what do we need to decide and understand before we set out.

Your journey will be yours alone. You will meet people along the way who understand a part of your journey, but nobody will understand the entirety of it, and nobody will walk it all with you. You will have your own unique learning to do, your own daemons and challenges to meet, understand and overcome. You will have wounds from early life that shape your thinking and feeling. You will have needs and ambitions that only you can meet.

Having spent years of my life supporting people who are walking their journeys, I can tell you that nobody has it easy. When we begin to shake off the illusions of our culture and dive deeply into the wild depths of ourselves, we find hard stuff. It can be scary. Many people spend years of their lives avoiding this journey, making perfectly logical excuses which are really based in the fear of standing naked before the reality of who they are. But by exploring Part 1 and choosing to dive into Part 2 of this book, you have chosen to stand in this place, to meet yourself, to finally drop the illusions and embrace the fear and the beauty of what lies beneath.

Part 2 of this book is quite long, with a lot of ideas, theories, truths and tools. In my experience of working with my coaching clients, some of it will have seemed obvious and straight-forward. Other bits might have seemed bizarre, outlandish, challenging or uncomfortable. The parts that seem obvious and the parts that seem weird will be different for everyone.

Whoever you are, you have work to do on yourself. I do, and I've been doing this stuff all of my adult life. I've had clients of all ages, and we all have learning and growing to do. It's the nature of wild humanity to grow.

But the words in Part 2 are designed to convey a very simple feeling. All of the layers of the attitude that is at the heart of this book are designed to bring you home to the person you were always meant to be. Being that person, being wild and naked and free of illusions and confusions, is the simplest state we can experience. No thought is necessary when we are at peace with the beautiful person we were born to be. We simply are, and we simply act.

We live in a complicated world which, in many ways, prevents our flourishing and happiness. We've grown up in this complicated, often toxic world, and we've adapted to it, learned to play its games and we've picked up wounds and complicated patterns of thinking, feeling and behaving in order to get along as best we can. That is the state of the modern, domesticated human. That's why there are so many words, ideas and bits of advice in Part 2 of this book.

What we are trying to get back to is simplicity. Coming home to ourselves, with forgiveness, gentleness, determination, curiosity and profound self-love, is a hugely restful experience. It is, in my experience, the foundation of profound confidence and strength. You know who you are and what you are, and this knowing gives you a rare ferocity and resilience. The journey of healing, learning and growing sufficiently to find this simplicity, peace and rest can be long and difficult. It may take months or years of your life, and some of the journey might be challenging, uncomfortable, painful, frightening or tedious. You will meet the same barriers over and over, and I've seen first-hand how maddening that can be. I've experienced it myself, and I continue to work every day to build my understanding, to let go of the illusions I've been taught and to embrace the loving simplicity of my wild self.

This is the most important journey you will ever undertake. You have been called to take it, and each crisis and moment of clarity in your life has repeated that call. Come back to yourself, it whispers. If you don't heed the whisper it will slowly become a shout. Come back to your true, wild nature. The world does not need more people who are hurt, asleep and desperately seeking validation. The world has far, far too many of those. The world, of which you are a part, needs you to shake yourself free, breathe deep and make choices motivated by an awakening mind and a wild heart. Its needs and your needs are in harmony.

The rest of this book is about what to do next. You will go through many awakenings in your life, and each time you come a little bit closer to the simplicity of wakefulness you will return to your daily life changed. I watch this happening in my clients. Naturally, we all grow and change in a regular, fluid way, but when we've spent years stuck in a particular place in our lives, the changes can be bigger and more dramatic. After we've been working together for a while, my clients come to sessions and say...

"I don't know what to do now. I don't enjoy the same things. Some of my friends and family don't understand me anymore, and I see them and their behaviour differently from the way I used to. I feel like I'm losing things and it scares me."

My personal calling in life, my purpose, is to share truth. I relentlessly pursue truth in all things, and I feel a calling to share what I find. That's my thing, and it's lead me to become a coach and it's lead me to write this book. But truth is not always gentle, and it is not always easy. It can be a lot to bear. I feel a responsibility to do more in this book than just tell you ways to come back to yourself. I want to offer some insights and ideas I have about how to cope with wakefulness, how to thrive as you begin to come home to the person you were always meant to be. I believe that we all have a right to happiness. Indeed, I've learned that when we are happy, we are our best selves and we naturally do things with more potency and more grace. Finding happiness in this journey is important, and ok, and worth making a priority.

How do we build happy lives, as awakened adults? That is the topic of the last part of this book.

We'll look at the joy that's waiting for you within the adventures and storms of your becoming.

We'll look at the traps and pitfalls that I've seen snare and waylay people as they're walking their hard, beautiful journeys towards self, and I'll give you some ideas about how to avoid them.

I'll offer you a load of tools and ideas to help you stand in your wakefulness with strength, calm and fulfilment.

We will look at the ideas of leadership and effective engagement, because in my experience everyone is at their best when they embody some form of leadership in their lives.

We will look at where all this is going. You are not alone doing this work. Millions of people all around the world are doing what you're doing. What's it all for, where might it lead, and how can this support you and nourish your life?

Deep joy

In this book, I have challenged you to fully explore the aspects of yourself. We've talked about the idea that you are made up of needs, wounds, shames, mind, body, emotions, spirit and a core "I" that sits at the heart of it all. We've looked at the choice to step fully into your personal power and of assuming responsibility for understanding and meeting your own needs. We've looked at stepping into adulthood and exploring ethics and honour. We've looked at recognising and side-stepping the toxic stories of our culture. We've remembered the essential place that the natural world plays in our lives and wellbeing. We've looked at adventure, courage, boundaries and connection.

You are called to engage with all of this. It's a lot. Recognising the changes you need to make is hard and engaging with your own growing, healing and learning requires commitment, focus and determined, sustained effort.

What's it all for? We've looked at the importance of it, both for yourself and others around you, but what will you, personally, get out of it?

In my experience, the answer to this question is a deep, astonishing, nourishing joy. I think it's important that we prioritise joy and that we connect with it regularly, that we welcome it into our lives even as we do the difficult work. I was called to undertake my own journey of awakening, and like everyone, I was compelled by the crises and turmoil of my own life. I didn't really expect to find joy waiting at the heart of it all.

Joy in silence and being

If you think about people you know who seem 'normal', what would you say they look forward to? What do they enjoy?

It's normal in our culture to enjoy mind-lead entertainment like TV, films and books. It's normal to look forward to peak experiences. The next weekend, the next break from responsibility, the next holiday, the next adventure. As a rule, modern lives are filled with noise. We fill our senses with conversation, music, TV, work, organising the home and structuring our lives. Each of these sources of noise make sense, in themselves, but take a step back and you'll see a life drowning in distraction. Each choice is rational and coherent, but masks a deep urgency to avoid quiet. Truth lurks in the quiet, unwanted, intimidating and denied. The realities of life, the quiet doubts we all carry, our shames and hurts, our painful memories and the secret beliefs about ourselves that are the mark of an unreflected life. So a normal life, a mainstream domesticated life, is stuffed full of noise and experience. Whether or not it's a happy life, it's comfortable, known and predictable. We remain stuck, safe and gently anaesthetised by the volume of sounds, images, tastes, smells and sensations of our lives.

You've chosen not to do this any more. You've chosen to pull yourself away from that story and face what lies in the quiet moments.

Once you have, and once you've healed the stuff that waits there (because a lot of it can be healed), you can relax in the silence.

I recommend Mindfulness to most of my clients. Certain core Mindfulness practices will be recognisable to anyone who's used a Mindfulness app or been to a Mindfulness class or retreat. The body-scan, for instance. Consciously noticing how each part of your body feels, from the little sensations in our toes that we never notice to the little feelings of air currents on the top of our heads. Meeting tensions and sensations in each limb and tissue. Slowly, consciously, mindfully scanning the body.

A slightly less common Mindful technique is Mindful Eating. In brief, this goes like this...

Take time to settle into a comfortable, alert, dignified posture in which you can meditate for a while. Take some deep breaths and take the time to notice what's going on for you. Notice the sensations of your body, notice the state of your mind (is it calm and peaceful or is it busy and babbling), notice any emotions that are present for you right now. Take time to bring yourself to this moment.

Take a small morsel of food. The last time I did this, it was a single square of chocolate. Take some time to look at it. Notice its details. Feel its texture between your fingers. Reflect on the journey this piece of chocolate has been through to reach your fingers. Can you smell it? Notice how your body responds. Take some time to be with the food before you eat it.

Next, pop it on your tongue but don't chew. Close your eyes and be attentive to what's going on. How does it taste? How is your mouth and the rest of your body responding? How do you feel and where is your mind going as you hold the morsel on your tongue? Be fully present with this moment and all the sensations it brings.

This is all before even biting down, chewing, swallowing, appreciating, reflecting. How different is this to the way most of us wolf down our meals? We are very busy people (often intentionally so, ramping up the volume and distraction). We do not have time for this.

But the value of this experience can be phenomenal. A lot of people report that the single square of chocolate they eat during their Mindful Eating exercise is the most delicious meal they've ever had.

It's so simple. By slowing down, bringing attention to something as simple as eating, and Mindfully taking the time to be fully present to a simple experience, it becomes immensely more delightful.

What happens if we bring this kind of attention to other things? Breathing. Walking. Cleaning. Visiting beautiful places. Spending time with our friends. Resting. Work. Sex.

The truth is that, given the way many of us are raised and educated, we fear what might lurk in silent moments. Sometimes this is justified. Sometimes our fears are inflated by our long habit of avoidance. But along with painful things, a lot of delight waits for us in silence.

Once again, I urge you to regularly develop your Mindfulness skills. Take a course, join a class, download an app, find free Mindfulness meditations online. Allow yourself to connect with the delightful joy that waits for you in the quiet moments.

Joy in connection

According to Brené Brown, we are mentally, emotionally and spiritually hard-wired for connection. Her research has clearly shown that a person who has a sense of meaningful connection is happier, less stressed and has a longer life expectancy than those who do not connect in a meaningful way.

When I was young, I was getting into photography and I used to enjoy taking interesting, well-composed landscapes. My father said to me, "take photos of people you love. They will be the photos you want to come back to look at." I didn't really understand what he meant then, but I've learned that he was right. The memories we treasure, the experiences we most value, are those we shared with the people to whom we feel a strong, meaningful connection.

As social animals, connection is huge for us.

Not all connections are made equal. Some connections will be simple and shallow, and ones you appreciate nevertheless. You might connect with co-workers or colleagues in a simple way every day, and this is something you really treasure about your work. Other connections go deeper. People who understand you, people who see you, people who have peeked beneath the mask and still choose to love you. As we've explored, the more vulnerable we can bear to be, the deeper a connection has the potential to go.

Connections are not just with people, either. You can develop a strong and profound connection with a place. You can connect with nature, with the earth-mother, with plants and animals. You can develop a connection with the things you believe. You can connect with your ancestors. Each of these connections can be fostered, and can become just as important to us as connections with other humans.

I invite you to pour effort and energy into connection.

Are the people in your life, people who see you and love you? Are they your tribe? If not, where might you find your tribe? Where can you step outside of the comfort zone and go looking for a connection that will nourish you? How can you connect more deeply with your home, with the land, with your spiritual yearnings, with the subtle and profound callings of your heart?

Remember that connections of all kinds take time. Heart-warming, nourishing connection is based on trust, and trust can take time, effort and consistency to grow. If you go looking for it, by meeting new people, but spending time in nature, by exploring your beliefs, give it time. Bring determination and curiosity to bear on the nurturing of connection.

Ultimately, connection can be one of the sources of joy that gives real meaning to everything else in your life.

Joy in power

Of the four aspects of being human: mind, emotion, body and spirit, I have always been stronger in mind and emotion than in others. Give me an intellectual puzzle and I'm happy. But my upbringing and early life experience, and some self-consciousness about a tall and gangly body, meant that I was always shy in the physical aspect. It wasn't until my late 20s that I decided to do something about it. When I find something where I feel shy, insecure or lacking in confidence, I try to bring some time and attention to it. In the words of Sun Tzu:

"If you know the enemy and know yourself, you need not fear the result of a hundred battles. If you know yourself but not the enemy, for every victory gained you will also suffer a defeat. If you know neither the enemy nor yourself, you will succumb in every battle."

I started making myself go to the gym. I got into body building. I've found it a great parallel for coaching and personal development…

When I hit the gym, I intentionally take myself into a place where I will be tested and pushed. I have learned to love this challenge. I have good days and bad days: on the bad days I just try to keep myself fit and moving, to gently work on my mind-body connection; on good days, I push myself hard to excel and break my previous limits. I try to bring joy, presence and total commitment to my exercise. I don't just stick to movements and techniques that I feel comfortable about: I make myself work on my sticky and difficult movements. I try to learn from others and find new ways to push myself, grow and approach my workout. I put effort into rest and healing, because I know that without these I'll burn out, lose interest or pick up injuries which will be frustrating and which will hold me back.

It's all an amazing metaphor.

When I am in a good place with my training, my mind-body

connection is good and I feel strong. As I walk, sit and move I feel the power and coordination of my body. My muscles bunch and move. My movements are precise and focused. I earned this. Through my determined effort and curious attention, through hundreds of frustrating setbacks, failures, breakthroughs and embarrassments, I got to know my body well and now I can feel its power. I am physically strong, I can move with grace and I know that I can handle physically demanding situations.

I carry a physical power with me, because I have applied myself.

This is another kind of joy, and another source of confidence, that goes with the commitment to your own personal journey of awakening. As you do things that are hard, you will know get to know yourself better. You will succeed sometimes, you will fail at other times. But if you are determined and willing to experiment and learn, you will grow. You will get stronger. You will become part of the storm. You will carry that power in your heart and know that you are powerful. As you watch yourself grow or catch yourself doing something that you never thought you were capable of, you will find satisfaction, confidence and joy.

It can be a heady, giddy feeling, knowing that you are capable of great and terrible things. This is why a personal sense of honour is so important. You could hurt people and cause suffering as easily as you can succeed and prosper.

Bring joy into everything

These are three examples of ways that joy can become part of your life, in ways that aren't possible if you haven't done any personal work. If you haven't experienced Mindfulness, it can be hard to find the sensual delight of each moment; if you haven't learned vulnerability and clear boundaries it can be hard to develop joyful connections; if you have not chosen to be somebody who applies themselves and accepts their personal power, you will not see yourself growing through adventure and adversity.

What's stopping you bringing joy into every moment of your life?

Sometimes we don't do it because we forget joy. We're too busy.

Sometimes we don't do it because it doesn't feel appropriate.

Sometimes we don't welcome joy into a moment because we aren't doing something we enjoy.

But these things don't prevent you from having joy be a constant companion unless you choose for them to. In my experience, emotions do not cancel one another out. I've found that it's possible to feel many things at once, and joy can sit alongside anything. You can be bored and joyful; you can be angry and joyful; you can be in grief or sadness or despair…and yet feel joy from delight or connection at the same time.

I have been at funerals where tears of grief and sadness are flowing freely, and yet I felt joy at my connection with these people, at my memories of the departed, at the wonder and mystery of life and death.

I have taken part in ceremonies commemorating the great death of species and the peril of our world at this time of human-lead devastation, and at the same time felt joy and great gratitude for the gift of my chance to be alive, to connect with the earth, to be part of a group of people who understand and grieve with me.

I have been at the depths of my own despair, a great personal depression, the loss of something precious or beautiful in my life, and yet felt a little glimmer of joy that I am alive to experience any of this at all, that the sun shines and rain falls on my face and friends offer me love.

Joy is not something we need to wait for. It's something we can welcome into all our moments.

I invite you to consider how you might do this, in simple ways in your life.

Deep Joy

Traps for the unwary

This journey of coming home to the person you were born to be will open up all kinds of possibilities for you. As you do the work to bring your life into alignment with your power, values, vision and needs, you will grow to be somebody capable of great things. This journey waits for everyone, when the time is right for them, and a great deal of suffering and confusion arise from people misunderstanding the call to awakening for other things. Stuckness in life, frustration at a lack of progress, a lack of clarity around what you really want, ongoing conflicts or misunderstandings with friends or loved ones, episodes of depression or just a feeling that life doesn't fit properly, can all be signs that a person is being called to wake up, but is resisting or misinterpreting the call.

You would think that something so important to human flourishing would be at the very heart of our culture, with people and traditions in place to help us all thrive and embrace the fullness of who we are. As we've explored already, this isn't true. Our culture is often unhelpful and harmful to us individually, collectively and to the wider world.

However, our culture is all most people have to work with. Most people exist wholly within the culture and they will fight against things that might disrupt the mainstream stories. We've explored how most people exist as adult-children, and how they seek validation and reassurance, as if yearning for surrogate parents, through things like popularity, wealth, prestige and a very narrow vision of success. If you disrupt the story, you threaten the foundations of self-esteem, and this will tend to trigger upset, fear and anger from those dependent on the story to mask their own worries and insecurities. If you try to share your own journey with some people, you'll be met with judgement, ridicule, rejection or the advice to give up, calm down and conform.

Everybody is trying to do their best to live the best life they can, given the understanding they have and the depth at which they currently understand themselves and their personal challenges. But the net effect is that you will walk most of your journey alone. That is the price of being a conscious adult at this time. Unless you are very lucky indeed, you won't have many friends or partners who understand the fullness of your personal journey. You will face many daemons that nobody else can see, and you will have amazing moments of personal triumph which nobody else can really appreciate.

We all carry needs for connection, recognition and belonging. That leaves many of us in a hard situation.

You are called to wake up, to investigate your needs, to understand your personal wounding and their effects on your life, to fully embrace your power and accept how potent your choices are. You are called to return all of your power to the centre of your being and step forwards in full adult consciousness. The call will not go away, and you will not reach places of peace and joy without diving into the storm, within and without.

At the same time, you will probably only find a few people in your life who have the experience or the expertise to connect with you, to recognise your unique beauty and pain, and to bring you a sense of belonging. Many of us will go for long periods of time without any connections which meet these needs.

In the next chapter, I'm going to offer you some ideas about how to thrive and succeed in a world which does not appreciate the awesomeness of you.

In this chapter, I'm going to look at some of the pitfalls that exist for you on your journey. All journeys are filled with distractions and opportunities to turn aside and accept something that's easier than the truth. Each offers you a balm to the existential challenges of coming into full adult consciousness. Each has attracted a lot of followers, and these people will probably approach you and say to you, 'stop your search, stop walking the difficult path, settle for this instead'.

One of my great friends and mentors, Mac Macartney, tells the story of Jumping Mouse. If you search online, you'll find a video of Mac telling this story. It's a Native American story which follows the journey of a plucky little mouse who, in an unexpected moment of clarity, sees the sacred mountain in the distance when he jumps above the tall grass of his home. He knows in that moment that he must make his way to the mountain. He is called, he recognises the call, and he sets out on his journey. Along the way he meets another mouse who knows that the mountain exists, but they tell him to stop his difficult and painful journey and to stay with them instead. The ancient European story of Parcifal (Sir Percival of the Arthurian legends) tells the same story. Parcifal seeks the grail, again a metaphor for wisdom and awakening, and he goes through great hardship and meets people on his quest who tempt him to stop and turn back, or to settle for something less than the grail.

This book is written with compassionate non-judgement. I talk about people who are addicted to the story of our culture, who rely on it for the reassurance and affirmation that it brings, but I can't bring myself to judge them. Even when our culture is singly responsible for the annihilation of the natural world, for putting the future of our children and all children in danger, I know that very few people actively choose to destroy the world. Some people have the freedom, the opportunity and the knowledge to recognise the call to growth and personal power and responsibility. Some people don't.

At the same time, some people who begin a journey of awakening stop short of embracing their full adult power and instead find connection, recognition and belonging in other things. As a person committed to helping my clients understand their own needs, I know it isn't my place to judge anyone who abandons the quest for adulthood in the hard and lonely moments.

However, the world desperately needs more adults who know themselves and who take responsibility for the consequences of their choices. In this chapter, I offer the list of traps for the unwary, as gentle warnings to you as you walk deeper into yourself and your own potential…

Silo thinking

Silo Thinking is a term from academic research, but it's the perfect phrase for this problem. For as long as there have been big groups of people, we've clustered into smaller groups with different ideas and beliefs. Often these differences are subtle – differences in priorities for what we think is important, different tastes in clothes or entertainment, different accents or regional traditions.

Sometimes our differences lead us into conflict. One group of people believes that the most important thing is family and close relationships within their sub-group of society and they choose to persecute or reject people they think are threats to these relationships. One group builds up an organisation around one interpretation of transcendent truth, and their need to be right drives them to attack people who don't share their beliefs. One group gets huge satisfaction and validation by cheering for footballers in green, and their shared identity leads them to attack people who cheer for footballers in blue.

We've always done this.

But today, we have better tools to section ourselves off into our sub-groups, particularly by religious and political affiliation. Social media, tailored web searches and news channels that share our political inclinations can easily lead us to live in little bubbles of reflected reality. We're exposed, every day, to people who say and believe the same things we do. We chat to each other about how obviously right we are, how evil the other side is. Gaps widen. We live within cut-off 'silos' of thought, sure that we're right, rarely challenged. As each group refines the language of their own rightness and the idiocy and evilness of the other side, we're equipped with insults and rhetoric when we finally do meet up with people from other groups. Sure enough, our pre-prepared conflicts flare up and we become more even entrenched.

That's what Silo Thinking means: letting ourselves be shut away in bubbles of reality that reassure us that the world is the way we think it is.

It's comforting, it's supportive, it brings us succour and identity. It's also just a comforting illusion. It's just a way to shut ourselves away from challenging differences. We close ourselves off from sources of learning, we support the building of division and we allow ourselves to slide deeper into beliefs that our way of thinking is the only way.

When I was in my mid-20s, I was setting up my first big business venture, and I needed somewhere cheap and convenient to rest and sleep during the brief hours when I wasn't working. I ended up lodging with a friend of the family, a very loud, jolly, outspoken man who was completely sure of himself and his world-view. He was a Thatcherite capitalist and talked loudly about Ayn Rand's philosophy. I'm British and politeness is very important to me, and besides we were sharing a house and I didn't want to make it uncomfortable by pointing out flaws and contradictions that my philosophical training let me see in his statements about the way the world is. One day, I needed to pop to London and he was driving that way, so we spent a few hours in a car together. We couldn't dance around it any more: the great debate began. We fenced, we jibed, we shouted, we swore, we got angry, we laughed.

After that journey it went on for many months. I learned so much!

I saw the lies and deceits that can lurk at the heart of the left-wing politics which I tended to like. I learned a lot about the value of personal freedom and how market systems can balance themselves when individuals are free to pursue apparently selfish goals, bringing wealth and prosperity for everyone. I love learning and I had the first stirrings of a deeper, more challenging love: my love of being proved wrong. Did I agree with it all? No. But I didn't see the 'other side' as evil or stupid any more. My own beliefs became much more balanced and realistic for having been challenged and critiqued. I am hugely grateful for my time spent living in that house.

I urge you to fight against Silo Thinking. Don't let it consume you. It's so easy at this time in history, but the consequences for us individually and communally can be terrible.

So cross boundaries. Listen to your enemies. Leave your prejudices at the door. Let yourself be wrong. Be open to learning and growth.

If you'd like to find some guidance and inspiration to break out of your silos, one of Brené Brown's more recent books, Braving the Wilderness, touches on the topic of polarised thinking and what you can do about it.

The religious deal

When you come to explore your spiritual dimension, you might want to dive into religion. Most religions have been around for a long time and they exist to help people connect with spiritual meaning and transcendent experience. Some offer pathways towards the divine. Some offer tools to explore the self in a rigorous and graceful way. Some help us find deeper significance in our connection with the natural world.

I have spent most of my life studying religion. After a lot of experiences from a lot of directions I've come up with this definition for a religion: they are the political structures that grow up around a spiritual revelation.

An individual, or a succession of individuals, see something transcendent, divine or revelatory, and they bring this back to people. But most people are not interested in engaging with the challenging journey towards spiritual awakening, they're just looking to meet their basic needs for community and affirmation that they're doing the right things. For every person involved in a religion who can teach you things about spiritual discovery, there tend to be a hundred people who are only there to identify with a political or community organisation. They will say the words, sing the songs and practice the rituals, but they will not understand your journey.

Interacting with religions, of any kind, can be helpful to understand your own spiritual needs. However, while you may find tools to explore divinity or meaning, and you'll get companionship in your search for understanding, you will also meet rules, expectations and the emotional needs of others. As a rule, these things aren't separated in religions.

Religions will tend to mix together the search for meaning with political and cultural dogma and personal emotional needs. A religious teacher may often mix up their spiritual quest with their own needs and push these on their followers in the belief that they're bringing only enlightenment. It's a deal you're expected to make with them. Yes, they will give you experiences and techniques to explore your own relationship with transcendence, but you will need to abide by their rules.

If the rules make sense to you and if they coincide with your own personal values, go for it. If they don't, I caution you to take what you need from a religion without fully falling into it.

It's all about choice, of course. Choose to engage in a vulnerable, curious, determined way if that feels right for you. But don't surrender your choice just because the needs of others demand that you do. You are not here to save anybody: that's not your job.

Reward/punishment thinking

On the journey towards full adult power, you must surrender your childhood perspective. It's the death of innocence we talked about in Part 1 of this book. The world is filled with adult-children who cause harm because they refuse to take adult responsibility for their needs. You are called to wake up, to walk the harder path that leads to your full potential.

This doesn't happen quickly, or cleanly, or totally, all at once. Bits of childhood thinking will linger until you've had the time and the freedom to explore them all and make some conscious adult choices about what you'll do instead. It can take years, and these years will be effort well spent.

One of the really common belief structures that can linger inside the beliefs of an emerging adult is the belief in reward/punishment thinking. It can be a big problem.

This problem is summed up really well in the opening chapters of *Nonviolent Communication*, which we have looked at before…

"The concept that certain actions merit reward while others merit punishment is also associated with life-alienating communication. This thinking is expressed by the word *deserves* as in "He deserves to be punished for what he did." It assumes "badness" on the part of people who behave in certain ways, and it calls for punishment to make them repent and change their behavior. I believe it is in everyone's interest that people change, not in order to avoid punishment, but because they see the change as benefiting themselves."

Most adults don't think about this consciously, most of the time. It tends to be an unconscious or semi-conscious process that constantly worries about doing the right thing (because people who do good things are rewarded for it) or doing the wrong thing (people who do bad things are punished).

While justice is an important thing for adults to consider, we aren't talking about justice here. We're talking about lessons learned in early childhood that if I do the right thing, my parents will reward me, and if I do things that are wrong, my parents will punish me. As we grow up, this morphs into a belief that good people are rewarded and bad people are punished.

This can cause us to make choices that we might not otherwise make. For example, we might spend our whole adult lives avoiding things that would be really good for us, because our parents disapproved of those things and we are still, unconsciously, afraid of their punishment or disappointment.

If you think this might be a belief and pattern that you carry, try to begin noticing its effects in your life and bring self-parenting skills, compassionate non-judgement and determination to bear in moving away from them and into more conscious, adult behaviour.

The temptation towards superiority

If you've ever spent any time in personal development groups, you'll probably have encountered a lot of smug superiority. People who devote a portion of their energy to understanding themselves deeply will end up with knowledge that other people don't. It can be very easy to fall into the trap of thinking yourself superior to others who haven't done this work and who don't know their own needs or the potential of their own power.

In this book we've effectively done a lot of talking about 'us' and 'them'. You are called to undertake personal development work, and you've recognised the call and you're taking action. A lot of other people, the vast majority of people, haven't and aren't.

First of all, don't let yourself fall into the trap of thinking this makes you better than anyone else. We are *all* called to take this journey. Crises and moments of clarity exist to remind us, again and again, of this intrinsic human truth. But the moment that we finally get it, when we finally recognise the pattern that's been staring us in the face and demanding that we begin to change, are generally a matter of luck, opportunity or privilege. Somebody who takes regular breaks and holidays, taking them away from the hubbub and noise of their lives, is more likely to notice. People who know people who have already done some of this work are more likely to realise that the journey is waiting for them. Try to stay humble. Your first stirrings of awakening were not the result of superior potential. You were offered the same reminders that everyone is offered, and you noticed.

Somebody once taught me an idea about community that really stuck with me. A healthy, stable community is like a sphere. The shape of the sphere is maintained by all the points on its surface, all working together, all contributing to pulling and pushing and maintaining the stability of the shape. The sphere would collapse if one of the points wasn't making its unique contribution. In a community, each point on the sphere is a person, with their own unique gifts and specialisms. A community needs people who keep the lights on, the floors clean, the water flowing and the food on the table. A community needs people who organise, structure and keep everything in its proper place. A community needs leaders and thinkers and designers and creatives. Each person in a community is important. The modern idea of hierarchical power structures arises from dysfunctional societies built on adult-child thinking and the need for rewards and punishments. A healthy organisation or community does not value its leaders more highly than its workers: all are seen as contributing something unique, important and special.

You have a certain kind of knowledge, and by reading this book you have a lot of opportunities to dive more deeply into your learning and growing, to unleash everything that you are and to overcome all the things that have always held you back. We are people who do this kind of work, who seek this kind of learning for the incredible potential it brings us. But again, this doesn't make us better than other people. We make our contribution within our communities and organisations, but we are dependent on others to make theirs.

Humility is really important in your journey. The temptation to see ourselves as superior because we have better skills at understanding ourselves or communicating our needs can lead us to miss out on opportunities for learning. As I love to say, every day is a school day. Every person you meet has something to teach you, and every situation brings opportunities for learning. As much as you can, leave ego at the door and look for the learning in every experience.

Despair

One of the things I've learned through my own journey of awakening and through long years of supporting my clients through theirs, is that despair can be addictive.

If the journey that has been waiting for you was easy, you would have taken it years ago. It is precisely because it contains fears, doubts, insecurities and questions that will shake you to your core that you have resisted the call, and it's those same things that contain the gold for you, the beautiful gifts that will catalyse your growth. Resisting or delaying the call is normal. We all do it. It's so nice to rest in places where we are comfortable, even if we know that the comfort is an illusion.

So when you take this journey, you're going to meet moments of despair.

Deep Joy

In his book, *The Sickness Unto Death*, Soren Kierkegaard says:

> *Just as the physician might say that there lives perhaps not one single man who is in perfect health, so one might say perhaps that there lives not one single man who after all is not to some extent in despair, in whose inmost parts there does now dwell a disquietude, a perturbation, a discord, an anxious dread of an unknown something, or of a something he does not even dare to make acquaintance with, dread of a possibility of life, or dread of himself, so that, after all, as physicians speak of a man going about with a disease in him, this man is going about and carrying a sickness of spirit, which only rarely and in glimpses, by and with a dread which to him is inexplicable, gives evidence of its presence within…*

> *Therefore it is as far as possible from being true that the vulgar view is right in assuming that despair is a rarity; on the contrary, it is quite universal. It is as far as possible from being true that the vulgar view is right in assuming that everyone who does not think or feel that he is in despair is not so at all, and that only he is in despair who says that he is. On the contrary, one who without affectation says that he is in despair is after all a little bit nearer, a dialectical step nearer to being cured than all those who are not regarded and who do not regard themselves as being in despair.*

The moments of despair can be brief, or they can last a long time. I have sat with clients whose despair was complete and overwhelming. You might confront a deep trauma, a pain, wound or sadness that you've been carrying for a long time, and despair that you'll ever be healed or feel whole again. You might notice yourself doing something that you swore you'd never do again and despair that you'll ever move on. You might begin to appreciate the scale and nature of your own shadow, that essential and intense part of yourself that you would be ashamed to show anyone else, and you might despair that all this darkness lies within you. You might look at the shape of your life, or the state of the world, and despair that you will ever find happiness or peace, or that the world will ever know hope or justice.

I can tell you that despair is important. The journey into darkness, uncertainty, fear and the unmaking of all your assumptions has always been recognised as a vital part of the journey into soul, into the deepest aspects of yourself. It isn't a bad sign, however painful or scary it might be at the time. If you engage consciously, with determination and curiosity, to walk the path of empowered adulthood, and you don't meet despair that shakes your very foundations, then I'm sorry to say you still have a long way to go. It's normal, it's ok. It's an important step in the coming home to the fully empowered, fully real self. Sometimes things need to be thoroughly unravelled and unmade before healing and growth can begin. However dark it may seem, I encourage you to walk the path that lies before you and trust that your heart knows where it's going.

However, for all its horrific fascination, despair is just a feeling. Try not to become fixated by it. I've met many people who began their own journey of awakening but became trapped by despair, by the overwhelming, beautiful revulsion of it.

Sometimes we get trapped because it's just such a strong feeling that it blots out all conscious thought or other emotion. At its worst, despair can be overwhelming, transfixing and world-defining. We see everything through the lens of despair and, whether we notice it or not, we can end up fighting to stay with the feeling, pushing out warming, positive feelings as we hold despair close. In a funny way, we find solace and belonging in our identification with our bottomless pain.

At other times, we stay in despair because it feels right. We have met great truths and they brought us despair, and so we can associate the despair with the enlightenment of the truth. To push away despair would be to deny the things that we have discovered about ourselves, about our relationships or about the world.

It is easy to fall in love with the purity and pain of despair. However, just because truth brought you despair does not mean that despair is the truth. Just as we began this journey with me urging you to remember both determination and curiosity, so I urge you to remember those core virtues now. Even when despair seems keen and right, even when it becomes a companion that you know well, hold it lightly. Be curious about it, rather than subsumed by it. It is just one truth in a world of truths. It is just one feeling in a world of emotion. You are just as entitled and worthy of joy as you are of despair.

When despair threatens to overwhelm you, I invite you to remember simple pleasures, to focus on little moments of joy and delight, and to seek comfort and ask for help from those you trust. Don't let yourself get lost in the overwhelming nature of your experience for too long. Force yourself to hold it lightly. Break it up with nice experiences. Let people tend to you and offer you kindness, and don't push them away unless you absolutely need to. If you need to, find professional help: somebody who will create a safe space for you to explore the learning that your despair brings without you becoming paralysed by the intensity of the feeling.

Darkness is an important part of the journey, just as delight, bliss and revelation are, but if you notice that you've fallen in love with the darkness, devote as much energy as you can towards letting in the light. Because while despair is a necessary step, it will hold you back from growth and power if you let it overwhelm the rest of your experience.

On dialectics

In our stories and fantasies, in books and in movies, there are often simple answers. Characters follow a plot that has a neat conclusion.

In the real world we have to be very suspicious of simple, shallow answers. So many aspects of our lives are being reduced to catch-phrases and throw-away lines. It's usually the mark of an unreflected life that somebody uses these kinds of banal sayings which sound good until you begin scratching the surface. If something can be easily summed up in a few words, it's probably manipulative nonsense. They make for good headlines, but bad answers to important questions.

Real life is a messy business, and we know that peace is found in the storm. We engage with risk, adventure and change, relinquishing our hold on simple certainties, because we know that human beings are at their best when they embrace the messy realities of life.

One of the tools I really value in exploring deeper questions are dialectics. Dialectics are conversations between ideas, which lead to higher understandings. The German philosopher Hegel summed it up that...

Thesis	+ Antithesis	= Synthesis
(an important idea)	(another idea, equally important, which seems to contradict the first idea)	(a higher conclusion)

This is set against traditional notions that there's only one right answer to any question. When you're doing maths, there's only one right answer. When you're exploring the great questions of being, meaning, life and death, it's more complicated than that.

Using dialectics in personal development means holding two contradicting positions about something that's very important to you, without making a final decision that either is right. You allow yourself to explore both, in the knowledge that there's a tension between one idea and the other. In the words of Aristotle, "it is the mark of an educated mind, to be able to entertain a proposition without accepting it."

It's the tension itself which can lead you to a higher truth. This is a very uncomfortable thing to do (earlier in this book we looked at cognitive dissonance), but it's a necessary tool if you're going to develop subtle and effective solutions to existential challenges.

Thinking in this way is about commitment to deep truth instead of reassuring but simplistic answers.

You will meet a lot of opportunities to try out the idea of dialectics as you explore questions that are important to you, but I think there are certain pairs of contradicting truths that we all meet at this time in history, and I think that exploring both truths and the tension between them leads us to understand ourselves in the world better. For example...

Responsibilities to self	vs	Responsibility to others and to the world
We are each responsible for our own wellbeing, health and flourishing. Sometimes this means putting our needs above those of others. "You cannot pour from an empty container"		We are here to contribute to the healing of the world, to be a force for good. We want to love and support the people we care about.
Vulnerability	vs	Resilience
To show up just as we are, without masks or defences, is an act of courage and a necessary part of our flourishing and wellbeing.		In the face of the demands and challenges of our lives, we must be strong and resilient so that we don't become overwhelmed and burn out. Sometimes doing this requires being thick-skinned.

Will – making things happen	vs	Surrender – appreciating the journey
We explore the vision that we want to build in our future and decide on the results that we want, then we make good choices that carry us towards that vision and those results. We are resolute and determined, with strong, focused willpower.		Some situations cannot be forced, and we spoil or neglect important things when we push on relentlessly. Sometimes we surrender, trust, let go of the reins and bring ourselves with uncertainty and vulnerability to a situation.
Beauty	vs	Horror
When we are Mindful, grateful and fully present in the moment, the simple beauty of experience can be breathtaking.		Looking at the way that people treat one another, or the harm that we do to other living beings, and all the ways that we hold ourselves back from happiness and fulfilment, can seem horrific.

Coping with wakefulness

Moments of revelation and awakening are generally peak moments. It feels good and exciting to finally understand something important and profound. However, once you unlock a truth, you then have to live it. This can start as an exciting challenge: a new way to approach your life, a new plan, maybe a new job or a new relationship, a new home or situation, a new chapter to your life, a clean page full of possibilities. Once the moments of beginning and creation have passed, there is just life. There are days and nights in a new reality where nothing special is happening. Once the excitement of learning has passed, and once we have settled into the challenge of integrating new knowledge into our lives, the next challenge begins: staying the course.

In this chapter I'm going to offer a few bits of advice for how to handle being a conscious adult in the world of adult-children. You will often be unsupported. Sometimes, you will be tempted to return to the answers of your childhood. Sometimes, the core wounds that you carry will undermine your progress. Sometimes you will get tired, and it will seem hard, or lonely, or unfair. These things are part of the price we pay for coming into our full adult power.

I work with my clients to unlock lives of adventure, but I don't sell them a fantasy that all of life is going to become made up of peak moments. Life is mostly made up of the spaces in between, so finding beauty and contentment in these moments is one of the most important components in a happy life. So many books and courses about personal empowerment leave this out. But after surging into action, I have seen so many people fall short of their full potential because of the unexpected challenges that wait for them in the quiet time after that initial explosion…

High quality rest

Resting is a skill. We tend to live stressful lives, and this stress take a toll on the body, mind, emotions and spirit. Stress is so normal that it can even be something that implies success and prestige. The consequences of sustained stress and depletion are understood by modern medicine, but again these consequences are so commonplace that we don't tend to think of them as problems. But given enough time and enough stress, worry and anxiety, your capacities will degrade and, inevitably, you will become unwell. Immune systems become less effective when a mammal is stressed, it will make bad choices and it will become more prone to chronic diseases. I urge you to choose to prioritise rest. Whatever you are trying to achieve, whatever your vision and your personal goals, you will do better when you are rested.

Of course, if you can adopt the attitude in this book then you will be more resilient. If you are determined and curious, embracing your full adult power, paying attention to your needs, engaging with the storm in a positive and results-oriented way, then you will cope much better with stress. But even then, rest is important.

Not all forms of rest are equal. What forms of rest nourish you best? What moments leave you feeling restored, revitalised and relaxed? Now compare these to the things you tend to do when you have the space and time to rest. Do they match up?

I encourage you to reflect on the kinds of rest that work best for you, and to make them a priority in your life.

Prioritise – manage your energy and choose your battles

By now you either have a vision for the future you're going to build, or you have some of the early ideas that will form part of your vision.

What matters is results. What matters is that the choices you make each day carry you a bit closer to that vision. But you don't have to do it all at once.

If you have an attitude of determination and curiosity, the manifestation of your vision becomes inevitable. It will arrive. You will make it happen. It's only a matter of time.

When you are making plans and deciding what needs to be achieved in sequence to make your vision come true, consider the resources you have available. You have a certain amount of time and a certain amount of energy. You have people in your life that you can rely on to a certain degree. You have all kinds of practical resources. Take care how you use them.

Try not to rush to the results you want, and try not to fight every battle, right every wrong, make every change and learn every lesson, all at once. It's ok to work thought things systematically, to be realistic about the number of things you can handle at once. Of course, if you notice that you keep choosing the things you'd rather do, or if you keep putting difficult things off, that's something to be resolute. But if you have the proper attitude of determination and inevitability, you can trust yourself to return to some things later.

For example, I enjoy New Year's resolutions. I try not to set more than three, but I make sure they're big, challenging goals that will require hard work and learning from me. They're chosen as part of my larger vision: they'll form foundations, or they'll force me to develop in ways that make my vision more possible. Three may not sound like a lot, but that's the point really. One of my goals for 2018 was to write this book, despite working three jobs and creating a new life in Brighton, UK. To write this book I needed to do a lot of research and reading, a lot of planning and a lot of bouncing ideas off friends and colleagues. It forced me to codify the 15 years of learning and training that goes into my coaching work, into a finite number of pages and a core list of ideas and principles. It's been good for me, and it forms the foundation for some more steps I'll take.

Decide what is most important and do that first. Decide what you can realistically achieve, given the resources and time you have, and achieve it. Don't let yourself despair if there is lots to do. Don't get mired in plans that turn out not to work: be flexible in your methods but inflexible in your goals.

Order the plans you make and the work you do in a way that will best lead to the results you want.

Play easily, play often

Sometimes, we resist the call to adult power because being an adult seems boring. Adults don't play and don't have fun. Do they?

Yes, they do, and I encourage you to make time and reserve energy for play.

What does play mean for you? Do you have hobbies? Would you like to? If you think about yourself having fun, doing something unproductive that brings you happiness, what do you see yourself doing?

Some of the wisest, most aware, more empowered people I've known have also been the most playful. I have had good friends who were priests or business leaders, who were quick to laugh, often silly and who didn't take themselves too seriously even though they were deadly serious about their work and their path. To be adult does not necessarily mean to be dour and humourless.

We've looked at self-parenting and building a relationship with your inner child. One of the ways that this relationship can support you is helping you discover free, fun play. Take your inner child by the hand and go be playful. Move your body in ways that feel free and good for you. Dance in whatever ways nourish you. Be silly with friends. Play structured games. Play sports. Go to comedy nights or do other things that make you laugh (laughter yoga is a thing, try it!). Find hobbies that fill you with joy. Rediscover the wild.

Clearly define and manage your wounds and trauma

Do you know what early-life wounds you carry? Do you know your ancestral wounds and the hurts that are passed down in your family from parent to child? Do you see the hurts the underpin our culture, which lead us to hurt one another? Do you understand the traumas that you carry in your body, which bring you physical pain and which influence your choices?

Personal wounds are one of the biggest influences on our choices. If you want to embrace the full power of your freedom to choose, you will need to meet, understand and, as far as possible, heal your core wounds and traumas.

Psycho-spiritual wounds can be found through counselling, coaching, personal development work and through exposure to other ways of living (such as travelling to other cultures).

Physical traumas can be uncovered by engaging with bodywork therapies and by exploring the work of Peter Levine (we looked at his book Waking the Tiger earlier). There are a lot of kinds of bodywork therapy out there, from the mainstream to the exotic, and many variations on each kind as each practitioner brings their own experiences and training to the work. If you suspect that you're carrying physical traumas that influence your thinking and feeling, I encourage you to engage with healing them to whatever extent is possible for you right now. Gently, with determination and curiosity, engage with your trauma and its resolution.

As we've discussed, some wounds can be healed. Others may always be with you but can be managed. Your wounds are never an excuse for your behaviour: you are responsible for your words, choices and actions and your personal sense of honour forms the first and strongest gate on your choices.

The more clearly you know the wounds you carry, the easier it is to manage them. You can look out for the tell-tale signs that your choices are being influenced or made by your wounds, and you can learn ways to calm them or meet their needs in healthier ways. It may be that some of your wounds are just too intense to be controlled in certain situations, so you might need to withdraw from those situations until they calm and you can try again. Whatever you need to do, it's ok so long as it meets your personal sense of honour.

The important thing is knowing and understanding. Don't let things lie undisturbed because you fear what will happen if you look underneath. Find safe, supported ways to understand the wounds and traumas you carry, so that you become more free to act with power and focus.

Remember the four dimensions of being

You are a complex, beautiful, messy being. In Part 1, I listed some of the core things that make up the human person, but one idea was the four dimensions of being. I learned this from a Native American tradition, and it's been very useful in my coaching work and my personal journey.

If you are made up of thought, emotion, body and spirit, and if each of these aspects is independent of the others, then you will be at your healthiest and most balanced if you pay attention to all your aspects.

If you think of each of these aspects of yourself, consider how confident you feel in each. Do you feel strong in mind but less sure in physicality? Do you consider yourself to be emotionally sensitive and aware, but not very academic and intellectual? Your natural affinity for each dimension will tend to correspond to how much energy you tend to put into it. This is something to pay close attention to.

I encourage you to make time for exploring your weaker aspects. Don't let them atrophy too much, or this weakness will begin to affect the whole of you. Seek balance in your different dimensions.

Return to the things that helped you wake up

Often there will be things that marked big steps in your journey of personal awakening. People, places, events, books, objects or other things that catapulted you in the right direction, which catalysed our adventures. Maybe they were a beginning for you, or maybe you were already on the path but they were important in speeding you on your way.

If you find yourself struggling to keep the momentum up, or if your commitment to your journey wanes a bit in the face of a long messy period of your life, then returning to things that have inspired you in the past can be very helpful.

This might be meeting up with helpful people, visiting inspiring places, re-reading helpful things or taking part in new courses. However, this sometimes requires planning or lots of energy, which might not be things you have at the times when you need some motivation. So another things you can do is to find symbols that capture the feeling or energy of the things that have supported you in the past.

In my meditation space at home, I have a range of objects that were gifts from beloved or treasured people, or which came to me at times of great significance, or which remind me of something very important to me. When I make time to meditate, I sometimes connect with these objects and I draw strength from the reminders they bring.

You may want to make a similar space in your home, which contains your touchstones: your reminders of what's most important. Your vision board can go in the same space, and all the other writing you do as part of your personal work.

Wherever possible, don't go alone. Build a support network.

Who are your allies on your journey? Who gets it? Who cheerleads for you and helps you become the best version of you?

As we've discussed, more and more things in our culture have been reduced to commodities and being alone and lonely is becoming more and more common. For many of us, it's become normal and something we expect and anticipate.

So it's very important that you foster connections, friendships, relationships and a feeling of community that nourishes you and supports you to grow and develop into a fully adult, fully empowered version of yourself. You should consider including this in your vision, and then working out a plan to make it happen.

How can you meet people who will understand the journey you're on?

How can you get support to keep moving in good directions, digging deeper into yourself, consistently moving into adult choice and reflecting well on things that are truly important?

Where can you go where you will be recognised, accepted and welcomed when you speak with vulnerability and honesty?

It may be that people, groups or places exist that you can go to. But it also may be that if you are looking for a place to support you, and you find it doesn't exist, then that's because you're meant to create it. You don't need expertise. You don't need to pretend to have answers. You just need to say, in whatever way makes sense for you: I am looking for a community, I am on a path of personal discovery and empowerment, and I want to spend time with like-minded people. What you are looking for, is looking for you. If you feel this need, so will others.

The important thing is, to whatever extent feels possible for you, not to go it alone. Certain bits of your journey will be private by necessity, but the rest can be shared. Consider who your people are, who your tribe is, and where you might find them.

Develop good habits

This is just a quick reminder to reflect regularly on the things you do with your time and energy. Are your habits ones that support your growth and flourishing, or are they hangovers from older, less healthy times in your life? Where do you need to begin letting go of old habits and developing new ones?

You can easily assess your current habits by keeping a habit journal for a week. What do you actually spend your time doing? Where did the hours of the day go? What did you do that cost you energy and what left you feeling energised and alive?

There are a lot of books out there about analysing your current habits and building new, better ones. A great practical book is *Making Habits, Breaking Habits* by Jeremy Dean, or for an idea of habits that can be really effective, pick up a copy of the best-selling *The 7 Habits of Highly Effective People* by Stephen Covey.

Rediscover the wild

How many of us can really say we understand wildness? With our busy urban or sub-urban lives, can we genuinely say that we have a connection with the natural world? We tend to agree that it's important, and we like the idea of it, but what does it actually mean?

How do you connect with nature? What are the next steps that you need to take to bring yourself home to the reality of your connection with the land? You might not have a clear answer to these questions, but you might have a gut feeling and that's a good place to start.

Because, as I've explored in this book, our connection with nature is often the missing link, the elephant in the room, the aspect of our personal development that we don't really think of as personal. I've said that a part of us doesn't reside within us, and isn't within our power to understand or control, but belongs to the land. We are a part of nature, an off-shoot of a great tree, and we owe our existence and our daily lives to its wellbeing. Our personal development, if cut off from nature, is only ever partly complete. We will always be missing a part of ourselves.

Nature is not a fantasy. The way it appears in books and movies is usually just an idealised or fantastical version. Nature is out there, outside of our comfortable homes and our controlled environments. It waits for you. How will you embrace its teachings?

Channel your outrage

Life is a messy business, and sometimes it's hard. We protect ourselves in a lot of ways, and we've looked at some of those ways in this book. One of the things we protect ourselves from is the hurt and outrage at things we know to be wrong.

There are plenty of things in the world that are wrong. Injustice exists everywhere, on a personal level, in relationships and out in the wider world. Once you've done the work to clearly define what you stand for (your personal values and sense of honour), you may find that you notice more things that you object to. The way some people treat you, or the way they treat each other. Crimes or injustices that you witness. The exploitation of the vulnerable by the powerful. Cruelty. The suffering of people or things that you love dearly. Systemic injustice, where a government or organisation is structured in a way that causes unfairness or suffering.

As a rule, we ignore these things. This gets harder and harder as you grow and evolve. You will develop the vulnerability to show up as you truly are, and to express yourself directly and clearly. You will have a clear sense of right and wrong. You will develop your empathy skills so that you feel the hurt of others more keenly. And, of course, your personal power, your ability to make empowered choice and your level of confidence will grow, leaving you far more able to act and take a stand against things you know are wrong.

You may find yourself correcting people who have always treated you poorly. You may find yourself speaking up more often. You may find that the news upsets you more than it used to. You may feel called to get involved in charity or activist work. You may feel more part of the world, with a drive to contribute in a positive way.

Moreover, you may just look at the world and see the scale of the wrongness that exists. A common response to this is rage. Indeed, rage is one of the four core signs of growth that I have noticed in my clients as they've come more fully into their own consciousness and power, along with grief, vulnerability and love.

Outrage is an almost inevitable part of this journey. I have seen two possible responses to it: one is to work hard to avoid or smother it because it's uncomfortable and challenging, and the other is to regard it as another call: this time, a call to action. We tend to be very busy, and we tend to have already committed much of our energy, so the idea of championing causes can seem like a burden we don't have the resources for. It can also be easy to confuse a genuine call to action with the Rescuer role from the Karpman Drama Triangle: we can easily feel that the obligation to fight for things we know are right is essential for us to earn self-esteem. Taking action for that reason will be harmful for you, because it'll reinforce your identity with a shallow, fragile kind of self-esteem instead of stepping into your authentic, beautiful, messy adulthood.

But if you find a cause that you believe in, if your outrage drives you to take action, then I encourage you to investigate what action you can take without overcommitting or burning out. You do not need to save the world on your own, or all at once. You do not need to take the sins of the world onto your own shoulders. But consider what you can do, if you find outrage burning in your heart, and begin to take action.

Confidence is your power to choose

Confidence is something you earn when you take action. Often, we think we need confidence in order to take action, and this becomes a catch-22 situation. My belief is that you don't need confidence to get started. You are capable of great things, some of which will be beyond your current imagination. You can say things to people that you never thought you could, you can do work that you always believed is beyond you, you can feel a tremendous sense of inner strength and you can bring wealth of all kinds into your life. This doesn't begin with confidence. Confidence will be what you pick up along the way. You will look back, one day, and realise how far you've come, and you'll be blown away by the things you've become comfortable doing.

Confidence, as we explored in Principle 1, begins with the realisation of choice. You have chosen the shape of your life, and you could make new choices at any time. If you believe you can't, if you believe you're trapped and incapable of changing or growing or escaping your current reality, then that's a choice too. You are free to choose. That remarkable idea lies at the heart of self-empowerment.

As you walk your path, pay close attention to the choices you're making. Are they good ones? Are you letting yourself overlook a choice because you think it might be too hard?

Remember the phrase we looked at earlier: what would you do if you were a little bit braver?

Once you identify something that you can only do if you were a bit braver than you are now, choose to do it. You may not be ready for it, you may not be brave enough, or smart enough, or strong enough. Do it anyway. Begin moving, holding your fears close and being fully conscious of them. Sometimes you'll succeed, sometimes you'll fail. Keep going. You will be amazed by what can happen, and you will be amazed by how much your confidence will grow.

Hold death close

This too shall pass: that's one of the core lessons that death teaches us.

If you are going through something hard, you know that it won't last forever. Stay engaged, stay conscious, be resolute and determined. Things will change and move on, and better things will arrive in your life. Work hard to ensure that when change comes, it carries you in directions that you want.

If you're in a moment of joy, connection or triumph, you know that this won't last either. Treasure what you have, be present in the moment and savour the beauty of now. Don't be too quick to rush on to the next thing or live in the expectation of moments to come. Be here, now. Stay present and stay grateful.

We've looked at our culture's response to death: to sideline it, shut it away, pretend that we can live forever until suddenly it arrives and fills our final moments with terror, confusion and tragic loss. Engaged, conscious adulthood calls us to hold death close, to feel its presence in our daily lives. Knowing that everything and everyone will pass away, that we only have a finite number of moments an that some precious things will disappear, never to be seen again, forces us to focus on what really matters. We do not have forever, we do not have the energy or the opportunity to experience everything and we cannot protect those we love from the effects of time.

Use the reality of death to hone your choices and to empower your sense of gratitude for what you have here and now. It will pass, all things will pass, and finally you too will leave this precious physical existence behind. How will you use the time that has been given to you?

On stoicism

If you would like to continue to explore the core attitude that's at the heart of this book, the philosophical school of stoicism offers a lot of the same teachings. In this book I've tried to take you down lots of different avenues of thought and development, and I've written the 12 Principles because I believe that each of them is necessary to build and maintain a healthy adult whole. But the core feelings of determination and curiosity were summed up well by the ancient founders of the school of stoicism.

Many stoics and their followers have been famous people. One of the most famous books of stoic philosophy is *Meditations* by Marcus Aurelius who was, at the time, the Emperor of Rome. Bill Clinton famously admired Marcus Aurelius, while Wen Jiabao, the former prime minister of China, has said that he has read *Meditations* over a hundred times. Today, stoicism is enjoying a revival and a lot of people are finding inspiration and support from this most practical of philosophies.

At its heart, stoicism is about an approach to life which is level-headed, moral and empathetic. It's about finding calm and equanimity in all situations, and about putting ego in check so we can live with dignity and fortitude. It's a collection of ideas and principles but it's also a list of practical tools to instil a logical, measured approach to life. Although it emerged in ancient Greece and has been generally popular in Europe, stoicism bears striking resemblance to Buddhist teachings and other works from around the world, which to me suggests that it carries wisdom that's of use to people in all times and places.

Above all, I think the true value in stoic philosophy is the resilience it brings us. It gives us reasons and reminders that help us stay centred through our successes and during moments of hurt, injustice or struggle. It helps us stay focused, calm and determined, which is very important when we're steadily working to make a vision come true.

I'd invite you, if this very short introduction intrigues you, to explore stoic philosophy and see if it can help you to stay centred as you navigate the messy adventure of life. Marcus Aurelius' *Meditations* are a good way in, if you feel ok engaging with words written over a thousand years ago. If you'd prefer a more modern, accessible book about stoicism, Massimo Pigliucci's *How to Be a Stoic: Using Ancient Philosophy to Live a Modern Life* is a popular and well-written way in.

Deep Joy

Leadership, engagement and service

In his book, *Finding Earth, Finding Soul: The Invisible Path to Authentic Leadership,* Mac Macartney describes true, authentic leadership as being the willingness to take a stand for what you believe.

A person who has done the work in this book, who has reflected deeply on their own nature, explored their own personal power and freedom, who has considered their own core values and ethics, is capable of great things.

In a work setting, an empowered adult has advantages that other won't have. You will be less influenced by the pressures and needs of those around you. Your motivation won't come from unreflected needs for safety or esteem, but will arise out of your quest for your own vision. This will give you an energy and drive that others will struggle to match. You will know the *why* behind all your choices, and this will bring a clarity and momentum that will carry you far, and you will be able to articulate it clearly and with confidence, which will bring you respect and trust, so long as your work is aligned with your values and vision.

Outside of work, your focus, vulnerability and clear boundaries will attract people and opportunities that will bring you happiness and fulfilment. You will steadily work towards the happy life in your vision, and you will notice incremental, inexorable improvements that will make joy a more and more common part of your life. Your gratitude and positive, results-oriented attitude, backed up with determination and curiosity, will make you interesting to others who share your approach and will make you pleasant to be around.

If you look at this state as a whole: positive, grateful, results-focused, empowered, boundaried, vulnerable, brave, ambitious, it describes the kind of leadership that Mac talks about in his book.

You may think of yourself as a leader, or you might think that leadership would never be part of your journey. I suggest to you that you are becoming a leader, simply by doing this work. Even if the life that you are building, based on the vision that you've created, is quiet, fairly solitary, working at something that's of great value to you but rarely seen by others, you will do this with authenticity and focused determination, bringing a quiet leadership to your work. If you are more of an extroverted person, or if you feel drawn to work or a lifestyle that involves a lot of people, your unleashed personal power and healthy personality will move you into positions of leadership in one way or another.

Bad leadership, the kind that it's hard to do once you've done this personal work, involves traditional hierarchies, reward/punishment thinking, the application of force, the hoarding of power. We've all seen bad leadership like this. We've seen managers, business owners and community leaders who are using their positions of privilege to meet their own petty emotional needs.

Good leadership, as expressed by Mac in his book and by dozens of other researchers and experienced leaders, if often invisible. To quote *Max DePree: "The first job of a leader is to define reality. The last is to say thank you. In between, the leader is a servant."*

You are already beginning to define reality by learning to create strong, positive visions for the reality you are going to create. This is what great leaders do for the people they lead: they hold the vision for where things are heading, and they convey it to others in a way that makes them feel engaged and motivated.

In the last chapter, I talked about a model for organisations or communities as a sphere, which is held in shape by the efforts of everyone in the community. A true leader is a servant. They understand that their role is to hold the vision and support others to make it come true. In any organisation, a leader cannot achieve anything alone, they depend on everyone else's skills and experience. They coordinate and organise everything behind the vision, and they remove barriers to making it come true, then they get out of the way and let others do their part. At the end, they say thank you. If they're doing their job well, a leader is barely noticed, and everyone in the organisation is left with a feeling that they made their contribution without interference.

Leaders like this tend to create success in organisations, communities, companies, charities, relationships, friendships and in their own lives. It requires all sorts of skills, because a leader has to be strong, emotionally resolved, brave and highly conscious, but they are exactly the skills that you'll develop by following the principles and advice in this book.

Whether you identify with the word on not, your own personal growth will leave you as a leader in your life.

Whatever you end up leading, whether it's a division in a company, your own business venture, a smallholding, a protest group or an intimate relationship, you will need to answer to the demands of other people. We are all inter-connected. We depend on others for support, money, energy, resources or for the richness of inter-personal relationships of all kinds. Our inter-connectedness is a blessing, and it's something we need to manage carefully.

We've spent a lot of this book looking at psycho-spiritual needs, boundaries and vulnerability. This is complicated enough within ourselves, but it becomes much more complicated when we're in relationship or in community. It becomes very important to be clear on your own needs, so that you can notice when your choices, words and actions begin to be driven by meeting the needs of others.

Above all, ensure that your leadership is a positive force in the world. Are you a leader who does things and takes part in things that are aligned with your values and your personal sense of honour, or do you leave your honour at home so that you can do things that meet your other needs? If it's the latter, do you have a plan to either move yourself away from dishonourable things, or to shift the organisations or communities of your life towards a life that will feel honourable and ethical to you? What does your form of leadership model and exemplify for others: for your children, for other adult-children who are trying to wake up and for other true adults who are your peers?

None of us are islands, and our inter-connectedness is the hardest and most rewarding thing we will ever engage in. As your personal power, consciousness and understanding grow, I encourage you to consider what kind of a difference you are making in the world, because you will begin to have more of an effect than the average person. Your conscious choices will have a bigger effect in the world than the unconscious choices of another person.

What will you stand for, and what will you bring about in the world?

On service

As we grow in confidence, and as we take brave steps into our full adult potential, we become bigger, more substantial people. However, as we work on a sense of gratitude for the blessings in our lives, and as we remember that we are just a part of a wider, wild world, we will be more aware of how small we are.

I've found that the life that waits for conscious, empowered adults is a life of service. We become committed to things, we learn to be fully present in each moment, and in those moments we often find that we want to contribute, to give back, to embody our gratitude for this wild and precious life. This life of service, in whatever shape it takes, isn't an obligation, but rather a joyful outpouring of the calling of our hearts.

Doing the work in this book allows us to become the authors in the stories of our lives, instead of living out the story that our parents wrote for us, or our culture prepared for us, or that other people expect us to live. We are free to write our own story.

What would the title of your story be? What will the plot be? Who are the main characters? Who are the good guys and who are the bad guys?

If a life of service feels good and right to you, I invite you to reflect on what you are serving. If you are not giving your energy and your effort to a purpose with joy and gratitude, what are you giving it to?

Allow your story to be one that you feel proud and glad for. Write a great story. Not anybody else's idea of greatness: you are not here to meet my needs or the needs of anybody else, unless you choose to. What is great to you, what is beautiful and significant and worthwhile and endowed with tremendous value and importance to you?

Deep Joy

Tipping point

We have reached the end of our time together and I'd like to thank you for allowing me to share some of my insights with you. The ideas in this book were born out of my years training in philosophy, spiritual traditions and through my work as a life coach. Deep Coaching, the unique kind of coaching that draws on all of my training and learning, helps my clients to take the difficult, frightening but hugely rewarding steps into full adulthood and full mastery of themselves. I watch people come to life more fully every day and it's always an exciting, humbling thing to witness.

In this book I have tried to make it clear why a profound journey of personal awakening is so important, why a commitment to the journey is necessary and some of the things this commitment brings us. I have offered ideas, inspiration and guidance based around the 12 Guiding Principles of Deep Coaching and I hope you have found them useful. Finally, I have spoken a little bit about the challenges that lie ahead for anyone who commits to coming home to their true selves, and some of the ways we can meet these challenges.

One of the things that sets Deep Coaching apart from many other models of personal development and schools of learning and healing, is that it balances the power of personal freedom and choice with the necessary responsibilities that come with being human. Instead of just focusing on your personal needs and goals, I have also talked about honour, responsibility and a connection to the wild world. What I've tried to convey in this book is that there's no contradiction here, nor do you need to practice them one at a time. It's my belief that when we understand ourselves and our own needs and nature well, we will come to the realisation that contributing to the flourishing of the world is in our own best interests. Injustices may or may not affect you now, but they will at some time. Supporting others now will mean you are more likely to receive support when you need it. Developing a deep and loving connection with the natural world will inspire you and other to take steps to defend it – something that's so important and necessary at this time of uncertainty and destruction.

When we live in a way that's mindful of our needs and the calling of our hearts, we naturally want to be a force for good in the world.

You may already be connected with organisations or groups that are working to transform the world in positive ways. It may be part of your work or it may be something you do as a volunteer or in an informal way.

I want to leave you with the wider change that I see coming in human culture, a change that will manifest itself if we can keep our personal and cultural daemons in check. The early 21st Century has seen a lot of victories in the West for the forces of fear, separation, prejudice and adult-child thinking. As we begin to feel the impacts of climate change and as the damage and imbalances that our culture has caused around the world begin to have an effect, our economies destabilise and the myth of progress begins to become less convincing. People begin to get worried, with their fears magnified and directed by news outlets and demagogues. Levels of stress increase, and as a species we begin to devolve back to our more protective instincts. Where we are not awake, alive and conscious to these influences and pressures, we become more tribalistic and silo thinking becomes more commonplace. We easily demonise those who think differently and we're more likely to perceive threats to our safety and to our way of life.

Ultimately, my work and the work of everyone who is supporting people to understand themselves and their motivations more clearly, is a stand against this back-sliding into protectionism and small-mindedness.

The world of our longing

Each person in the world has a way of approaching their lives. When we speak to people, we expect and anticipate certain things from them. We expect and anticipate certain things in our lives, and we expect our lives to have a certain shape. We react to things in ways that we've practiced over and over since childhood. Few people ever leave behind their early-life responses to the world, to one another, to themselves.

This, I've suggested, is the problem. The prison that keeps us locked in place is a certainty that the way things are now is 'just the way things are'. We expect and anticipate too much. We live in comfort zones, rarely happy but generally reassured by predictability and by knowing where we stand.

I have offered you tools and ideas to break out of this prison. Our freedom of choice extends to virtually every corner of our lives, and our choices and personal power can transform everything we experience.

As we allow certainty to fade and instead embrace a life of adventure and consciousness, the way we approach the world at large can change. We are born into a particular time in history. Our culture is a certain way, what is popular and what isn't is a certain way, we live in certain communities with certain prejudices, our home countries are at war or they aren't. Each generation has to endure its hardships and its successes. Most people at different times in our past would have believed that things would always be that way. 'Just the way things are' isn't new, it just happens to be more deeply ingrained right now thanks to the power of silo thinking and the skilled manipulations of marketing experts. But in each generation, there were people of vision, people who refused to accept 'just the way things are'. Those people, most of whom are forgotten by history, shaped the world we live in today.

You will be one of those people. To whatever extent is right for you, you will be a force for change in the world. I've said that the journey towards personal awakening and coming home to your true self is, by extension, embracing the power to influence others around you. You will be a leader, to some extent.

It becomes important that, alongside building your personal vision and exploring your personal values, you enquire into the world that your heart longs to live in. What would it look like?

Initially, we can be tempted to return to the beliefs and views of our youth, of our parents, of mainstream culture. This is always true until we have reflected on something and rejected the temptation of 'just the way things are'. Once that falls away, what does your heart long for? What world would you create if you had the power? How would it be?

In the schools of learning which support the growth of human potential, this is called the "world of our longing". It is a vision for a good, healed, whole world. In countries across the globe, groups of people are working to bring it about. Activists and political dissidents. Leaders, writers and teachers. People are working for positive change in business, in politics, in law, in communities and in popular ideas about the environment, about justice, about what is true and right.

This work is going on all around us, often invisibly. People of vision, who share some of your longings for a better world, are devoting their lives to the birthing of this world, and to the death of toxic, hurtful ideas and assumptions.

A version of history

Versions of history are stories that have been accepted by the people of the time. Some things that we are told happened, didn't happen. More often, things are left out or twisted to have a meaning that works for the people of the time. The dark ages weren't dark at all. They were often times of learning and social development, but because the Romans were popular at the time the phrase "dark ages" was coined, we made the assumption that the departure of the Romans must have been a terrible thing. Often history is edited to make the rich and powerful into central characters and the rest of the population into simply a backdrop. History is also tailored to suit the prejudices of the time. Victorian historians travelled the UK rebuilding or often completely redesigning ancient sites of ritual to fit their idea of what those people were like. Right now in the United States, a lot of history being taught in high schools tells that the Native Americans were glad about the arrival of the settlers, that they happily handed over their land to the technologically superior, more organised, more deserving European arrivals. The Trail of Tears is often left out entirely.

So, history is what you make it. For every objectively true, carefully researched event that definitely took place, there are a dozen interpretations of what it means, and those interpretations will shift over time to suit the needs and prejudices of the culture.

I want to offer you my view of human history, through the lens of personal development and the potential for human awakening and flourishing.

The history of humanity has been a long, hard, slow struggle towards enlightenment and psycho-spiritual evolution. Fighting against this have been the forces of fear, separation, selfishness, short-term thinking and the hoarding of power.

Today, we have incredible potential to transform the world into something positive, nourishing and beautiful. There is no technological or economic reason why anybody should live in poverty, should live in fear of persecution or war, should die of easily preventable disease. There is no technological or economic reason why women in the world should be denied education, freedom of choice or equal levels of power with men. There is no technological or economic reason why anyone should do work that is meaningless, harmful or crushing to the spirit. We have the knowledge and the resources to do away with all of these things, and to find out what the world might be like without them, what we could really achieve as a species.

Of course, we don't do this. Our politics, our prejudices, and in general, the efforts and fears or those who refused to break free of 'just the way things are' holds us back. We continue to fight, to steal and hoard resources, to persecute and segregate ourselves.

Above all, we are at war with the natural world. Our earth-mother, who gives us life, food, air and everything we need to thrive, has been savagely attacked by our culture: a culture that only exists to serve and protect those of us who haven't done the personal work to wake up and embrace our true power and potential. I've mentioned Derrick Jensen's work, and if you want a really searing, unflinching perspective on the injustice and devastation that our civilisation has wrought, and continues to wreak, on the natural world, I invite you to read his harrowing book: Endgame.

The tipping point

We are more interconnected than ever before. We have better access to information, and we have the possibility of social mobility: we escape from lives that severely limit our freedom and potential. Somebody born in poverty can work themselves out of it, and people born into homes steeped in fear, violence, prejudice or addiction can break generational cycles and become free to live different kinds of life. None of this is easy, but it is possible, and it's more possible today than it's ever been. We have more chances to access and unleash our personal power than we ever have before.

As ever, the forces of fear and separation are fighting back, and we can easily lose all we've gained. Economic differences can shrink, opportunity can shift back to the rich and powerful and we can easily be manipulated into thinking that separation and fear are good things.

But more of us are waking up. More people are doing the work to come back to the true nature of our potential, to the responsibilities of being human, to the full richness of this messy and beautiful life. It's happening all around you, and I believe that one day we will see a tipping point where fear and separation will stop being fashionable, where the petty games we play and the masks we wear in a desperate bid to be accepted and liked, will stop being the norm. I believe that a time of freedom and enlightenment is possible.

This might sound like a fantasy. It might sound like my dream that has nothing to do with you. But if you feel a stirring to be part of the birthing of the world of our longing, then I encourage you to look around and begin linking up with other like-minded individuals. Groups and organisations exist all over the world to support you to engage, from charities doing good work, to political parties to personal development groups and organisations offering nature-connection ceremonies. Follow the calling of your heart. Work to rebuild the lost arts of community. Reverse the damage done to our inter-connectedness. Know your neighbours.

At some point we will have to reconsider the myths and core beliefs of our culture, as we get closer to the tipping point. Our stories will have to change, and the things that we congratulate or damn people for will have to change. Who, really, are our heroes? What kinds of things does a hero do? Are they really people of violence and self-gratification, or are they women and men who follow the calling of their hearts to be part of the birthing of a better world? People who wear their messiness and realness on the outside, with vulnerability and courage, rather than wearing polished masks to seem impressive, to meet the expectations of a hurtful culture. Who are our villains and who do we vilify in our stories? Are they really benefit frauds or petty criminals, the people who act or believe differently from us, or are they the people of power and influence who allow injustice to go unchallenged and who support the raping of the natural world for short-term benefit? At some point, we will have to rewrite our myths and tell better stories to each other.

For now, I invite you to contribute in good ways whenever you can. Spend your money in ways that will support the birthing of the world you want to live in. Cast your votes based on hope and on holding power to account, rather than on the cynical, short-term visions of petty demagogues. Think, in the Native American way, of the wellbeing of children, human and non-human, for the next seven generations, and building your plans and hopes accordingly. Expect true leadership, empathy and humanity from those in power.

Walk the three paths of your journey. Do the inner work to meet the true person that you are, to understand the mysteries and realities, the shadows and the gifts, that go into making of the unique being of you. Do the work on your relationships: grow your courage to be vulnerable and your healthy boundaries so that your can engage in the difficult, rewarding adventure of friendship, intimacy and inter-connectedness with others. Walk your path of outer work: have good effects in the world, make contributions that align with your values, bring determination and curiosity to the long hours you put in to the work that you choose to do.

Never imagine that this journey has an end. There is always more to learn, deeper truths to find, more healing and connection to do. While we hold to a vision and a set of goals, while we are moving in good, positive, healthy directions and making empowering choices for ourselves that build lives of happiness and fulfilment, we know that this life is an adventure, change and discovery. It is the journey that matters. Destinations are simply moments of recognition where we're shown how powerful we truly are by the beautiful and impressive life that we have made for ourselves.

Bibliography

Recommended books

Books I have talked about, which I think everyone could learn from

Coming Back to Life: The Updated Guide to the Work That Reconnects by Joanna Macy , Molly Young Brown, et al. (2014)

Daring Greatly: How the Courage to Be Vulnerable Transforms the Way We Live, Love, Parent, and Lead by Brené Brown (2015)

Die Wise: A Manifesto for Sanity and Soul by Stephen Jenkinson (2015)

Endgame Vol.1: The Problem of Civilization: The Problem of Civilization and Endgame Vol.2: Resistance by Derrick Jensen (2006)

Finding Earth, Finding Soul: The Invisible Path to Authentic Leadership by Tim Macartney (2007)

How to Be an Adult: A Handbook on Psychological and Spiritual Integration by David Richo (1991)

Iron John: A Book About Men by Robert Bly (1990, repub 2001)

King Warrior Magician Lover: Rediscovering the Archetypes of the Mature Masculine by Robert Moore and Douglas Gillette (1992)

Making Habits, Breaking Habits: How To Make Changes That Stick by Jeremy Dean (2013)

Nonviolent Communication -- A Language of Life by Marshall B. Rosenberg (2003, repub 2015)

Self-Parenting: The Complete Guide to Your Inner Conversations by John K Pollard and Linda Nusbaum (1987, repub 2018)

Swim Wild: Dive into the natural world and discover your inner adventurer Hardcover by Jack Hudson (2018)

The 7 Habits of Highly Effective People by Stephen R. Covey (1989, repub 1999)

The Hero with A Thousand Faces (The Collected Works of Joseph Campbell) by Joseph Campbell (2012)

The Language of Emotions: What Your Feelings are Trying to Tell You by Karla McLaren (2010)

The Way of the SEAL: Think Like an Elite Warrior to Lead and Succeed by Mark Divine and Allyson Edelhertz Machate (2016)

The Way of the Superior Man: A Spiritual Guide to Mastering the Challenges of Women, Work, and Sexual Desire (20th Anniversary Edition) by David Deida (2017)

Wild Power: Discover the Magic of Your Menstrual Cycle and Awaken the Feminine Path to Power by Alexandra Pope and Sjanie Hugo Wurlitzer (2017)

Wild: An Elemental Journey by Jay Griffiths (2008)

Works consulted

Other sources of inspiration behind this book

A Game Free Life: The definitive book on the Drama Triangle and Compassion Triangle by Stephen B. Karpman M.D. (2014)

A Little Book on the Human Shadow by Robert Bly and William Booth (1988)

Dark Side of the Light Chasers: Reclaiming your power,

creativity, brilliance, and dreams by Debbie Ford (2001)

How to Be a Stoic: Using Ancient Philosophy to Live a Modern Life by Massimo Pigliucci (2017)

Meeting the Shadow: Hidden Power of the Dark Side of Human Nature (New Consciousness Reader) by Connie Zweig and Jeremiah Abrams (1990)

The Children's Fire: Heart song of a people by Mac Macartney (2018)

The current status of urban-rural differences in psychiatric disorders, Acta Psychiatr Scand. 2010 Feb;121(2):84-93

The Outsider (Penguin Modern Classics) by Albert Camus and Sandra Smith (1942, repub 2013)

The Sickness Unto Death: A Christian Psychological Exposition of Edification and Awakening by Anti-Climacus (Classics) by Soren Kierkegaard and Alastair Hannay (1849, repub 1989)

Unlimited Power: The New Science of Personal Achievement by Tony Robbins (2001)

Bibliography

Next steps

1. If you enjoyed this book, help others enjoy it too!

Please leave a review on Amazon and Goodreads

2. The core of my work is still one-to-one coaching, either in Brighton in the UK, or by video call.

If you'd like support for your own journey of healing and awakening, get in touch.

About the Author

Alexander Butler grew up in the South West of England and then escaped to London to attend university. He studied Philosophy, Religion and Ethics at Heythrop College, University of London.

Since then he has run businesses and worked for ethical organisations that make a positive contribution to the world. He's worked to study and understand the human condition from as many angles as possible. He's worked alongside therapists from different disciplines, studied business, learned from priests, Sufis, shamans and Buddhists. As the world began to wake up to the impending environmental disaster, he studied the reasons that people (especially leaders) do not take action. At Embercombe, an inspirational centre for personal and leadership development, he was taught how to coach clients and support people through a process of self-enquiry and healing. Eventually he was asked to begin teaching and coaching, and he's been doing this ever since.

Alexander now lives and works as a coach in Brighton on the South Coast of England. He works with clients in person and online, and he helps them to radically redefine what's possible, using the wisdom contained in the 12 Principles and the rest of his 20 years of training and learning.

Deep Joy

Printed in Great Britain
by Amazon